Microsimulation Techniques for Tax and
Transfer Analysis

GORDON H. LEWIS
RICHARD C. MICHEL
Editors

Microsimulation Techniques for Tax and Transfer Analysis

THE URBAN INSTITUTE PRESS
Washington, D.C.

Library of Congress Cataloging in Publication Data
Microsimulation techniques for tax and transfer analysis / Gordon H. Lewis and
  Richard C. Michel, editors.
    Papers presented at a conference held in October 1987 at the Urban Institute in
  Washington, D.C.
    1. Taxation—Simulation methods—Congresses. 2. Transfer payments—
  Simulation methods—Congresses. I. Lewis, Gordon H. II. Michel, Richard C. III.
  Urban Institute.
  HF2279.M53   1989   336.2′001′13—dc20   89-24832
                                                                   CIP

ISBN 0-87766-433-1 (alk. paper)
ISBN 0-87766-432-3 (alk. paper; casebound)

Urban Institute books are printed on acid-free paper whenever possible.

Printed in the United States of America.

9 8 7 6 5 4 3 2 1

Distributed by:
            University Press of America
4720 Boston Way   3 Henrietta Street
Lanham, MD 20706   London WC2E 8LU ENGLAND

THE URBAN INSTITUTE is a nonprofit policy research and educational organization established in Washington, D.C., in 1968. Its staff investigates the social and economic problems confronting the nation and government policies and programs designed to alleviate such problems. The Institute disseminates significant findings of its research through the publications program of its Press. The Institute has two goals for work in each of its research areas: to help shape thinking about societal problems and efforts to solve them, and to improve government decisions and performance by providing better information and analytic tools.

Through work that ranges from broad conceptual studies to administrative and technical assistance, Institute researchers contribute to the stock of knowledge available to public officials and private individuals and groups concerned with formulating and implementing more efficient and effective government policy.

Conclusions or opinions expressed in Institute publications are those of the authors and do not necessarily reflect the views of other staff members, officers or trustees of the Institute, advisory groups, or any organizations that provide financial support to the Institute.

CONTENTS

Foreword   xiii

Preface   xv

**1 Introduction and Overview: Issues and Problems
in Microsimulation Modeling**   *Richard C. Michel and
Gordon H. Lewis*   1
  Static and Dynamic Microsimulation Modeling   1
  Databases   9
  Imputation and Matching   13
  Timeliness   18
  Validity   22
  Design   26

**2 The Historical Development of the Transfer
Income Model (TRIM2)**   *Randall L. Webb, Richard C.
Michel, and Anne B. Bergsman*   33
  Why Do Microsimulation?   33
  Policy Analysis in the Late 1960s: RIM   36
  TRIM: A Software Framework for Microsimulation   38
    Flexible Modular Structure   40
    Parameterization   41
    Data File   41
    Filing Units and Status Definitions   42
    Documentation of Methodology and Self-
      Documenting Runs   43
    Efficiency   44
    Table Generation   45
    Good Programming Techniques   45

Organization of Personnel   46
Policy Analysis in the 1970s: TRIM, MATH, and
    CBO   46
KGB: Echoes of RIM and Breathing Space for
    TRIM2   50
TRIM2: A More Complete Framework   52
    Flexible Modular Structure   53
    Parameterization   53
    Data File and Operating Efficiency   54
    Filing Units and Status Definitions   56
    Documentation of Methodology and Self-
        Documenting Runs   56
    Table Generation   57
    Good Programming Techniques   57
Policy Analysis in the 1980s: What Has TRIM2
    Done for Us Lately?   58
Recent Uses of TRIM2: Two Case Studies   61
    TRIM2 and Tax Reform   61
    TRIM2 and Welfare Reform   63
Software Support for Policy Analysis in the 1990s   66
    Ease of Use through Interactive Job Set-up   67
    Improving the Accessibility of TRIM2 for
        Nongovernment Projects   68
    Making Results of TRIM2 Simulations More
        Easily Available to Policy Analysts and
        Policymakers   69

**3 Microsimulation as a Policy Input: Experience at
Health and Welfare Canada**   *Richard J. Morrison*   77
    MAPSIT   79
        Microsimulation as Example Generation   80
        The MAPSIT Package   81
        A Descriptive Example   83
        A More Analytic Example   86
        MAPSIT in Its Educational Role   89
    SIMTAB   89
        Microsimulation for Cost and Clientele
            Estimation   90
        The SIMTAB Package   92
        SIMTAB Descriptive Analyses   95
        Analytic Simulations with SIMTAB   97
        SIMTAB as a Policy Tool   99

MAPSIT and SIMTAB Together   100
Summary   101
Appendix: The SIMTAB Data Aging Model   103

**4 The Development of the Dynamic Simulation of
Income Model (DYNASIM)**   *Sheila R. Zedlewski*   109
Development of the Original DYNASIM Model   110
Policy Applications of the DYNASIM Model   116
Events Leading to DYNASIM2   117
Development of the DYNASIM2 Model   120
Policy Applications of DYNASIM2   123
Futuro Poaaibilities   129
Addendum: Other Microanalytic Models   132

**5 PRISM: Dynamic Simulation of Pension and
Retirement Income**   *David L. Kennell and John F.
Sheils*   137
Overview of PRISM Methodology   137
Comparison of PRISM and DYNASIM   144
PRISM Model Assumptions   146
Demographic Assumptions   146
Labor Force and Economic Assumptions   147
Pension Coverage Assumptions   151
Retirement Decision Assumptions   152
Employer Pension Plan Assumptions   153
Individual Retirement Account Assumptions   158
Assets in Retirement   162
Supplemental Security Income Program Benefits   163
Illustrative Results   165
Poverty among Elderly Living Alone   165
Income Distributions in Future Years   167
Average Incomes in Future Years   168
Pension Receipt in Future Years   169
Levels of Income   170

**6 A Method for Simulating the Distribution of
Combined Federal Taxes Using Census, Tax Return,
and Expenditure Microdata**   *Richard A. Kasten and
Frank J. Sammartino*   173
Measuring Aggregate Family Income   174
Simulation Methods   176
Adjustments to the Data   176

Aging the Data   178
Simulating Combined Federal Taxes   178
Distribution of Income and Taxes in 1977, 1984,
    and 1988   179

7 Micro-Macro Linkages in Economic Models
Joseph M. Anderson   187
Why Link Micromodels and Macromodels?   188
    Use of Macromodels or Projections to Control
        Micromodels   189
    General Equilibrium Feedbacks and Interactions   190
    Microeconomic Basis of Aggregate Behavior   191
Examples of Micromodel-Macromodel Linkages   193
    Household Income and Tax Simulation Model
        and Wharton Econometrics Long-Term
        Macroeconomic Model   194
    Household Energy Price Impacts Model—Data
        Resources Incorporated Quarterly Model—ICF
        Energy Market Models   203
    Use of Pension and Retirement Income
        Microsimulation Model (PRISM) to Calibrate
        ICF Macroeconomic-Demographic Model   208
    Integrating DYNASIM2 with ICF Macroeconomic-
        Demographic Model   210
NIA Macroeconomic-Demographic Model—An
    Aggregative, Microeconomic-based Approach to
    Economic Modeling   212

**8 Microsimulation and SIPP: Can We Use the New
Longitudinal Data?**   *Pat Doyle and Harold Beebout*   221
The Promise of SIPP   221
    The SIPP Data   222
    Challenges and Problems in Using SIPP for
        Microsimulation   223
Overcoming Problems in Microsimulation
    Applications   223
    Problems in SIPP Applications   224
    Potential Solutions   230
    Cross-Sectional Applications   232

Longitudinal Applications   233
Conclusions and Future Directions   234

About the Editors   241

About the Contributors   243

Tables

1.1 Simulating a Reduction in Tax Rates   3
4.1 Program Blocks Operational in the Original
     DYNASIM Model   114
4.2 Program Blocks Operational in the DYNASIM2
     Model   124
4.3 Applications of the DYNASIM MODEL: 1977–87   126
5.1 Assumed Real Earnings Differentials   149
5.2 Percentage Distribution of Workers by Industry
     of Employment Assumed in PRISM for
     Selected Years   150
5.3 Pension Coverage Assumptions   152
5.4 Probabilities That Married Individuals Will
     Choose to Elect the Joint and Survivor's
     Option, by Size of Benefit   155
5.5 Savings Plans Participation Assumptions   157
5.6 IRA Adoption Assumptions for Noncovered
     Workers, by Age and Family Earnings Level   159
5.7 IRA Adoption Probabilities for Covered Workers
     in 1982, by Family Income and Age of Worker   160
5.8 Probabilities of Contributing to an IRA in a
     Given Year Once Selected to Adopt an IRA   161
5.9 Percentage of Elderly Living Alone with Incomes
     Below the Poverty Level   165
5.10 Growth in Number of Elderly Persons, 1987–
     2020   166
5.11 Income Distribution of Elderly Receiving Income   167
5.12 Percentage of Elderly Receiving Income, by
     Source   168
5.13 Percentage of Elderly Receiving Pension Income   169
5.14 Average Income for All Elderly Living Alone
     (1987 dollars)   170

6.1 Distribution of Family Income from Each Source
     of Income, by Population Decile, with
     Corporate Income Tax Allocated to Capital
     Income   181
6.2 Distribution of Family Income from Each Source
     of Income, by Population Decile, with
     Corporate Income Tax Allocated to Labor
     Income   182
6.3 Distribution of Family Income and of Federal
     Tax Payments by Population Decile, with
     Corporate Income Tax Allocated to Capital
     Income   183
6.4 Distribution of Family Income and of Federal
     Tax Payments by Population Decile, with
     Corporate Income Tax Allocated to Labor
     Income   184

Figures

3.1 The Child Benefit System. Comparative Child
     Benefits: 1984 and 1979   85
3.2 Child Benefit System Components, Ontario
     2-Parent, 2-Child Family, 1987   87
4.1 Structure of DYNASIM   111
4.2 Structure of DYNASIM2   121
5.1 Flow Diagram of Pension and Retirement
     Income Simulation Model (PRISM)   140
5.2 Data Sources Used to Create ICF Pension/Social
     Security Database   142
7.1 Linked Energy Market-Macroeconomic-
     Household Microsimulation Modeling System   204
7.2 Structure of the Macroeconomic-Demographic
     Model of Health Care Expenditures   214
7.3 Demographic Groups in the Macroeconomic-
     Demographic Model of Health Care
     Expenditures   215

FOREWORD

The Urban Institute has been deeply involved with the development and use of microsimulation as a policy analysis tool since 1968, when the Institute was established. It is thus with particular pleasure that I write this foreword to our newest book on the subject.

Microsimulation modeling allows the analyst to use the rich microdata now available on individuals and families, within a model of a large-scale social system constructed from a great many assumptions about demographic and macroeconomic changes, to analyze the effects of program change. The effects on individual families with particular characteristics can be simulated. So can the effects on the income distribution as a whole. Early microsimulation was restricted to modeling the effects of cash transfers. Later development has added in-kind transfers and, finally, the positive tax system.

The advent of microsimulation has transformed the analysis of tax and transfer programs and the terms of the social policy debate. In the early and mid-1960's, when many of the War on Poverty and Great Society Programs were passed, only very crude estimates of the costs of programs were possible. Almost no systematic information could be obtained about characteristics of the population that would be eligible for a new program or program change, who among the eligibles would be likely to participate, or who would be the gainers and who would be the losers if the change were implemented. Twenty-five years later, such information is taken for granted both inside and outside government because of the advent of microsimulation.

The Urban Institute has played a considerable part in bringing about this change. For twenty years Institute researchers have been involved in the development of both static and dynamic microsimulation modeling. Static models have richer program detail, are more economical to run, and are the tool of choice for analyzing the short-term effects of policy change. Dynamic models, structured to accommodate behavioral change over time are particularly well suited for analyzing the long-term effects of policy and non-policy variables.

Our static modeling work grew out of the first microsimulation model ever developed, which was used by President Johnson's Commission on Income Maintenance (the Heineman Commission) to assess alternative family income maintenance programs, such as the negative income tax. This model was brought to the Institute and developed over many years into what is now called TRIM2 (Transfer Income Model).

Dynamic microsimulation modeling is the brainchild of Guy Orcutt. Orcutt joined the staff in the late 1960s, organized a team, and under his leadership the Dynamic Simulation of Income Model (DYNASIM) became a functioning policy analysis tool in the mid-1970s.

Twenty years after the beginning of microsimulation modeling, many large models—some static, some dynamic, and some a mixture of the two—are used daily for policy analysis. This volume describes the histories and current structures of several of the most widely used models here and in Canada. I hope that it will provide a valuable source for experienced model users and a good introduction to the field of microsimulation for readers interested in learning about the technique and its uses.

William Gorham
President

This book is the result of the Conference on Software Systems and Income Transfer Policy held in October 1987 at The Urban Institute in Washington, D.C. The conference was initially scheduled to be held in St. Louis as part of the annual conference of the International Association for Mathematical Modeling (IAMM). The plan was to devote a session of that meeting to software systems and income transfer analysis, allowing some of the principal designers and users of software systems developed for microsimulation to describe their models and discuss plans for future development. It quickly became clear, however, that the subject warranted more than a one- or two-hour block of time. As a result, we decided to organize a separate meeting and to move the conference to a location convenient for a majority of the participants and other attendees. This meant that we opted for Washington, D.C.

We wish to express our thanks to the authors and the discussants, and our appreciation to The Urban Institute. The discussants deserve special thanks for their useful commentary on these papers: Reuben Snipper (U.S. Department of Health and Human Services), Roberton Williams (Congressional Budget Office), Kevin Hollenbeck (The W. E. Upjohn Institute for Employment Research), Wendell Primus (Committee on Ways and Means, U.S. House of Representatives), Richard Michel (The Urban Institute), and David McMillen (Bureau of the Census).

In addition to these discussants, Steven Caldwell provided a commentary on the conference as a whole and addressed a series of questions about the past and future of microsimulation. Using an economic argument (an unusual approach for a sociologist), Caldwell suggested that the extent to which microsimulation is used can be understood from the standpoint of four factors: the perceived benefits of the information generated, the cost of using microsimulation to generate the information, the cost of using alternative techniques to generate appropriate information, and the financial resources of actors who might value the information. Perhaps the most interesting conclusion he drew was that the dramatically declining costs of computer power and the possibility that much more powerful computers will become available may point to a larger microsimulation community, not just in the federal government but in state and local governments and among university researchers. If that is correct, then the nature of the software systems and the kinds of changes that are needed are of even greater importance.

Special thanks are due William Darby (Washington University, St. Louis), who, as part of planning for the IAMM sessions, provided the initial impetus for the miscrosimulation conference, and to The Urban Institute, which served as host. Because of the generosity of the Institute, the papers that were prepared are able to reach a larger audience.

Gordon H. Lewis
Richard C. Michel

Chapter One

INTRODUCTION AND OVERVIEW: ISSUES AND PROBLEMS IN MICROSIMULATION MODELING

Richard C. Michel and Gordon H. Lewis

In organizing the microsimulation conference held in October 1987 at The Urban Institute, we sought to include the major models being used by the United States government. Because a significantly different approach to microsimulation has been taken in Canada, we also invited participation from Richard J. Morrison, a key analyst in Canada's Department of National Health and Welfare. The models discussed in this volume (TRIM2, HITSM, DYNASIM2, and PRISM on the U.S. side; and MAPSIT and SIMTAB on the Canadian side) do not represent all of the models used, but they are major simulation programs used regularly for analysis of transfer systems in the United States and Canada.[1] Other models not yet used as extensively include the method for simulating the distribution of federal taxes, described by Richard A. Kasten and Frank J. Sammartino in chapter 6 of this book, and the Macroeconomic-Demographic Model (MDM) of the Retirement Income System, discussed by Joseph M. Anderson in chapter 7.

Conference participants were asked to address the history of their model, the current status of that model, and the kinds of software changes that should be made to enhance its use. Not surprisingly, the resulting papers covered a good deal more material as well, centering on several themes: the use of static versus dynamic models, the nature of the databases required for successful modeling, imputation of values when the database is incomplete, the timeliness of microsimulation, validity of the results, and issues of design. The remainder of this introductory chapter surveys these issues in turn.

STATIC AND DYNAMIC MICROSIMULATION MODELING

The field of microeconomic simulation includes a wide variety of modeling approaches. Of the models that have experienced ongoing development since the concept of microsimulation was introduced in the 1950s, two generic types have been most demanded by government users: *static* models, which have been used most often to examine the potential impacts of detailed changes to tax and transfer programs, and *dynamic* models, which have been used most often to examine long-term impacts, particularly in the area of retirement issues in the 21st century. These two types of models form the bases for the chapters in this volume.

What distinguishes static from dynamic models? To understand this, one must know a little about how simulation modeling operates. Most of the models in widespread use, and the majority of those discussed in this volume, have their foundation in surveys of households. Other models, such as the MAPSIT model discussed in chapter 3, are not based on survey data.[2]

The household databases that have proved most enduring as the primary inputs into microsimulation systems are large surveys of a nation's general population (in this volume, the surveys are for either the United States or Canada). These surveys contain extensive, but not necessarily exhaustive, demographic and income information on the members of a household. In a sense, each record is like a loan application to a bank, which asks for details about every household member.

This detailed information becomes the raw material for microsimulation models. The need for simulation on these databases arises because this raw material is frequently inadequate to test the broad effects of a policy change or to examine the distribution of existing benefits. For example, most general U.S. household surveys containing demographic and general income information do not collect tax data for each individual or family. To add taxes to the data files, it is necessary to use the demographic and income information on the general survey to calculate a tax liability for a given year. This calculation is a simple simulation.

Apart from missing whole classes of economic variables, general household surveys in the United States often reveal problems even among the variables they include. For example, aggregate benefits from government programs to low-income families and persons are consistently "underreported" when compared to actual program data.[3] To obtain the correct amount of benefits, it is essential to create procedures that assign the "missing benefits" to people. These procedures are also simulations. Furthermore, once the simulation of an actual tax or transfer program is set up and new or revised variables are added to the file, changes in policies such as a decrease in tax rates can also be simulated simply by adding variables representing those new policies.

How these simulations are carried out on household data files is what distinguishes microsimulation from other kinds of simulation, such as models of natural events that forecast the destruction of the ozone layer. These latter simulations use aggregate data and either project them forward in time or alter the value of a variable in an explanatory model. In contrast, microsimulations operate directly on independent variables contained in the individual records of a household data survey.

An example of this is shown in table 1.1, a simple household record in which a husband, wife, and child together form a tax filing unit. The household survey data indicate that both spouses have earnings and that the husband has a small amount of interest income. The household survey, however, did not collect information on the amount of taxes the family would owe. We have simulated tax liabilities under two simple hypothetical tax systems. In the system labeled Option 1, which is assumed to be current law for this family, all

Table 1.1 SIMULATING A REDUCTION IN TAX RATES

Data on Household Record		
Male, age 33, household head		
Female, age 31, spouse of head		
Female, age 6, child of head		
Income Variables from Survey		
Male		
Earnings	$27,000	
Interest	300	
Dividends	–0–	
Welfare	–0–	
Female		
Earnings	7,700	
Simulation of Tax Liabilities		
Assume the couple files jointly:	Option 1	Option 2
Standard deduction	$3,500	$3,500
Per-person exemption	$1,000	$2,000
Combined tax rate	30%	15%
Tax liability to be added as variable on household record	$8,550	$3,825
Average tax rate (taxes divided by gross income)	24%	11%

income is taxed at 30 percent after taking a standard deduction and a per person exemption of $1,000. Option 2, which is assumed to be a proposed change in current law, clearly represents a significant tax reduction. The proposal doubles the per-person exemption to $2,000 and halves the overall tax rate to 15 percent, but leaves the standard deduction the same as Option 1. The results are as expected: Option 2 tax liabilities for this family are $4,725 lower than the current-law in Option 1.

In a microsimulation model of taxes, the current-law tax liability (here $8,550), would first be added as a new variable to the household record. The simulation of the proposed change creates a new tax liability variable (here valued at $3,825), which is also added to the household record. The key here is that variables on the household record are altered, either by adding a new one or changing an existing one. If the simple simulation program in table 1.1 were in place, for example, one could also simulate the tax effects of the husband receiving a 10 percent increase in his earnings simply by substituting the new earnings figure in the calculations under either Option 1 or Option 2 or both.

In microsimulation models that operate on large household surveys, these calculations are repeated thousands of times, once for each tax filing unit in the survey. Of course, the input data (earnings, age, race, sex, relationship to household head, etc.) are provided in much more detail. The March Current Population Survey (CPS) in the United States contains about 60,000 household records with more than 150 variables describing demographic characteristics such as race, education level, and marital status; labor force characteristics; and more than a dozen income sources. The actual simulations of items such as taxes are made even more complex by a variety of factors, including the presence of more than one tax filing unit in a household (e.g., Aunt Mary may file her own tax return because she is not literally a dependent of the household head).

The simulations themselves are also more complicated than shown in table 1.1. As U.S. citizens know, the federal income tax rules are much more intricate than the rules implied in Options 1 and 2, and involve multiple tax rates at different income levels, itemized deductions, various income exclusions, and sundry credits. Organizing the parameters (that is, the standard deduction, per person exemption, etc.) in a complete simulation of U.S. federal income taxes involves many more lines of computer code than implied in the table.

A brief diversion may be useful here to clarify another bit of terminology. Throughout this volume, and others on microsimulation, models are referred to as micro*economic* simulations. In part, this is because an economist, Guy Orcutt, originated the idea of the purpose of simulation among policy analysts. But Orcutt's original idea of the purpose of simulation was to get a better sense of the impacts of economic behavior, such as gaining or losing a job, in the household sector of the economy.[4] And although many models have now expanded to simulate events or policy changes that are not purely economic, the fundamental value of the modeling lies in its ability to illuminate the distributional effects of changes on all or part of the household sector of the economy.[5]

Having seen how a microsimulation model operates directly on the household records, we can return to the question of what differentiates *static* from dynamic modeling. In brief, a *static* model assumes that the individuals within a household will not change their behavior in response to policy changes or to other events. For example, in a static model the hypothetical family in table 1.1 is assumed not to change its behavior with respect to work when a new tax system, such as Option 2, is implemented. However, if some theories about economic behavior were true (e.g., that lower income tax rates lead to increased work) we might expect the family to respond in some way. The wife, for example, might increase her earnings by either moving to a higher paying job or increasing her hours of work with her current employer.

A *dynamic* model attempts to capture at least some of these behavioral reactions, either in response to changes in policy or to economic and demographic events. In table 1.1, for example, a simple work–response assumption might be that every percentage point reduction in the average tax rate would lead to a half percentage point increase in earnings. In the case of the hypothetical family in table 1.1, gross earnings are $34,700 before Option 2 is implemented, and Option 2 reduces the average taxrate by 13 percentage points. Under our simple assumption, earnings (a proxy for work effort here) should rise by 6.5 percent, or about $2,255 for either the husband or the wife. Clearly, responses to tax rate changes are more complicated than this, with secondary and primary workers affected differently and the macroeconomy and level of family income playing large roles in determining individuals' ability to increase or decrease their work effort. But this is the kind of behavioral response that dynamic simulations attempt to capture.

In real life, of course, many different events are occurring nearly simultaneously. An individual's response to tax rate changes, for example, may be affected by whether the wife in a family is pregnant,

by whether either spouse is entering a period of retirement opportunity, by whether a worker's employer is in a period of financial
decline or growth, and so on. An individual's decision may be affected by all these events, and each individual may weigh the importance of the events differently. Furthermore, response times are
likely to vary among individuals, with some reacting quickly and
others more slowly. As a consequence, these decision processes are
quite complex, and the ideal model to simulate them reflects this
complexity to the extent feasible given data availability, computer
technology, and econometric methods.

Largely because of constraints imposed by both computer technology and limited knowledge of behavior at the micro level, the
dynamic simulation models in use today must simplify the decision
processes in various ways. One obvious simplification is to assume
that events are sequential rather than simultaneous in nature—for
example, that only one policy change is occurring at a time and that
all other factors are fixed while that change happens. A second simplification is to assume that behavioral responses occur quickly.
Thus, tax rates are lowered, then individuals respond, given a fixed
set of other characteristics, such as the unemployment rate or the
pregnancy of the wife, and so forth, *if* these are considered important.
This sequencing of decisions is computationally necessary since the
computers on which simulations are run perform the calculations
sequentially. Because of the need for this computational simplification, however, a principal requirement for the success of dynamic
simulations is a thorough understanding of what specific behavioral
responses to events will be and what variables most affect those
responses across individuals.

Unfortunately, our understanding of how individuals behave is at
best incomplete and in many cases superficial. Even when theoretical
alternatives can be agreed upon, there is limited consensus on quantitative ways to characterize that behavior. For example, detailed
information from the Vital Statistics of the United States and from
Bureau of the Census surveys would seem to provide a good basis
for simulating fertility, mortality, marriage, and divorce over time.
But Vital Statistics data provide only limited variables, usually just
age and sex, from which to build an explanatory model. Yet we know
these demographic events are also affected by other variables such
as income, parents' education levels, and numbers of children already born. Cross-sectional data from Census surveys provide some
help but are limited because they do not provide data on the same
families over time.

Our knowledge of labor supply behavior, including retirement, may be somewhat better. Several specialized surveys of the retired population, for example, have given us reasonably good notions of how and why individuals retire. In contrast, our understanding of work effort responses to changes in either tax or welfare policy is not good. Related to the previously mentioned case of simulating a decrease in tax rates, for example, is the U.S. experience with the Economic Recovery Tax Act of 1981, which reduced marginal tax rates considerably, particularly among higher income taxpayers. Supply-side economists of the period argued that the reduction in tax rates would increase work effort to a sufficient degree that total tax revenues would rise even in the face of dramatically lower tax rates. Although some individuals may have responded by increasing their incomes, the net effect was not a massive growth in federal income tax revenues, and the U.S. federal government was left with a large structural deficit.[6]

In part because of similar certainties and lack of agreement among analysts about specific sets of behavioral responses to policy changes, dynamic models have not achieved dominance over static models in the policy arena. Today, far more funding from both government and private sources is provided for the application, development, and maintenance of static models than dynamic models. But interest in dynamic modeling or in modeling that blends the two approaches has grown in recent years as developments in the computer software and hardware industries have driven down the cost of computation and made it otherwise possible to simulate complex events.

In this volume, three chapters explore the development of various modeling systems, analyze the events that drove development in one direction or another, and speculate on future directions. In chapter 2, Randall L. Webb, Richard C. Michel, and Anne B. Bergsman examine the intriguing history of the development of the TRIM/MATH family of static microsimulation models and the impact of these models on cash and in-kind welfare program policy and on tax policy. The authors show how the coincident trends of increasing demand for quick turnaround estimations and advances in software development have combined to accelerate and complicate development of static models in the last 20 years. In some sense, the enormous success of TRIM and MATH in shaping the public debate on distributional and cost issues in these programs has paved the way for many other modeling developments outside these two systems.

In chapter 3, Richard J. Morrison describes the growth of static

microsimulation modeling development within the Canadian Department of National Health and Welfare. Two models, MAPSIT and
SIMTAB, the former of which is based on simulations using a synthetic database and the latter of which is based on the Canadian
Survey of Consumer Finances (SCF), were developed governmentally
and are used in conjunction with one another to inform policy discussions. The Canadian case differs from the U.S. case, however, in
that demand for the model results has not spread outside of the
Department of National Health and Welfare (such as to the mass
media). One consequence has been that the type of distributional
analyses so intrinsic to U.S. congressional reports on legislation has
not been institutionalized in Canada's policy process.

Chapter 4 in this volume, by Sheila R. Zedlewski, describes the
evolution of the original DYNASIM model. As Zedlewski notes, although early versions of the model were elegant and theoretically
sound, the heavy computational requirements made complete system
runs on large surveys too expensive to run. Furthermore, validation
of the early versions showed that the behavioral algorithms when
left unadjusted over time led to results that did not track well with
actual aggregate data. Early versions of the model therefore incorporated procedures to align the DYNASIM aggregate results to macro
forecasts, with which many model users felt comfortable. Subsequent
software improvements by Guy Orcutt and by Zedlewski and Jon
Johnson at The Urban Institute reduced the costs of running the
model considerably. Zedlewski concludes that recent DYNASIM applications have focused on the model's greatest advantage, its ability
to make long-range projections. She also argues that recent advances
in computing power are making this type of microsimulation more
feasible and more widely available. Nevertheless, we believe that
the absence of good data and good research on behavioral responses
continues to limit the issues to which the dynamic simulation results
can be successfully applied.

Other chapters in this book focus on the results of model applications of either static or dynamic models or hybrids, and give readers a sense of what the various model types can do. In chapter 5,
David L. Kennell and John F. Sheils use the Pension and Retirement
Income Simulation Model (PRISM) to analyze a variety of issues
affecting the elderly population over the period 1987 to 2020. PRISM
is a semidynamic system that ages cohorts of adults represented in
the 1978 CPS through use of cell probabilities taken from Census
birth, death, and marriage projections.[7] It includes some behavioral
estimates, such as retirement responses. The chapter shows how

long-run simulation estimates can be used to analyze the economic situation of groups far into the future.

In chapter 6, Richard A. Kasten and Frank J. Sammartino demonstrate the abilities of a static model to simulate detailed effects of current and proposed tax laws. In the chapter following, Joseph M. Anderson discusses how a model can be built that allows interactions between microlevel events and the macroeconomy. Anderson describes several such models and gives examples of their application, but those that are most fully interactive actually use a cell-model approach to household-level simulations.

DATABASES

As noted earlier in this overview, most microsimulation models use household-level surveys as the basic input into their estimation systems. Some, like MAPSIT, operate without survey-based data, but even these models require a synthetic database of prototypical households or families.

The previous discussion of the differences between static and dynamic models noted that the original grand purpose of microsimulation systems was to duplicate the economic and demographic decisions of the household sector. Since these decisions are a function of a broad array of household and individual characteristics, including personal history, the ideal database would provide all the variables important in these decisions over a long period of time; in other words, it would be a *longitudinal database*.

For a variety of reasons, collecting such information is a formidable task. First, the expense of surveying households to obtain the richly detailed data necessary for extensive behavioral analyses often limits the initial size of the sample. Yet, small sample sizes make it difficult to analyze the characteristics and responses of the subgroups that are frequently critically important in policy analyses. Second, sample-attrition problems further reduce the size of a sample over time. Third, significant computational and data management problems are inherent in manipulating microlevel longitudinal data. These problems have limited the ability of researchers even to access the data, let alone perform more sophisticated analyses of them. As a result, relatively few longitudinal data collection efforts have been conducted in the United States and other countries.

The most complete longitudinal survey of U.S. households is the

University of Michigan Survey Research Center's Panel Study of Income Dynamics (PSID). The survey, which began in 1968 and continues today with only modest changes,[8] collects demographic information and retrospective annual income data from a sample of about 5,000 U.S. families. It allows one to see changes from year to year in the composition and economic status of these families and thus to observe their behavior. In a general sense, the PSID would seem to provide a perfect database for building a dynamic microsimulation model by using the actual observed behavior of families to project their futures and those of other families. Yet, the PSID data have never been used directly in a microsimulation system.[9]

The reasons for this are varied, but some of them illuminate the difficulties associated with collecting and organizing the appropriate data for simulating the economic activities in the household sector. The first major problem with the PSID is that its sample is often too small to yield reliable estimates for some of the subgroups, such as the "working poor" or even the poor generally, which are often the subjects of analyses desired by researchers, government policymakers, and private foundations.

The sample-size problem is compounded by a second and complicated issue of sample representativeness over time, since the representative weight of a particular family in 1968 might not be the same weight in 1989. For example, when significant demographic shifts occur among the general population or when the family composition changes (such as in the case of divorces), the initial sample weights will simply be wrong at later dates. This makes untenable the notion of a single longitudinal weight for a family over long periods. Yet, assigning multiple weights to a single family over time compounds the conceptual and computational problems in extrapolating from the observed behavior of an individual family to the aggregate behavior of groups.

A third major problem is that the PSID, to minimize the response burden on the participating families, has simplified and collapsed some of the income detail, making it difficult to analyze particular programs. As Webb, Michel, and Bergsman argue in chapter 2 of this volume, the demand in the United States for increasingly detailed simulations of specific programs during the 1970s created significant barriers to the widespread use in the microsimulation community of any database with such income question simplifications.

As a result of these and other problems with using the rich PSID data, all of the early versions of both dynamic and static microsimulation models were based on *cross-sectional* rather than longitudinal surveys. This remains true today. Cross-sectional surveys have significant practical advantages over longitudinal surveys. They are relatively inexpensive to implement; a wide variety of information can be collected without being a continuing burden to the sample families; and, the point-in-time representativeness of the sample is fairly easy to calculate.

The cross-sectional survey most widely used in the United States is the previously mentioned March Current Population Survey (CPS). As a nationally representative sample of about 60,000 U.S. households, the March CPS collects detailed demographic information for the survey date, detailed income information for the calendar year prior to the survey, and detailed labor force information for both times. Because of the presence of this information and because the CPS has used a fairly consistent format since the late 1940s, it became the survey of choice for early microsimulation modeling systems.

Most of the U.S. models described in this volume use the March CPS as their basic input data. In the TRIM2 system (see chapter 2), the CPS database is edited and reformatted to make it consistent over time and more efficient prior to performing tax and transfer simulations. The DYNASIM model (Zedlewski, chapter 4) uses the 1973 March–May match of the CPS, which was further matched with longitudinal earnings histories from Social Security records.[10] DYNASIM then adds a series of complex behavioral algorithms to the system to create a longitudinal file into the future. The Kasten-Sammartino tax model (chapter 6) begins with a raw March CPS and supplements the core data with data from two other cross-sectional microlevel surveys. The HITSM and MDM models described by Anderson (chapter 7) also use the March CPS as their basic input, albeit with some modifications. The tax and transfer results from the HITSM system, for example, are controlled to meet certain program and employment data subtotals. The MDM model, because of the complexity of its macroeconomic interactions, uses detailed cells from the CPS and does not therefore operate on the actual microrecords.

There are two exceptions to the use of the March CPS. Among the U.S. modeling systems, the PRISM model (Kennell and Sheils, chapter 5) uses a May 1979 CPS survey that contained detailed pension data. This file, which, like its March cousin, is a cross-sectional one, has been matched to Social Security Earnings Records by the U.S. government, thus producing a file containing detailed earnings, though not total income, histories.[11]

The second exception, or, more precisely, set of exceptions, comes from the Canadian models described by Morrison in chapter 3. As discussed earlier here, one Canadian-based model, MAPSIT, uses a synthetic database, rather than survey data. Although this database can be as detailed as the developers desire, the MAPSIT model stands apart from the other models in this volume because it does not attempt to weight its results to population totals. The other Canadian model, SIMTAB, is founded in survey data, specifically the Canadian Survey of Consumer Finances. The SCF is the Canadian equivalent of the U.S. March CPS, containing detailed demographic and income information and thus allowing analyses of a broad array of tax and transfer programs.

Because of the practical considerations already noted here, cross-sectional surveys have gained a strong foothold as the preferred databases among the current array of models. Yet, they have significant problems of their own, which are largely associated with their inability to shed light on the way people behave when demographic, economic, or policy events occur. Furthermore, even in cross-sectional surveys, trade-offs are made with respect to the detail of information asked for. Thus, the broadest of surveys frequently lack data that are essential in analyzing particular programs or events.

In the United States, a recently implemented survey called the Survey of Income and Program Participation (SIPP) represents an effort by the federal government to both improve understanding of dynamic household behavior and provide more detailed information on household economic variables. The SIPP is an ongoing longitudinal survey that collects detailed *monthly* economic, labor force, and demographic information from sample families over a 32-month period. The SIPP in many ways corrects for the deficiencies of both the CPS cross-sectional surveys, which have no longitudinal information, and the PSID, which collects longitudinal information only on an annual basis. Initially, many analysts thought the SIPP would replace the CPS as the most widely used survey among microsimulation modelers. Alas, like other surveys, the SIPP has many significant drawbacks, not the least of which are its relatively small sample sizes.

Pat Doyle and Harold Beebout have been pioneers in analyzing the difficulties of using the SIPP and in identifying its potential utility to household dynamic studies, including microsimulation. In chapter 8 in this volume, these authors provide an excellent in-depth discussion of both the promise and problems of the SIPP.

Although the SIPP will provide many insights into both intrayear and interyear household dynamics, it seems clear now that it will not become the principal database for the current array of microsimulation models. Cross-sectional surveys will continue to be the dominant input files. The next section discusses how the developers of microsimulation models have developed clever, if not perfect, methods for getting around the limitations of these cross-sectional surveys.

IMPUTATION AND MATCHING

Nearly all the chapters in this volume provide examples of how the analysts and programmers who work with microsimulation models have enhanced their models through the use of multiple data sources. In general, a microsimulation model begins with a sample survey as its core input database. The core database contains a large but often incomplete set of variables that are critical for performing the simulations desired by the analysts. To create a new database that completes the input variable requirements, model developers supplement the variables on the core database with information from other microdatabases.[12]

This variable supplementation takes three generic forms. *Exact matches* link records from two databases that contain complementary variables and share a common set of households. *Statistical matches* link records from two databases that contain complementary variables but do not necessarily share a common set of households. *Statistical imputations* use statistical techniques such as multivariate regression to assign estimated variable values to the core database from another database that holds complementary variables. The core database that is being supplemented is known as the *host database*, and the database from which new variables are being drawn is known as the *donor database*.

Analysts agree that exact matches of records are generally preferable to other techniques when one file is used to supplement information on another. The reason for this is intuitive: if one has supplementary variables on the donor database for the same set of households or families as are on the host database, this is equivalent to dramatically expanding the survey questionnaire. In addition, when both the donated and host variables are available for exactly the same time frame, no noise other than sample noise is introduced into the variable values. In the case of either statistical matching or imputation, additional error would be introduced in the assignment of a donated variable value because of the unexplained variation inherent in stochastic procedures.

The availability of exact matches is entirely dependent upon the number of data sources with overlapping samples. Among the most common forms of exact matches in the United States are those that use government-generated databases—such as tax return forms from the Internal Revenue Service—as a donor database and those that use the overlapping samples of the monthly CPS.

The government-generated donor databases are not surveys but complete universes of all persons, families, or households who are required by law to file certain sets of information.[13] If these sets are truly universal, the donor database can be matched to almost any survey that samples a subset of U.S. persons, families, or households. Two such universal databases have been used over the past two decades to accomplish exact matches: the Social Security Earnings Records database, which provides earnings histories (up to a taxable maximum) on all U.S. workers, and the Internal Revenue Service tax return records, which provide a variety of income and deduction/ expenditure data for all tax filing units.

The matching of CPS files is possible because of the nature of both the questionnaires and the monthly samples. A CPS is taken every month to measure unemployment rate trends. In addition to the basic questions necessary to tabulate the unemployment rate, a supplementary set of questions is attached to some monthly surveys to collect additional information. This information varies monthly. For example, the March CPS, as discussed earlier, collects detailed information on income, labor force participation, and in-kind benefit receipt for the previous calendar year. Because the supplements change from month to month, it is desirable for some purposes to link the samples from different months.

Although the set of households sampled varies from month to month, there is substantial overlap for contiguous CPS months. The entire sample consists of eight rotation groups, each containing one-eighth of the regular monthly sample, which is about 60,000 households. Two of the rotation groups (i.e., one-fourth of the sample) leave the sample every month and are replaced by two others. An exact match is thus possible for a subset of the records for monthly surveys within four months of one another. For example, the March sample has a 75 percent sample overlap with both the February and April samples, a 50 percent overlap with the January and May samples, and so on. Although the overlapping sample is not necessarily representative of the U.S. population, an exact match of this sort can sometimes add considerably to the power of analyzing certain issues.

Given the apparent desirability of exact matches, why doesn't everyone use them? As always, there are numerous barriers to creating exact matches on a regular and consistent basis.

For example, there are several basic problems with the intra-CPS matches. As previously noted, they are only possible within a limited span of months, which constrains the ability of individual analysts to find donor and host databases that provide the desired combination of variables. Since not every month contains supplementary questions and only the March income supplement is taken every year, it is possible that there is no complementary information on CPS surveys that are available for exact matches. Moreover, the sample overlap between months for which matches are possible diminishes rapidly, and it is unclear how representative the subset of matched households is. A March–June match would only yield a 25 percent overlap. The diminishing overlap problem is compounded by sample attrition, which occurs in spite of the efforts of the Bureau of the Census to reduce the survey burden on individual families by using the rotation groups.

The major problem with the matches to large government databases is one of privacy. The use of government databases that are developed for such purposes as calculating Social Security benefits or determining tax liabilities is restricted by law to those general purposes. Privacy restrictions prohibit the release of these files to any persons not required to know their content. This is understandable, since no one wants the public to have unlimited access to records of his or her earnings' histories or income tax returns.

To succeed, of course, any exact matching procedure requires that each household or family have a unique and universal matching variable, such as a Social Security number or a name and address. Such information, if available to the public (including researchers), would clearly allow the identification of individual households. The result is that the only offices that have the ability to perform exact matches from government data files are those that have administrative responsibility for the programs for which the government data are collected. It is not, nor should it be, a priority of these offices to provide such matched files for research purposes, and thus few matches have been done that are available to the general analytic community.

Both of the long-range projection models described in this volume, DYNASIM and PRISM, rely on exact matches of CPS files with Social Security Earnings Records. The PRISM model, described in chapter 5 in this volume, uses the most recent exact match available outside of the government.[14] PRISM uses several exact matches to analyze pension, retirement, and income issues. The model's developers began with the May 1979 CPS, which contains supplementary questions on pension coverage. Unfortunately, however, the May 1979 CPS lacks the complete set of total income and labor force variables that appear on the annual March CPS. Thus, it was necessary to perform an exact match for a portion of the file with the March 1979 CPS.

In addition, PRISM developers also needed data from the Social Security Earnings Records, which provide earnings information up to whatever the maximum taxable earnings were in a given year. Earnings records between 1951 and 1977 had been previously matched by the government to the March 1978 CPS. This exact match file was then linked to the March–May 1979 matched file to provide the basis for the PRISM simulations, creating a unique quasi-longitudinal file for analyzing pension and retirement issues.

Unfortunately, exact matches are not perfect. The matching techniques can limit sample sizes in cases like the intra-CPS sample overlap problems discussed earlier. The Social Security Earnings Records themselves provide earnings information only up to the taxable maximum, which changed inconsistently over the 1951–1979 period. Although this does not affect Social Security analyses in either PRISM or DYNASIM, it does limit the ability to evaluate longitudinal changes in total earnings and income. And, as the PRISM experience shows, the number of exact matches required to create a complex database can be daunting and represents a cost barrier to regular updating.

These kinds of deficiencies have troubled other exact matches as well and, combined with the infrequency with which exact matches are produced by the U.S. federal government,[15] have caused microsimulation analysts to rely more heavily on statistical matching and imputation procedures.

Statistical matching is accomplished by linking the records of similar households, families, or persons from different surveys. How similar the matched households are often depends on the purpose of the match. The general procedures for statistical matching begin with the determination of the variables that are coincident to both the host and donor databases. These coincident variables form the basis for the match. Examples of some common coincident variables include sex, age, marital status, state of residence, and total income.

The analyst decides which coincident variables are most important in performing a match. For example, if the purpose of the matched file is to analyze women's fertility issues and the donor file contains variables not on the host file that are critical to this analysis, sex would obviously be an important matching variable.

The match begins with the definition of a function, sometimes called a distance or difference function, which specifies the variables that will form the basis of the match. Each variable is assigned a penalty value, and the purpose of the function is to minimize the sum of penalty values between records on the host and donor databases. When this sum is minimized, two records are matched to one another, essentially adding all of the desired variables from the donor database to the host database.

In some cases, the penalty values assigned to variables may be infinite. In other words, if two records on the host and donor files do not match on a variable with an infinite penalty value, that particular records match is rejected. Such would be the case in the previous example for the sex variable: an algorithm would not match a male record from the donor file to a female record on the host file under any circumstance.

The value of statistical matching is that if there are a number of donated variables that are of value to the analyst, one can be sure that they are at least consistent with one another. And if the coincident variables are also numerous, thus minimizing the penalty value on which the individual record matches are based, one can have some confidence in the consistency of the donated variables with the host variables.

Statistical matching, however, is not widely used, and there are no examples of such matching in this volume. Part of the reason for this is that it can be expensive. If both databases are extremely large, convergence to minimum penalty values can be very computer intensive. On the other hand, if either the host and donor sample sizes or the number of coincident variables are small, the procedure can result in matching two records with very high penalty values.

For these reasons, among others, most microsimulation model developers have used statistical imputation procedures to link donor and host databases. The principles underlying imputation are not dissimilar to those underlying statistical matching. A set of coincident variables on both donor and host databases is identified and used to generate estimates of the donated variables to assign to records on the host database.

These estimation procedures range from the very simple to the very complex. Simple imputations might involve bivariate cross-tabulations from a donor database, which are then used to assign mean values of a single donated variable. More complicated imputations might involve the simultaneous imputation of several continuous donor variable values to a host database using advanced econometric models.

Statistical imputation has several important advantages to microsimulation modelers. First, it is efficient. Once an imputation equation or methodology has been developed on the donor database, a simple algorithm will assign the donated variable values to the host records, using a minimal amount of computer time. In addition to being inexpensive, imputation also lends itself better to updating than either exact or statistical matching. Second, imputation functions based on statistical techniques such as regression provide a virtually infinite set of donated variable values. That is, unlike statistical matching, the imputed variable values are not restricted to only those observed on the donor file: estimation allows us to fill in the blanks. Finally, imputation often allows analysts to take advantage of methodological developments in statistics and econometrics that are continually being developed at academic research centers and that often permit us to overcome data deficiencies.

Nearly every model described in this volume includes a number of statistical imputations. The variety of donor databases used for these imputations is considerable, and in some senses the validity of many of these simulations is dependent upon the quality of the imputation procedures. The chapters included here provide ample evidence of the resourcefulness of microsimulation model developers, who are constantly attempting to enhance our ability to understand economic behavior in the household sector through the clever integration of data from multiple sources.

TIMELINESS

Since a major function of microsimulation is to provide policymakers with information they can use to evaluate alternatives during their deliberations, timeliness is an issue of great concern. A timely result, however, depends both on particular aspects of timeliness and on the purposes for which microsimulation results are needed.

Time is a factor in microsimulation in a number of different ways, depending on whether one focuses on the time it takes to set up or convert a model for analytic use, or to generate results on the computer, or to analyze the results and generate a report. These stages in producing an analysis are not of equal length. Each stage can vary greatly in the time that is required, but on average, more time is required to get the model ready than to run the model or to analyze the results.

The first step in most analyses is to set up the model so that it accurately represents the system to be analyzed. This may require as little as changing a few parameters or as much as writing large sections of new code to specify the nature of programs being included for the first time. In either case, the model is not actually executed until the analyst and the programmer believe that it is ready, at which time they begin the process of checking the output to see if the model ran successfully. *Success* in this case refers to whether the model computed the transfers correctly in a programmatic sense, not simply whether it compiled and ran. If the model did not run successfully, the analyst and programmer make further modifications, rerun the model, and reexamine the output. Only when the examination shows that the model has run successfully can the analyst confidently begin to prepare a statement of results.

Since one can loop through "modify, check, modify, check, . . . " for a long time, a modeling environment that facilitates development of clear, understandable models can contribute substantially to reducing the total time it takes to complete an analysis. Several features that facilitate clear and understandable models are: (1) good documentation, (2) use of a programming language that is easy to read, (3) checking for internal errors and consistency, (4) good diagnostics, (5) support of modules that can be independently tested and linked, and (6) extensive use of parameters that can be set without changing the code. Chapters 2 and 3 in this volume discuss these and other approaches to efficient modeling.

Finally, the importance of timeliness depends on the kind of analysis that is being done, which is often related to whom it is being done for. Analyses of legislative proposals are often requested to be produced in weeks or days, sometimes even hours. On the other hand, analyses for private organizations, academic researchers, and other "third parties" may have time frames of multiple months. Internal analyses to explore the ramifications of alternative designs for social programs can often be virtually open ended, but then again, they may be needed the next day.

Evaluating the "timeliness" of models is not a simple matter, and the issue arises in several chapters in this volume. Webb, Michel, and Bergsman, in chapter 2, point out that in terms of response to legislative initiatives it was critical for TRIM to be replaced by TRIM2.

The authors contend that if TRIM, as opposed to TRIM2, had been the only model available to The Urban Institute when it was asked to evaluate the tax reform proposals in 1985, the analysis could not have been done on time. But even TRIM2 had a somewhat mixed record: in the case of tax reform, TRIM2 was able to provide results when needed, but in the case of the welfare bill proposed in 1987 by Representative Harold Ford of Tennessee, had the deadline for the analysis not been delayed several months, even TRIM2 might not have been able to deliver the analyses needed. TRIM2 successfully responded in both of these cases, but the successes resulted from correctly anticipating needed analyses, on the one hand, and unexpected delays, on the other. Thus, even the improved coding and documentation in TRIM2 has not led to a modeling system that can always respond in cases where time is of the essence.

Whereas chapter 2 focuses on getting a model ready to run, Zedlewski, in chapter 4, provides insight into the problem of actual run time, a considerable concern for those interested in dynamic (longitudinal) models. Zedlewski points out that the earlier version of DYNASIM could take from 4 to 12 hours to complete a single year's projection. DYNASIM2, on the other hand, can project the next year's population in all of its detail, taking only 7 to 11 minutes per year. These reductions, ranging from a factor of 30 to a factor of 70, are truly impressive, but even at 9 minutes per year, a 40-year analysis would still take 3 hours. For many research projects, this amount of time would not be trivial.

Although several factors may have led to the development of Anderson's Macroeconomic-Demographic Model (MDM) of the Retirement Income System, described in chapter 7, the result is a model that he characterizes as running quickly, although MDM's speed relative to that of DYNASIM2 is not clear. As in the case of DYNASIM2, the basis for MDM's speed appears to be the method used for aging the population and for aligning other characteristics by using results from macroeconomic analyses. Anderson justifies the development of MDM in part on its speed and reduced expense of operation, compared to microsimulation models that rely solely on record-by-record manipulation of the database.

Another way in which models have evolved to provide detailed results in a timely fashion has been the trend toward specialization and the development of special purpose models. Although these sound like similar issues, they have different origins and effects. What they have in common, however, is that they both facilitate the production of timely results.

By *specialization* we mean the elaboration of a general model to handle a special function. One example of this occurs in the case of the differentiation that has developed between TRIM2 and MATH. After the creation of the MATH model, for example, there was a fairly early concentration of efforts on using that model to carry out analyses of the Food Stamp Program. In part, this may have been the result of funding availability at the time, but the effect has been that the analysts using MATH developed a comparative advantage in the food stamp area. The advantage appears to derive from the development of databases tailored to the specific needs of food stamp analyses. This specialization, or division of labor, between MATH for food stamp analyses and TRIM2 for Aid to Families with Dependent Children (AFDC) analyses, is detailed by Webb, Michel, and Bergsman in chapter 2.

Another kind of specialization is represented by the experience in Canada, where two different and complementary modeling systems have been developed: one for "example generation" and the other for "cost and clientele estimation." The example generation model, MAPSIT, is used to achieve understanding of the combined effects of linked or interrelated programs. The analyses may be of a single system of programs or comparisons between the system representing the status quo and a system that includes a proposed change. MAPSIT's speed in generating results is illustrated in an incident in Canada in which a cabinet member, during a coffee break in a cabinet meeting, phoned an analyst with a request for several analyses, based on different assumptions than had been used in prior work on an income support proposal. The necessary solutions and tables were generated and the changes needed in the bill were identified and provided to the cabinet member before the end of the coffee break.[16] Not all analyses can be done that quickly, but MAPSIT, as an example generator, illustrates the speed that special purpose modeling systems can provide.

In chapter 3 by Morrison, timeliness surfaces through the use of MAPSIT as an example generator, but it is clear that MAPSIT is able to be responsive in part because of its clear code. One of the uses found for MAPSIT in Canada is that of training new policy analysts; the user interface for MAPSIT is sufficiently readable that the listed version of the code, which sets out the logical structure of the various transfer programs, has been used to train analysts in the operation of those programs.

The construction of special purpose models, on the other hand, appears to be driven less by the needs of developing special databases and more because existing models have failed to solve the problems at hand and because they are controlled by other organizations or agencies. In addition, special purpose models are built when it is faster to build a model that focuses on a specific problem than to enlarge the problem domain of an existing model to include the new problem. The KGB (Kasten, Greenberg, and Betson) model, discussed in chapter 2, is the premier example of this strategy at work.

When special purpose models are built, however, the bad news is the same as the good: the only problems they may address well are the special problems they were created to analyze, but unless the models are maintained carefully, which they often are not, they will become obsolete even before the problem ceases to be of interest. As soon as the creators are no longer actively engaged in the use of those models, the models are likely to fall into disuse. Again, this was essentially the case with the KGB model.

What is the lesson to be learned? That models, whether general or special purpose, are more likely to be worth their investment if they are well documented, if they are easily modified (to keep abreast of current program configuration), and if the costs of maintenance are not too high. One way to control costs appears to be to keep the analyst close enough to the model so that the number of people needed to update the models and to generate results can be reduced.

Still another aspect of time—the time it takes to get a database ready for use—is raised by Doyle and Beebout in chapter 8. Some of the problems they describe may be solved by a sufficient lead time, whereas others are problems for which only redesign of aspects of the survey would provide a good solution. In either case, database preparation has a major impact on timeliness. It also plays a major role in validation.

VALIDITY

Another area in which microsimulation has been the object of considerable criticism concerns validity. How does one know whether the results obtained are accurate? The problem of assessing validity is made difficult because of the various ways in which inaccuracies can occur. Sargent (1985) suggests that model validation requires attention to three different aspects of modeling: conceptual model validation, computerized model verification, and operational validation.

Conceptual validation refers to the manner in which the model is specified. Are the relations correct? Is the temporal sequence correct? Are the behavioral relationships properly specified? *Computer verification* refers primarily to the manner in which the program is written. Do the operations specified in the microsimulation accurately reflect the intent of the programmer and analyst? Finally, *operational validation* comes closest to what many observers would view as the crux of validation, whether the model produces output that accurately describes the state of the world simulated by the model. Demonstrating operational validity is often impossible, since the simulations typically refer to unobserved or unobservable states of the world, but in some circumstances tests can be devised that lend increased (or decreased) credibility to the simulation results. Such tests include the use of earlier data to establish the starting conditions and then letting the model estimate subsequent events to test whether the predictions are consistent with the actual outcomes.

Andrews et al. (1987) suggest still a fourth area of concern with model validation, concern with the validity of the input data. This concern, which Andrews et al. also credit to Sargent (1985), involves the accuracy of the initial database and modifications to that database, including matches, imputations, and aging.

None of the chapters in this volume addresses all of these aspects of validity, but most address some of them. Several chapters discuss problems of validity of the database, and some document in considerable detail the manner in which a particular database has been constructed, modified, and used. A surprising characteristic of these papers, however, is the relative absence of discussion of conceptual validity.

The lack of discussion of conceptual validity may result from the fact that most of the simulations discussed are static rather than dynamic. Dynamic modeling focuses one's attention on the nature of the assumed relationships. Even static modeling, however, often requires that one age the database, which explicitly or implicitly requires use of a conceptual model. If the aging is done by adjustments based on a set of known, aggregate values, then the conceptual model involves assumptions about independence or limited dependence of various variables. If the aging is done dynamically, then the model either requires an explicit statement about the manner in which events are related or implicitly assumes that events which are not linked are not related. In aging the database, however, the tendency seems to be to focus attention on the database, rather than on the conceptual model underlying the modifications.

Even in the case of static models, the situation is not so simple as it might seem. If the database did not require aging, would the problem be reduced to a simple accounting relationship? Could one directly calculate the effect of a programmatic change? The answer defies a simple yes or no; it depends on whether the policy being examined is likely to produce significant behavioral responses that go beyond those incorporated in the model. For example, when changes were made in the purchase requirement for the Food Stamp Program, the work done with MATH was reasonably successful in projecting the number of participants. On the other hand, if a new program were constructed or a program were extended to a population currently not eligible for it, it seems obvious that one would be hard pressed to justify confidence in the estimation of participation.

Among the authors in this volume who raise issues related to conceptual validity, Webb, Michel, and Bergsman, in chapter 2, for example, argue that microsimulation models such as TRIM and TRIM2 are better at producing relative rankings of the costs of programs than they are at estimating the exact costs of programs.[17] Haveman and Lacker (1984) suggest that these models are also better at costs than they are at participation. Although it seems perfectly appropriate to acknowledge the strengths and weaknesses of various models, to do so also raises the question of why a model works better for one type of prediction than for another, a problem still not resolved. The question also arises as to whether these general characterizations of the results of microsimulation are true of the current versions of these models.

Regarding operational validity, it is obviously impossible to evaluate predictions about the future from the vantage of the present, but several approaches can be taken. Haveman and Lacker (1984) suggest three methods: (1) calibrating the model for an earlier time period and running the model so that one can compare estimated characteristics with currently observed characteristics, (2) running the model with varying assumptions and parameter values, and (3) analyzing the assumptions and procedures within the model. This third alternative is essentially the same as addressing the question of conceptual validity.

None of these approaches has seen extensive use in the microsimulation area, although the first strategy has been used in a few cases (Betson, Bolton, and Chernick, 1986; Chow, 1977; Kormendi and Meguire, 1988). Haveman and Lacker (1984) follow the third strategy. We know of no examples of extensive or systematic use of the second strategy. The dearth of sensitivity analyses is probably due to the cost involved and the time required. The realistic possibility that microsimulation may find its way to advanced microcomputers or personal workstations, however, holds promise for significant change in the salience of cost and time.

Each of the previous strategies is appropriate when attempting to validate a particular model. In situations where there are competing models, however, one may also possibly conduct comparative analyses. Where different organizations and agencies use different models, as is the case in Washington, D.C., this possibility seems quite useful. In the present volume, Kennell and Sheils (chapter 5) discuss differences between PRISM and DYNASIM; Anderson (chapter 7) compares the Macroeconomic-Demographic Model (MDM) and DYNASIM; and Morrison (chapter 3) comments on the similarities and differences between SIMTAB and TRIM. In comparing MDM and DYNASIM, Anderson concludes that the outcomes appear to have been fairly divergent, to the point that it was obviously bothersome to the analysts, but no data are provided as to the actual estimates or the magnitude of the differences. In comparing TRIM and SIMTAB, Morrison's comments are primarily of a structural, rather than operational, nature, due to the difficulties that would be encountered in applying both models to the same database.

Two other chapters point to another way of addressing the credibility of models, if not their validity. Morrison (chapter 3) cites the use of SIMTAB to provide a cross-check on the results obtained from MAPSIT. Since the programming and the general approach underlying SIMTAB are quite different from those underlying MAPSIT, the fact that the two models gave essentially the same results was considered reassuring. Again, however, the reader will not find data on the actual size of the discrepancies, nor any metric for the measurement of similarity of results.

Chapter 2 discusses the possibility that TRIM might be run on a personal computer (PC) at some point, which would make it possible for different analysts to check one another's work. The strong likelihood that microsimulation will be available on microcomputers opens up the possibility for substantially increasing the amount of validity testing that will be done, not only because such work on microcomputers is nearly free, but because more analysts will have access to the capabilities of performing microsimulation and because when the work is done in academic settings, there is less sense of impending deadlines to drive out all but the essential tasks.

The final issue of validity concerns the validity of the database. Database validity includes issues of sampling, imputation, matching, and aging. Concern with validity at this level is one of the strongest themes in this book. Kennel and Sheils, in chapter 5, provide extensive detail on how their databases were modified. Both this and chapter 7, by Anderson, are exemplary in their explication of the substantive assumptions and the processes used in these models.

In describing their procedures, Kennel and Sheils discuss the operations they follow for adjusting PRISM's predictions so that they align with estimates of corresponding properties from macroeconomic models. Zedlewski (chapter 4) also discusses time series adjustments to calibrate DYNASIM2. Neither Kennell and Sheils nor Zedlewski provides data on the discrepancy between the unadjusted projections and the benchmark to which they were adjusted, although in reference to these models, Anderson suggests that the adjustments are "small" or "minor."

The chapters by Zedlewski, Kennell and Sheils, and Anderson raise an interesting issue concerning the adjustment of the outputs of the model. To what extent should the modeler adjust the outputs to match predictions from macromodels even where the macromodels have their own issues of validity? Zedlewski argues that to be credible within the policy analysis community, the outputs must conform to the currently accepted projections. If that is true, and if the level of validity for those latter projections is itself debatable, it is easy to see why some analysts would argue for limited or weak interpretations of the microsimulation results: use of rankings of effects rather than specific numerical results. Although the issue is not resolved, Zedlewski's contention concerning credibility of results provides a cogent defense of the alignment process and a starting point for further discussion.

DESIGN

What constitutes good design depends on the context—on the purposes for which the model was built; on the goals of the user; and on where the analyst is located relative to the actual running of the model.

Up close, so to speak, good design requires a clear structure to the program and an efficient code; it requires readily accessible documentation that will make it possible for others to understand and modify the model later on. Stepping back a little, good design involves issues such as developing a system that will allow the critical problems to be addressed and that will produce answers within the time constraints. Stepping still further back, there is the question of whether the modeling package will allow one to analyze not only current topics of interest but the topics likely to be of interest in the future.

At the innermost level there is, or should be, a concern not just with the code as it is to be written but with the program as it is to be used. This means, for example, not only that the code should be well documented, but that the model itself should facilitate the documentation of work that is done. When an analyst uses the model, the output from the model should include not just the calculated output variables but also either a concise statement about the nature of the parameters, the assumptions, the dataset and the modifications that were made to the dataset or an accurate, up-to-date (i.e., specific to the current analysis) reference of where this material is to be found. "It takes too much time" is of course the classic answer given by the programmer who fails to provide documentation. The programmer knew what the code meant when it was written and what the assumptions and parameter values were when the analysis was generated, but these things are seldom obvious to others, nor long remembered even by the programmers.

Also at the innermost levels are the problems of providing good diagnostics, deciding how "friendly" to make the program, and determining whether and how to use modularity. For example: Should the user be able to build models of his or her own or merely use modules that have been built by others? And if the user is to interact with the program, how should the user interface be structured?

At the next level out is the fundamental question of whether the modeling package addresses the questions that need to be addressed: cost and clientele estimates, participation rates in specific programs, effects on work incentives, and so forth. Further, there is the issue of detail: does the model allow one to switch from annual to monthly accounting periods to allow examination of the phenomenon at the latter level? Does it allow modeling of specific programs at various levels of detail? For some analytic purposes, for example, one may want to model the federal personal income tax program as a function simply of earnings, and at other times to model the calculation of personal income tax down to the level of each of the components of specific schedules. Does one want the analyst to be able to choose the level of detail appropriate for the current problem and the current database?

Other considerations at this middle distance involve flexibility with regard to the independent and dependent variable(s). There are times when the set of interesting dependent variables includes more than the number of units affected and the number of dollars transferred. Dependent variables such as the percentage of day care costs that are subsidized and independent variables such as the ratio of the secondary earner's income to the primary earner's income are also of interest in specific instances. One of the choices that must be made in designing a software system is whether to provide for this type of flexibility within the system or simply to permit the export of files into spreadsheet programs and other postsimulation, analytic packages.

At the farthest remove from day-to-day work with the models is the question of the problem domain for the model. Should the model be a model-building package in which the analyst can model different types of programs? Or should the analyst be restricted to picking from the set of programs that is "hard-wired" into preexisting modules? At one extreme is the program that is written from the top down and does one thing; woe be to the analyst who wants to solve a different problem. At the other extreme is the approach that assumes that the analyst will want to build different models with varying levels of detail over a wide range of problems. Obviously there are intermediate positions. One of these provides relatively fixed, but highly parameterized, modules and allows the analyst to choose appropriate subsets of the modules. An alternative position provides basic modules or submodels and allows the analyst not only to choose but also to modify the submodels as desired, while retaining the base model in an unaltered state in a system library.

This issue of modifying models versus building new ones is complicated further in that in building "new models," substantial portions of prior models may be used. In building the KGB model, for instance, much of the basic structure of TRIM was used, even though major new pieces were added. In this volume, Anderson (chapter 7) describes a model called HEPIM (Household Energy Price Impacts Model), which uses some of the methodology of HITSM. If large portions of previous code are being adopted and if the portions that are adopted have developed credibility within the policy community, the strategy would appear to be efficient and should prove useful. To the extent that the portions adopted are not separately identifiable or do not have a proven track record, however, such adaptation may prove less successful. In addition to the credibility of the prior code, however, a critical issue is how well the new or modified model is documented.

TRIM2 provides a good example of several aspects of the issue of model modification. Two aspects of the philosophy guiding the development of TRIM2 have been to provide modules that the analyst can turn on or off in focusing on different problems and to provide modules that make extensive use of parameters so that the analyst can evaluate different forms of the basic programs. Even with regard to new programs, such as programs for long-term care, it is relatively straightforward to construct new modules that interact with the basic TRIM2 model, although the programming and testing can still involve nontrivial amounts of time. On the other hand, if one wanted to analyze issues that involve longitudinal data (for example, pension issues that require earnings histories), the amount of restructuring and programming that would be needed in TRIM2 would be substantial.

Issues of design feature prominently in several chapters in this volume. Chapter 2, by Webb, Michel, and Bergsman, makes clear that in the development of TRIM2 considerable attention was given to design issues: documentation, parameterization, efficiency, table generation, and, in general, "good programming techniques." Similar concern is found in Morrison's description of MAPSIT and SIMTAB (chapter 3) and in Zedlewski's description of DYNASIM2 (chapter 4).

These issues of how broad, or flexible, or detailed a modeling package should be are not issues for which there are right or wrong answers. The choice to provide more breadth, or more flexibility, or more detail comes at a cost. The purpose here is not to attempt to resolve these issues of design but merely to highlight them and to suggest that the design questions raised will have a major impact on future development of software systems for income transfer analysis.

Notes

1. The models represented in this volume are more representative of the current models for welfare analyses than for taxation analyses.

2. These models use detailed sets of prototypical households or families, usually defined by income or earnings levels, to describe the effects of policy changes. Perhaps the most common example of this kind of analysis occurs when a proposal to change income taxes is made. Usually, the daily newspapers contain a table showing how individuals and families at various income levels would be affected by the proposal. These tables are the result of a simple form of simulation. MAPSIT and its predecessors

are more elegant and complex versions of this approach. For a more complete description of this approach and its uses and outcomes, see Lewis and Morrison (1987).

3. This "underreporting" may occur for many reasons, such as individuals forgetting that they received a benefit or underestimating the amount that they received, or it may result from sampling problems, since the low-income population is often difficult to survey.

4. See Orcutt et al. (1961).

5. It is, of course, also possible to build simulations of the business sector using surveys of firms and establishments. Efforts to do this are now underway in the United States and Canada, but no complete documentation on these efforts currently exists.

6. For the record, some supply-side theorists now argue that they never said revenues would increase sufficiently to eliminate short-run deficits, but, rather, that savings would increase to absorb the increase in the debt.

7. For example, the PRISM system uses exogenous control totals on an annual basis to determine the distribution of demographic characteristics. This contrasts with a fully dynamic model such as DYNASIM or MICROSIM in which the distribution is first determined by the endogenous equations and adjusted to controls only if the endogenous results are far off.

8. For a description of the initial sample, see the introduction in Morgan et al. (1974).

9. Many of the behavioral algorithms in DYNASIM and other dynamic models are based on analyses from the PSID, however.

10. This was the last public-use sample available that included a match with Social Security Earnings Records. Another match was attempted in 1978 but was felt by the government to be unsuccessful and was not released publicly. Since then, increased concern about the privacy of individuals has severely inhibited the government's activities in the exact match area. Some government administrators have indicated that they do not ever expect another exact match to be created.

11. This matched file was not made available publicly but was created as part of ICF's work for President Reagan's Commission on Pension Policy.

12. The exception to this generalization is the MAPSIT model, which, as noted earlier, is not survey-based but relies on a synthetic dataset of prototypical families.

13. This, of course, ignores the issue of illegal nonfilers, such as tax evaders.

14. As noted earlier, even this match was not available to the general community of users but was available to ICF because of contract work the organization was doing for President Reagan's Commission on Pension Policy.

15. There is the additional possibility that privacy concerns will prevent any future exact matches from being released to the research community.

16. Lewis and Morrison (1987), p. 242.

17. This was also suggested in the report by the U.S. General Accounting Office (1977).

References

Andrews, Richard, William Birdsall, Frederick Gentner, and W. Allen Spivey. 1987. "Validation Methods for Microeconomic Simulation." Graduate School of Business, University of Michigan, Ann Arbor. Photocopy.

Betson, David, Roger Bolton and Howard Chernick. 1986. "Review Panel's Report on the MRPIS Project." Working Paper. Department of Economics, University of Notre Dame, South Bend, Ind.

Chow, George. 1977. "Comparison of the SSI Portion of the MATH PBLAST (Mathematica) Module and the TRIM SSI (Urban Institute) Module." Working Paper. U.S. Department of Health and Human Services, Office of the Assistant Secretary for Planning and Evaluation. Washington, D.C.: Urban Institute.

Haveman, Robert H., and J. M. Lacker. 1984. "Discrepencies in Projecting Future Public and Private Pension Benefits: A Comparison and Critique of Two Micro-Data Simulation Models." Report SR-36, Institute for Research on Poverty. Madison: University of Wisconsin.

Kormendi, Roger, and Philip Meguire. 1988. "Dynamic Validation of the TRIM Welfare Simulation Model." Paper prepared for the U.S. Department of Health and Human Services, Office of the Assistant Secretary for Planning and Evaluation. Ann Arbor: School of Business Administration, University of Michigan.

Lewis, Gordon H., and Richard J. Morrison. 1987. *Income Transfer Analysis*. Washington, D.C.: Urban Institute Press.

Morgan, James N., Katherine Dickinson, Jonathan Dickinson, Jacob Benus, and Greg Duncan. 1974. *Five Thousand American Families: Patterns of Progress—An Analysis of the First Five Years of the Panel Study of Income Dynamics*, vol. 1. Ann Arbor: Survey Research Center of the Institute for Social Research, University of Michigan.

Orcutt, Guy, M. Greenberger, J. Korbel, and A. Rivlin. 1961. *Microanalysis of Socioeconomic Systems: A Simulation Study*. New York: Harper and Row.

Sargent, R. G. 1985. "An Expository on Verification and Validation of Simulation Models." In *Proceedings of the 1985 Winter Simulation Conference*, edited by D. Gantz, G. Blais, and S. Solomon, 15–22.

U.S. General Accounting Office. November 1977. "An Evaluation of the Use of the Transfer Income Model—TRIM—to Analyze Welfare Programs." Report to Congress. Washington, D.C.: U.S. Government Printing Office.

Chapter Two

THE HISTORICAL DEVELOPMENT OF THE TRANSFER INCOME MODEL (TRIM2)

Randall L. Webb, Richard C. Michel, and Anne B. Bergsman

WHY DO MICROSIMULATION?

Computer systems that model economic behavior have become an integral part of the decision-making process in both the business and public sectors. The most widely known of these model types is the macroeconomic model, which is used by such prominent organizations as Data Resources, Wharton Econometrics, and the Congressional Budget Office (CBO) to forecast elements of the U.S. economy. Macroeconomic models rely on aggregate data as a basis for making inferences about economic events. Frequently, these inferences are based on complex multivariate regression analyses and can involve the solution of systems of simultaneous equations.

However, macroeconomic models represent a conceptual dilemma for many microeconomists because the behavior of basic decision-making units within the economy (either firms or individuals) is not well represented by aggregate data. As a result, a family of models known as microeconomic models has been developed that attempts to portray the decisions of individuals or firms, generally in response to changes in exogenous factors. These models have their foundation in data that are collected at the decision-making level, that is, either the firm or the individual household, family, or person.

Microeconomic models generally were developed to move the computational algorithms closer to the decision unit. After all, an unemployment rate in the macroeconomy is not "decided upon" by any person or organization; it is, rather, the summation of the decisions of firms to create or abolish jobs and the decisions of individuals to enter or leave the labor force or to accept new positions or leave existing ones. A microeconomic model using individual-level data allows the analyst to observe or to estimate behavior directly, rather than to infer it from trends in summary statistics.

Micromodels are, of course, not a perfect substitute for macromodels. One major problem is that no existing database contains a complete and detailed description of the economic characteristics of even a representative sample of firms or individuals in the U.S. economy. Thus, to obtain a comprehensive profile of the characteristics of individuals, it is necessary to create synthetic or simulated variables.

The family of micromodels has many members, ranging from those that attempt to represent the entire economy in a general equilibrium framework to those that focus on only a small sector.[1] This chapter describes the development of three generations of one member of the latter subset of micromodels, a simulation model now known as TRIM2 (the Transfer Income Model, Generation 2). The general purpose of TRIM2 is to simulate the system of government taxes and transfers at the household or family level. The modeling process uses a rich but incomplete set of income and demographic elements on a national household database to create simulated variables. The variables that require simulation are either not well represented on the database or are not on it at all. TRIM2 focuses almost entirely on simulating variables related to income, taxes, or cash and in-kind benefits.

The demand for simulated transfer data by the federal government developed in tandem with the expanding governmental role in redistributing income in the post-World War II period. In the decades after the New Deal, and continuing through today, federal, state, and local governments set up a wide variety of programs to provide cash or in-kind assistance to various persons judged to be in need.[2]

As an outgrowth of President Lyndon Johnson's War on Poverty, the federal government began to consider ways to coordinate the programs that existed in the 1960s. In 1968, the president appointed a Commission on Income Maintenance Programs, one of whose tasks was to document the existing programs and the extent to which benefits from those programs helped alleviate poverty. The commission staff discovered that aggregate program data did not provide answers to some critical questions in determining whether and how much the income transfer system needed revising. In particular, there was little information on the receipt of multiple kinds of benefits by individual families. It was thus impossible to assess whether the collective support provided by various levels of government was being efficiently targeted and, if so, whether that support was sufficient to support the family. In 1969, the staff thus began to develop a new model to simulate the data it needed on an existing database that already provided rich details on many demographic and some income characteristics of U.S. households. The new model was intended to improve the understanding of the joint distribution of federal income taxes and federally funded transfers and to allow the commission to consider the potential cost and distributional impact of alternatives to the current system (McClung, 1970). It was the beginning of an odyssey that two prominent analysts later called "dreams in search of data."[3]

In the nearly two decades since then, the number of such simulation models has grown, and each model has taken a somewhat different course of development.[4] Surges in development have frequently been related to policy interests or initiatives, either pending or planned, at a sponsoring agency or foundation. The development of the models has therefore been constrained by the time available before the information was needed by decisionmakers as well as by more traditional financial constraints. Each successive policy initiative also demands increased detail over the previous effort. Thus, model developments have occurred not only in response to the need to simulate the cost and income distributional effects of specific new proposals but also to satisfy the desire for more detailed information on the impacts of existing programs on, for example, regional and demographic subgroups of families and individuals.

This chapter focuses on software advances and how they have interacted with policy needs and other user demands during the evolution of the TRIM2 model in the past two decades. Early in the development of this family of models, both analysts and programmers recognized the need for a generalized software framework within which substantive microsimulation software could be developed and run. The chapter pays particular attention to the requirements of such a software framework, to the approaches taken by the TRIM family of models in meeting these requirements, and to the importance of an institutional commitment to developing and maintaining such a framework even in the face of strong demands from policy initiatives for quick-turnaround estimates. The chapter begins by describing the antecedent of TRIM and TRIM2, the RIM model, in the 1960s and early 1970s, moves on to a discussion of the use of TRIM during the 1970s, and ends with the development of TRIM2 in the early 1980s.

POLICY ANALYSIS IN THE LATE 1960s: RIM

The RIM (Reforms in Income Maintenance) model was first designed and programmed for the President's Commission on Income Maintenance Programs in the summer and fall of 1969 (Wilensky, 1970). The commission used it to simulate various universal income-conditioned transfer programs that were being considered as alternatives to the existing welfare programs. The model also simulated payroll tax and federal income tax liabilities. This was "the first time that transfer cost estimates were produced for extensive economic, demographic subgroupings of the population in this country."[5]

In the winter and spring of 1970, the model was extended to simulate the administration's Family Assistance Plan (FAP), the initial U.S. House of Representatives version of FAP, and alternative proposals by Senators Fred Harris, George McGovern, Jacob Javits, and Charles Goodell. At that point, eligibility screens based on criteria other than income were introduced into the model. Further substantial modifications were made to the original model in the spring and summer of 1970 at the request of the Senate Finance Committee as it considered FAP, and RIM began awkwardly to simulate programs with different filing units. During the remainder of 1970 and through 1971, the FAP framework was extended further to incorporate proposals relating to food stamps, medical insurance premium payments, day care, and the 1971 House version of welfare reform contained in H.R.1. These simulations added complexity in filing unit definition and began to use state-specific benefit levels. Extensions to the model were also made to simulate proposals outside of the FAP framework, including an Urban Coalition package, various housing allowance proposals, and universal poverty line guarantee plans. The Urban Coalition package simulated 13 separate grant/tax program reforms in one pass of the file, severely straining the RIM structure and demonstrating the need for the flexibility to produce multiple simulations and the capacity to produce a large number of simulations efficiently, generally in a single pass of the file.[6]

A significant RIM development in January 1971 was the ability to use the 1969 Current Population Survey (CPS) file as well as the 1967 Survey of Economic Opportunity (SEO). The SEO was designed to provide data to address poverty-related policy issues. It contained particularly rich income data and oversampled the lower income strata, but by 1970 the data were four years old and were becoming less useful. The CPS was a somewhat less rich data source but had the major advantage of annual updating. Allowing RIM to use both files was achieved by reformatting the CPS into the SEO format. Thus originated the technique of using a common file format to extend the life of a model by allowing it to operate on new surveys as they become available.

The development of RIM was carried out at The Urban Institute under contract from the Office of Economic Opportunity (OEO) in the Department of Health, Education and Welfare (HEW),[7] with programming and computing responsibilities handled by The Hendrickson Corporation. RIM continued to be used at The Urban Institute through 1971. RIM was initially programmed on a CDC 3600 computer and later converted to a CDC 6600. TRIM was developed on IBM 360 computers, and all descendents of TRIM except for a UNIVAC version at the Treasury Department have continued to operate only on IBM mainframes.

The RIM model was used for about two years to simulate an impressive array of tax and transfer programs, but it had severe shortcomings of the kind that are frequently found in simulation models developed by a small group of people to meet immediate needs. The model suffered from inadequate documentation and lack of attention to the overall software framework. The following are excerpts from two contemporaneous evaluations of RIM.

It [RIM] was almost always used on a crash basis to cost out a particular plan. No work was done in between these crashes to improve the model, document it, or otherwise provide for its orderly development. As a result it became cumbersome to use as well as more expensive to modify. The cost per run grew with each modification. Because of a lack of adequate documentation, only two people were sufficiently experienced to implement changes to the model, and its reliability was questioned.[8]

The degree of generality embodied in the first version fell far short of satisfying later expectations for the model. No systematic method of defining filing units was built into RIM . . . An enormous number of decision rules must be set [sic] for a run such as H.R. 1 and it became more obvious that RIM had no simplified, general method of recording these decisions and relating them to others made in prior runs. Since the system lacked sufficient generality, each new request was typically programmed independently of prior requests . . . In retrospect, if any one thing is to be pegged as the reason for RIM becoming such an awkward monster, it would have to be the overeagerness of model users to place their resources into getting numbers in a hurry, rather than into achieving a higher quality system for producing those numbers.[9]

TRIM: A SOFTWARE FRAMEWORK FOR MICROSIMULATION

Out of the RIM experience came an improved understanding of the general software requirements for doing microsimulation. More important was the recognition of the need to invest the effort and resources to create a flexible, easy to use, well-documented software framework for microsimulation.

In August 1970 The Urban Institute decided to seek funding for development of a more satisfactory software framework for microsimulation, and a one-year contract was obtained from the Office of Economic Opportunity for $30,000 to deliver a new working model based on modifications to RIM. This initial effort was unsuccessful, but the institutional commitment continued, with HHS's Office of the Assistant Secretary for Planning and Evaluation (ASPE) providing an additional $50,000 and The Urban Institute providing almost $500,000 in internal funds over the next few years. Early in 1972 it was decided to abandon RIM completely and to develop an entirely new framework. That framework was TRIM, which was operational early in 1973 and was formally accepted by HHS/ASPE in June 1973.[10]

HHS/ASPE continued its institutional support for a microsimulation framework by awarding a one-year contract for "microsimulation maintenance" in 1974.[11] This was followed by a series of three-year contracts starting in 1975 at a level of approximately $200,000 per year. The Urban Institute has thus far won all of these competitive awards, whose contracts have called for maintenance, documentation, and further development of TRIM and for training ASPE staff in its use. These ASPE staff have developed considerable expertise in using the model and its output, but only a relatively small number of staff at ASPE and The Urban Institute have had sufficient experience with the model to actually set up runs or change the model.

The general functional requirements for a software framework for microsimulation were apparent in the evaluations of RIM and in the design of TRIM. These requirements are identified next, followed by more detailed discussion of the specific design requirements that derive from them.

□ Simulate a wide variety of tax and transfer programs, leading to the more specific requirement of modularity.
□ Simulate programs that use different filing units. Methods of defining filing units and other status indicators must be consistent both

across different parts of the model and over time, to allow the simulation of historical trends.

□ Allow examination of impacts on highly disaggregated population groups and accommodate the needs of diverse analytical questions. This requires use of a data file providing adequate sample size at the desired levels of disaggregation. This also requires recording of simulation results at the micro level and flexible tabulation capability.

□ Allow examination of alternative versions of a program and of the interactions among programs. This leads to the more specific requirement that it must be possible either to simulate multiple programs and multiple instances of a given program in a single run, or to pass data between runs, or, preferably, both.

□ Provide acceptably current estimates by using new surveys as they become available and by providing data-aging techniques. This and the previous requirement lead to the more specific requirement of a flexible common data file format that can be used for all surveys, to which variables can be added in a run, and that can be output from one run and input to a subsequent run.

□ Allow flexible specification of simulations, leading to the more specific requirement of extensive parameterization. Flexibility also requires that the computer code be easy to modify and to expand, to simulate new programs or make major changes in current programs.

□ Be understandable by analysts and programmers working with the model, with the results and methodology explainable and defensible to others. This requires excellent documentation of the methodology of the computer code and of the specifications of each run.

□ Provide quick enough turnaround of simulations to allow use in the heat of a policy debate. This requires ease of use, ease of modification, and execution efficiency. Ease of use is supported by parameterization and a user-friendly method of specifying parameters. Execution efficiency requires efficient code and an efficient file structure for handling the large data files used. Execution efficiency is also needed because of generally limited budgets.

□ Facilitate continual change to meet changing demands. This requires that the code be well structured, modularized, clearly written, and well commented, and that provision be made for error checking, debugging, and validation.

It should be noted that microsimulation modeling is essentially a data-processing task rather than a computational task. Complex data transformations and logical classifications and simple computations are performed on large quantities of data, and the results are summarized in various ways. Microsimulation almost never requires the solution of simultaneous equations or the evaluation of integral or differential equations, as might be required, for example, in a macroeconomic model or in the computer simulation of an oil refinery. Static microsimulation as represented by the TRIM family until now has also contained relatively few probabilistic determinations of behavior, as contrasted with dynamic microsimulation models such as DYNASIM, or discrete event simulations such as a computer model of the movement of shopping carts in a supermarket.

The general functional requirements just described were approached in TRIM via a number of design solutions that are discussed next.

Flexible Modular Structure

The flexible modular structure of TRIM and the ideas of extensive parameterization and of a flexible common file format for input and output are perhaps its most important and enduring characteristics. This structure of TRIM consists of a supervisor that controls a set of simulation modules or "master routines," each of which simulates a specific transfer program or performs a specific data transformation or input–output function. The user selects which master routines to execute in which order via parameters, thus allowing different programs or multiple instances of one program to be simulated in one run. Efficiency is served by executing only the master routines needed for a specific run. The flexible file structure allows runs to build on each other by passing variables from one run to the next via an output file. Internally within the model, all data about the current household, whether read from the input file or added by the master routines, are stored in a Family and a Person common block, allowing data to be passed from one master routine[12] to the next.

The ordered set of master routines to be executed in a run is called the "run sequence." The run is divided into three phases: initialization, processing, and summary. The supervisor repeatedly passes through the run sequence, calling each routine in turn. Each routine in the run sequence is called once for initialization. During the processing phase, the data for an entire household are read in, each master routine in the run sequence is called in turn to process that household, and the household is written to the output file, with the variables created by the master routines appended to the records. After all households have been processed, the run sequence is executed once more to allow the master routines to print their summary tables.

A general structure was designed for the master routines, in which each was modularized into sections for initialization, processing, and summary printing. A common technique was used for specifying parameters for the supervisor and for all master routines. This design allows new master routines to be added relatively easily and without disrupting the rest of the model. A user entry point is available to allow special-purpose or one-time programs to be included in a run.

Parameterization

Extensive parameterization was consistently cited as a design objective by the designers of TRIM, which used parameters to control most of the substantive aspects of the operation of the simulations and for overall control of the system. Parameterization allows the user to vary the simulation widely without recompiling the code, and is necessary to allow multiple simulations of the same program in a single run. Parameterization also initially promised to free the analyst from dependence on the programmer. However, policy proposals made in the U.S. Congress and elsewhere do not consider the problems of microsimulation and almost always manage to formulate some twist that cannot be handled by the existing parameters, so that programming changes are still frequently required.

A general method for defining system or program parameters was designed for TRIM. Each master routine had a number of parameters, with default values, so the user only had to specify those that differed from the default. Some parameters had defaults that varied by year. This feature was implemented in a number of ways: by an array of default values per year, by a separate block data subprogram for each year, or by a separate external file for each year. In part because the handling of parameters was not well standardized, this feature was not always implemented in an error-proof fashion. Each of the program simulation master routines could be called a multiple number of times, but there was usually an upper limit to the number of times a routine could be called in a single run.

Data File

The TRIM CPSEO common file structure was constructed to meet three goals: the ability to use new surveys as they became available (initially either the CPS or the SEO), the need to be able to pass data from one run to the next, and the need for an efficient file format. The CPSEO file structure consisted of a mapping strategy so that whichever file was used, a variable with the same name had the same codes. A common set of required data fields was identified—these variables had the same names and the same codes. Other useful variables were appended to the core set from each file.

Actually, the CPSEO consisted of two file formats—a character file format designed to make the data available to other researchers and a binary file format for efficient use in TRIM. At the time of the TRIM design, Bureau of the Census files were fairly dirty. It was common practice to clean up whatever data file was being used while extracting the data necessary for one's model, and it was thought that outside researchers would be interested in the results of the CPSEO recoding/clean-up procedure. In fact, few outside researchers were interested in the character format CPSEO files, but many were interested in using TRIM simply as a way to read and write CPS files, while adding their own processing in between.

The binary file format was designed for more efficient processing within TRIM. Coded data items restricted to values less than 256 could be packed into one byte on the file. The file structure had a number of header records describing the file and the variables it contained. Thus, the structure was extremely flexible in that each file could contain a different set of variables. This basic design has held up well for nearly 20 years of CPS files and has also been used with the 1970 Decennial Census Public Use File and the 1975 Survey of Income and Education (SIE) File.

The TRIM internal structure for the file data was less successful. It was a hybrid between a fixed structure and a flexible structure: variables in a core set were placed in fixed locations in common blocks, whereas simulation variables that were added could "float" in any free space. However, as more programs were added and as files were produced with many simulation variables, there was not enough free space because the core set included many variables not present on all files. A number of cumbersome features were added to circumvent this problem. The file structure could handle multiple occurrences of a given variable simulated by multiple executions of a master routine in a single run, but it was difficult to distinguish variables simulated in different runs.

Filing Units and Status Definitions

The desire for a single definition of status characteristics came from the fact that everything was computed "on-the-fly" in RIM. For example, the definition of a *child* for the same transfer program might be determined differently in different parts of the code. Thus there was a great desire to have prespecified definitions for each type of categorical eligibility. This gave rise to the "definer and status" routines, which were a type of preprocessing in TRIM, essentially setting up many categorical eligibility codes before the transfer programs were simulated. Consistency of status definition was generally implemented by creating status definer variables as part of the data preparation process and carrying these variables on the data files. MATH (described later in this chapter) subsequently implemented many status definers as FORTRAN functions that were executed whenever a definer was needed, thus trading off decreased file space for increased execution time.

One of the crucial uses of status definition variables was for defining filing units. Seven different "FLGUT" (pronounced "fligit") variables were created for defining units consisting of individuals, the whole household, families, and subfamilies, federal income tax filing units, and AFDC (Aid to Families with Dependent Children) or SSI (Supplemental Security Income) units. All seven FLGUTs and their subtypes were identified for each person in the household. Thus FLGUT3 might indicate that a person belonged to filing unit type 3 and that the unit was a subfamily. The FLGUT variables were the key to handling multiple filing unit types.

Documentation of Methodology and Self-Documenting Runs

The initial TRIM system documentation was impressive. It comprised three volumes: the *TRIM CPSEO Codebook*, the *TRIM Technical Description*, and the *TRIM Users Guide*, which were kept relatively up-to-date in the early days. In fact, both the *CPSEO Codebook* and the specifications contained in the *Technical Description* preceded the actual coding. TRIM itself, except for the supervisor, was coded directly from the specifications, which became the *Technical Description*. Only the *Users Guide* was prepared after the fact.

The *TRIM Technical Description* reflects the TRIM designers' attempt to create a "building block" structure of generalized components from which one could pick in setting up a simulation. In theory, one would choose a FLGUT type to define filing units, various status definers to determine eligibility, and various "tax" routines to compute taxes or benefits. In practice, this attempt at generality hid the fact that most of the definers and tax routines were very specific to a particular tax or welfare program. The *TRIM Technical Description* is organized by type of "building block" rather than by program being simulated, making it more difficult to understand specific master routines.

The *TRIM Users Guide* was organized by master routine, describing how to run each master routine and defining its parameters. The organization of the *Technical Description* and the formality of its specifications, combined with the splitting of the substantive description of individual master routines between the *Technical Description* and the parameter descriptions in the *Users Guide*, significantly reduced the usefulness of the impressive volume of the documentation.

The runs attempted to be self-documenting by printing all program parameters and file descriptions. Runs could be commented by text cards, which were also added to the output file. A later subgoal was to be able to print all yearly defaults in a given run if a switch was set, but this was implemented in only a few routines.

Efficiency

Efficiency was an important consideration in the early 1970s when computer costs were higher and computer resources more limited. The efficient file structure already described was one approach taken. Another approach was reducing memory requirements.

The aim was to lessen the number of runs by running several programs at the same time. However, the cost of runs would increase as the number of different programs loaded together increased, because cost is partially a function of the core needed to store the programs. The "virtual" operating system was not yet available, and TRIM was constantly pushing at the limits of available core. TRIM addressed these issues in several ways. First, only the programs actually used in a run would be loaded. An overlay structure was developed, so that the program code for different phases of the run would overlay each other, thus reducing the maximum core used in a run. Core was further reduced through use of a (permanent) workspace pool—each program requested blocks of space from the pool. The permanent workspace was typically used for program parameters for each simulation and for summary tables for each simulation. Different pool sizes were available, so that only the smallest size necessary would be loaded with the run. Temporary workspace came from another pool—each routine could use the same temporary space in any way it wanted. Temporary space was used for copies of the particular instance of the program parameters or for the computed variables before they were copied into the internal data structure.

Table Generation

Table generation was limited. Each master routine had hard-coded tables, with a few optional tables added later. The internal routine SUMTAB provided limited general-purpose table generation capability, and the external routine TROUT, which could read TRIM files directly, provided additional capability, but both were limited in flexibility and were difficult to use. The user entry point, TALLY, was also intended as a way to get special tabulations. Character data files could be produced by TRIM for tabulation in statistical packages, but this feature, too, was not easy to use. The complexity of the data structure, the multiplicity of filing unit definitions, and the wide variety of tabulations desired by analysts made it very difficult to provide a satisfactory flexible tabulation capability.

Good Programming Techniques

The success of any software system depends to a large extent on good programming techniques, among which are that code must be well structured, modularized, clearly written, and well commented, and that provisions must be made for error checking, debugging, and validation. These characteristics are particularly important in a microsimulation system that must be flexible enough to be changed continually.

The modular overall structure of TRIM, with a supervisor controlling a set of master routines and each master routine having sections for initialization, processing, and summary, was excellent and has continued to be used in TRIM2. Many operations common to many master routines, such as initialization, were handled in a consistent manner, frequently by commonly used subroutines. A utility routine library was provided. Attention was given at many points to error checking. Either all (or selected) variables for all (or selected) households could be printed at the end or at many points in the processing of the household for debugging purposes. Each master routine included debug prints that could be turned on or off.

However, the principles of structured programming were not yet widely recognized at that time, and all too frequently were violated in the design and coding of TRIM. Code was sometimes not modularized into manageable routines, and there were far too many instances of "spaghetti code"[13] and of code that was acceptably well-structured but was uncommented and not formatted for ease of reading. Some modules suffered from unplanned incremental development, resulting in unstructured code that was difficult or impossible to understand or validate.

Organization of Personnel

One of the reasons the first TRIM development effort failed was that the economists specifying the model were isolated from the analysts and programmers who were implementing those specifications. The computer personnel had lower status, no role in design, and an inadequate picture of the overall system. In the later, successful TRIM development effort, the computer staff was an integral part of the development team and contributed substantially to the design of both the software framework and the substantive simulations. This has continued to be the pattern in subsequent development of TRIM and TRIM2, and has contributed substantially to their success.

POLICY ANALYSIS IN THE 1970s: TRIM, MATH, AND CBO

As noted earlier, after the collapse of the Family Assistance Plan proposal in Congress in the early 1970s, the U.S. Department of Health and Human Services' Office of the Assistant Secretary for Planning and Evaluation (HHS/ASPE) continued its institutional commitment to the TRIM model. This commitment took two forms. First, as previously mentioned, HHS/ASPE awarded two successive contracts (1974–75 and 1975–78) to maintain and develop TRIM. Second, a core of economists and programmers within HHS/ASPE continued to run the model in-house to develop a welfare reform plan that would prove more politically acceptable than FAP.

The contracts, both of which were awarded to The Urban Institute, were designed to relieve HHS/ASPE analysts and programmers of the responsibilities for making routine changes to the model (such as annually updating benefit parameters) and for implementing major programming changes that required extensive testing and for which they had little time (such as programming a food stamp module). This arrangement seemed to work exceptionally well, and permitted HHS/ASPE analysts to develop a highly complex welfare reform proposal during 1974.[14]

The welfare reform proposal, called the Income Supplement Plan, relied heavily on simulations from TRIM to guide its development, particularly with respect to filing unit definitions and the level of benefit guarantees. The proposal was intended to be introduced during the final two years of the Nixon presidency but was sidetracked by the president's resignation in mid-1974. Nevertheless, key elements of the TRIM analyses became the basis for decisions made later when the Carter administration developed its two welfare reform proposals in 1977 and 1979.

The period from 1974 to 1975 was one of steady but not dramatic development in TRIM. For the most part, the developments corrected and made consistent the programming in the basic model. Some new substantive modules, such as one to simulate the new SSI program, were developed, but they relied largely on existing filing units and straightforward benefit calculations. In general, the changes that occurred during this period were subtle, and many were nearly invisible to analysts who were using the output of TRIM. After HHS/ASPE stopped working on the Income Supplement Plan in 1975, the TRIM model seemed to be headed for a period of relative disuse.

Two organizational developments in the mid-1970s changed the course of the development of the model and of microsimulation generally. The first occurred when a group of Urban Institute TRIM analysts was hired by Mathematica Policy Research (MPR), a policy research organization based in Princeton, N.J. MPR adopted TRIM and used it unchanged at first. As funding was obtained, the MPR version of TRIM was altered, and the model was renamed the Micro Analysis of Transfers to Households (MATH).[15] The entrance of MPR into the microsimulation field marked a major shift in the use of this technique during the late 1970s.

In the 1970s, The Urban Institute in general had significant support from private foundations and sole-source government awards. Government funding for research was plentiful, and the Institute often confined its fundraising to solicited grants and contracts. MPR's new MATH group, which was based in Washington, D.C., had no similar luxury and thus began an aggressive effort to market the MATH model. MPR met with considerable success, receiving development funds from such varied sources as the U.S. departments of Agriculture, Labor, and Energy as well as various states. Toward the end of the 1970s, in fact, the MATH model was a fixture in several government policy offices, and most of the substantive extensions of microsimulation techniques were being developed and implemented by MPR analysts.

The second institutional development that expanded the use of microsimulation in the 1970s was the founding of the Congressional Budget Office (CBO). Although the CBO's mandate from Congress was to advise it on budget issues, its director, Alice Rivlin, had a long-standing interest in the distributional consequences of legislative decisions. Under her direction, the CBO initiated projects to analyze not only overall budgetary costs of new proposals but their income and demographic distributional consequences as well. In 1976 and 1977, the CBO awarded contracts to MPR to, among other things, estimate the effects of using alternative definitions of income on poverty counts and to examine the cost and distributional impacts of a variety of welfare reform alternatives.[16] These analyses provided the CBO and Congress with a capability to replicate the kinds of extensive analyses that had previously been performed only for the executive branch of government. Ultimately, it was the CBO's cost and distributional analyses, not those of the executive branch, that became the standard by which legislative initiatives were judged.

The emergence of the CBO and MPR as major users of microsimulation had benefits that affected more than just those two organizations. For example, not only was The Urban Institute's TRIM model able to take advantage of improvements designed for the MATH model, but the visibility of the CBO analyses and the continued marketing and development efforts of MPR dramatically increased the demand for microsimulation of any program that affected persons or families. Microsimulation techniques both within and outside the TRIM and MATH frameworks were successfully applied to such disparate government programs as food stamps, unemployment insurance compensation, child nutrition benefits, housing allowances, energy credits, and state income taxes. Less successful attempts were made in the areas of social services, education, and medical insurance. Policy proposals in many of these areas were considered incomplete unless they contained a discussion of which groups would gain and which would lose as a result.

While MPR was successful in marketing MATH to a number of government agencies for development of a wide variety of programs, it did not have a funding source like that of the HHS/ASPE TRIM maintenance contracts to support the maintenance and documentation of the model or the further development of the software framework. To meet this need, MPR created a "MATH Users Group" for periodic users of microsimulation results to be kept informed of developments being funded outside their own agency. For an annual fee, an agency would receive a copy of the model, a complete set of documentation, quarterly updates of the code and documentation, and a limited amount of technical assistance. For a period, the MATH subscription service was quite successful, raising funds even from nonusers of the model. Even ASPE, which was generously supporting the TRIM model, had a subscription to MATH.

The Treasury Department began using its own version of TRIM in 1973 when The Urban Institute TRIM project director returned to the Office of Tax Analysis (OTA). The OTA wanted to use TRIM to supplement the in-house tax model (still in use today) in providing estimates for proposed federal income tax legislation. The Treasury Department contracted with The Hendrickson Corporation, which had handled the programming of TRIM, to convert TRIM to run on the department's UNIVAC computer. Gradually, the Treasury version concentrated on expanding the FEDTAX module, which was used instead of the tax model when proposals were made to expand the types of taxable income (types not on the tax model data file, which was derived from actual tax returns). TRIM was also used where family relationships were important in the proposed legislation, such as requiring information about taxable dependents. Because Treasury assisted HHS by providing estimates related to taxes, HHS assisted Treasury by having The Urban Institute write a conversion program to convert the yearly TRIM computational files from the IBM format to a format readable by the UNIVAC. This task was performed under the 1975 TRIM maintenance contract.

The Treasury Department's TRIM was linked to the Tax Model in another important way: the federal income tax units were statistically matched to those in the Tax Model data file. Thereafter, both models could use data from either file, although TRIM had more flexibility in the way it could retrieve data from either database, and it still had all the household relationships, which could not be represented in the Tax Model.

While the Treasury Department's version was expanding the FED-TAX module, the MATH Model was developing and expanding the food stamps module, FSTAMP. Treasury was a member of the MATH Users Group and regularly updated its model with selected software from the MATH model under a maintenance and support contract with The Hendrickson Corporation. The Treasury's TRIM then became a hybrid of the TRIM and MATH models.[17]

All of this activity created a boom of sorts in the microsimulation business, which helped support both the MATH and TRIM models and caused at least one other major research firm, the Stanford Research Institute (SRI), to begin a microsimulation development effort (later aborted).

This golden age of demand for microsimulation analyses left the models substantively much broader than they had been in 1973. But, as in the development of RIM, the pressure for quick turnaround of cost estimates and the rapidly expanding policy agenda to which the models were being applied left little time for clear-cut documentation or efficient and structured programming. By 1977, when President Jimmy Carter took office, no users of microsimulation results, including the CBO, actually had staff who knew how to reprogram the models, and thus the users were dependent upon analysts and programmers at either MPR or The Urban Institute to do so for them. This situation worried many officials in government policy offices, especially in HHS/ASPE, which had lost many of its former TRIM experts, for it meant that the government would be dependent upon the responsiveness of private contractors even during intensive periods of legislative activity.

KGB: ECHOES OF RIM AND BREATHING SPACE FOR TRIM2

The fear of dependence on private contractors was realized in 1977 when President Carter decided to embark upon a major welfare reform initiative and turned to HHS/ASPE to produce the official administration cost and distributional analyses in a short time frame. No analysts were left in HHS/ASPE who understood the then-existent TRIM model, which had been complicated by ad hoc developments since 1975. Furthermore, the current-law bias and rigidity of the TRIM structure did not seem to lend itself well to the innovative public-jobs-and-cash strategy favored by many policy officials within the administration. HHS/ASPE therefore decided that analysts within the agency would develop a model that could be run within HHS/ASPE for the official estimates. The result was the creation, over a period of about five weeks of intense work, of a new microsimulation model named KGB for its developers, Richard Kasten, David Greenberg, and David Betson.[18]

At the same time that KGB was being implemented, the HHS/ASPE project directors of the microsimulation contract embarked upon a strategy to make TRIM more user-oriented and more efficient by redesigning the model's software to be more adaptable when policy initiatives arose.

KGB was intended as a relatively simple model to be used in-house for a specific project. It used data files derived from TRIM and included simplified tax and transfer program simulations in addition to the jobs component. The model was heavily used and extensively modified, but there was never time for documentation or to develop a generalized software framework. Operating efficiency was also a problem; in fact, the model sometimes brought down the whole computer. KGB was usable only by its creators and their research assistants, and its use ceased when its creators left HHS/ASPE.

KGB was similar in many ways to RIM, in that it was developed by a few people for a specific purpose with little documentation and no consideration for software framework. It was not flexible and was usable only by the persons who created it. Its life span of roughly three years was also about the same as RIM's.

The KGB experience further echoes the RIM experience. TRIM was not used for the 1977 welfare proposal largely because it still exhibited some of the problems found earlier in RIM. TRIM was regarded as difficult to understand and to use. It had a flexible structure to facilitate modification, but its complexity and the difficulty of understanding much of the actual code inhibited understanding and modification. In fact TRIM, like RIM and KGB, could be effectively used and modified only by a relatively small group of people. TRIM was extensively documented, but the documentation was not easy to use and did not provide sufficient tutorial material for new users and analysts. TRIM also did not provide an adequate vehicle for the type of short-term, intense development required by the welfare reform effort.

In spite of the institutional commitment to TRIM represented by the continuing microsimulation maintenance contracts issued by HHS/ASPE, a key element of institutional commitment or involvement was missing. HHS/ASPE staff were not thoroughly familiar with the model and not fully capable of using and modifying it for a new policy simulation effort. This was due to three primary factors: the inherent difficulty in understanding such a model; the fact that TRIM did not yet meet the needed level of flexibility, documentation, and ease of use; and the fact that the tenure of government analysts is frequently less than the extended period of use required before a person can effectively use a model of this complexity.[19]

Even during the KGB period, ASPE's commitment to TRIM continued, and in 1978 a second three-year microsimulation maintenance contract was issued. This time, however, it included specific tasks calling for major improvements in the efficiency and usability of TRIM. The use of KGB rather than TRIM for the Carter welfare reform effort may have actually contributed to the development of

TRIM2, because, over the next two years, KGB absorbed the heavy day-to-day simulation work, providing breathing space for the development of TRIM2.

TRIM2: A MORE COMPLETE FRAMEWORK

The short-term success of the KGB model focused attention on technical flaws of TRIM and caused analysts at both HHS/ASPE and The Urban Institute to rethink the structure of the model. Although the TRIM framework for microsimulation was a major improvement over RIM, enduring to this day in the MATH model, it still had major shortcomings, most of which were echoes of RIM. The commitment of HHS/ASPE to maintain a framework for microsimulation continued, and the microsimulation maintenance contract awarded to The Urban Institute in 1978 called for major improvements to TRIM. A feasibility and design study was begun in fall 1978 and resulted in a design paper by Randall Webb in March 1979. Development work began in mid-1979, and TRIM2 was operational by the end of 1980.

The shortcomings of the original TRIM that were exposed by the KGB experience were concentrated in the areas of operating efficiency, ease of use by analysts, and ease of modification and development by programmers. The new maintenance contract recognized these problem areas and included tasks devoted to improving operating efficiency, improving printed output, and developing new kinds of output. The original design of TRIM2 responded by calling for three central features: interactive set-up of simulation runs, a more efficient data structure, and flexible, interactive manipulation and presentation of output. Three major support features would be required: a comprehensive data dictionary, standard methods for storage of parameter values and of summary output data from runs, and standardized procedures for initializing simulation modules. The design also called for adding the capability to store on one file and process in one run data aged for multiple years and economic scenarios. In addition to standardizing the initialization phase, the design called for a standardized format for all subroutines and enforcement of the principles of structured programming in the coding of all TRIM2 routines.

Only portions of this grand scheme were implemented, with interactive job set-up and interactive manipulation of output being the primary deferrals. TRIM2 consisted almost entirely of new code. The following are critical new features developed for TRIM2:

□ A new, flexible, and efficient structure for the data files and efficient routines for reading and writing that structure.

□ A central database, the Central TRIM2 Directory (CTD), in which are stored all variable definitions, all parameter definitions for all simulation modules, and default values for all parameters. It was envisioned that the variable directories of data files and the summary output from runs would also be stored in the CTD, but these features have yet to be developed.

□ Standard procedures for handling all types of parameters based on the CTD. All access to input and output microdata file variables is via parameters. Most of the processing of parameters during the initialization phase is handled by the supervisor. The initialization phase work for a simulation module, formerly representing as much as half of the code of a TRIM master routine, is almost completely automated, vastly simplifying the programmer's job.

The subsections following examine TRIM2's features in more detail, using the categories listed earlier in discussing TRIM. Note that in some categories there was great change, but that in other areas the TRIM design solutions endured.

Flexible Modular Structure

The basic TRIM structure of a supervisor calling a run sequence of simulation modules selected by parameters and the division of the run into initialization, processing, and summary phases were retained. Some of the restrictions in TRIM were lifted in TRIM2. The number of simulation modules in the run sequence and the number of times a given module can be executed in one run are limited only by the aggregate storage available. In recent years run sequences with more than 25 simulation modules have occurred with increasing frequency.

Parameterization

The processing of parameters was standardized and automated based on the CTD, and a free format was developed for entering parameters. All parameters for all simulation modules are fully defined in the CTD, including text documentation of each parameter. The following types of parameters are allowed: text, logical, integer, real, 8-character string (for using mnemonics for specifying options), and variable specifications. A parameter can have one value or an array of values. The array may be specified as having one or more values per state using the 56

"FIPS" state codes. A parameter can have a single default value or can have default values that vary by year. Default values are also stored in the CTD and indexed by year if so specified. Special sets of values for a given parameter can be generated, stored in the CTD, and referenced by name in a run.

In setting up a TRIM2 run, the user specifies values for any parameters that are not to take their default values. For parameters with yearly defaults, the year represented by the data file is used unless the user specifies that the defaults for another year are to be used. The supervisor routines handle the reading of the user parameter values, the fetching of default values, the storage of all parameter values internally, and the printing of all parameter values for run documentation purposes. When a simulation module occurs multiple times in the run sequence, the supervisor ensures that the parameter values for the different occurrences are kept separate. Within the simulation module, the parameter values are accessed by the common block "/TEMPRM/," which is reused by each module. During initialization, the module must establish the mapping of parameters into /TEMPRM/. The initialization phase code can be as simple as an array of parameter names and a call to the mapping subroutine, as compared with the many pages of code required in TRIM. In subsequent phases, the supervisor takes care of restoring the contents of /TEMPRM/ for each module in the run sequence.

In addition to simplifying the processing-phase programming chores and providing automatic run documentation of parameter values, the storage of parameters in the CTD also allows automated documentation of simulation modules, as discussed later in this chapter.

It should be noted that although the free-format TRIM2 parameters are far more user friendly than the fixed TRIM format, the mode of parameter specification is still essentially batch punched cards. Interactive set-up of jobs was not undertaken, but the groundwork for this development was laid.

Data File and Operating Efficiency

The new data file structure, along with the routines to process it, is certainly the single most important development in TRIM2 and is responsible for most of its efficiency gain and much of its increased flexibility.

Input/output costs were a substantial portion of the total costs of running TRIM, so that this area was the primary focus of efficiency efforts. It was noted that of the 200 to 400 variables on a CPS file, a range of only 20 to 80 are used in any given run, and many are rarely used. The design effort looked for ways to eliminate infrequently used variables from the file, to read from the file only those variables needed for a particular run, and to write out only variables created in the run. At the same time, the importance was recognized of easily retrieving any variable when it is needed. The solution was to allow the user to select which variables to write to the output file and to allow TRIM2 to read up to four files in parallel to provide access to variables that are on one file but not on another. Thus from the original 400 variables, an "active" file of perhaps 50 to 100 variables would be created and used for most runs. An output filo could consist ot the active variables from the input file plus newly created variables, or only the new variables. When necessary, the original full file could be read in parallel with the active file to retrieve additional variables, or the active file could be read in parallel with the file of new variables output from a previous run.

A number of other techniques were devised to improve the efficiency of the file. Each household is now stored as a single record to minimize the actual file accesses. Within the household, variables are stored by variable rather than by person or family to improve the movement of a selected set of variables from the record into the common blocks. Variables are compressed into one byte, four bits, or one bit whenever possible. Assembly language routines handle the transfer of data from the records to the common blocks.

An important new feature of the new file structure is that variables representing different years and different economic scenarios can be stored on the same file and that output variables created by different executions of the same simulation module can be easily distinguished. Each variable is identified by a four-part identification consisting of a variable name such as WAGES or FLGUT3, a simulation name identifying the particular simulation module execution that created the variable, the economic scenario, and the year.

Benchmark runs done in 1981 indicated that the cost of reading data from TRIM2 files was between 12 percent and 62 percent of the cost of an equivalent TRIM run. The variation depended primarily on the number of variables on the file and the number of variables actually read. Even when TRIM2 read from two files in parallel, the cost was only 50 percent of the TRIM cost.

Comparison of TRIM and TRIM2 costs for actual simulations is more difficult, because the substantive simulation modules in TRIM2 were generally very different from their TRIM counterparts. The

FEDTAX module did remain very similar across the two models for a time, and FEDTAX runs generally cost about 50 percent less in TRIM2. The AFDC module in TRIM2, on the other hand, was dramatically different from the equivalent TRIM public assistance module (PBLAST). Because TRIM2 AFDC used a monthly accounting period, it consumed more central processing unit (CPU) time. Thus, some of the increased input/output (I/O) efficiency of TRIM2 was used as an opportunity to do more complex simulations without raising costs.[20]

Filing Units and Status Definitions

Since many of the status definition variables were actually specific to a single simulation module, TRIM2 dropped many of these variables and made the status determinations at run time in the module. Most of the FLGUT variables were retained but were substantially reformatted.

Documentation of Methodology and Self-Documenting Runs

The TRIM2 documentation consists of three components. The *TRIM2 Reference Manual* describes the overall structure of TRIM2, the Central TRIM2 Directory, and the file structure, and also provides a tutorial in how to use TRIM2. This is a relatively stable document, with a few chapters revised each year. *TRIM2 Codebooks* contains the TRIM CPS codebook, which is revised yearly as each CPS is converted for use in TRIM2, and codebooks for any other surveys that are converted. Both documents are maintained on a word processing system.

The third document, the *TRIM2 Simulation Modules*, consists of two or more looseleaf binders with one chapter for each simulation module. An auxiliary program called MRDOC (pronounced Murdock) reads from the CTD, from stored text about the module, and from the comments in the actual computer source code for the module subroutines to produce the chapters of *TRIM2 Simulation Modules*. The text portion of the documentation of each module is maintained via a word processing system and describes the methodology, the structure of the module, and any special instructions for using the module. The automated system allows an up-to-date version of any chapter to be produced at any time.

TRIM2 maintains a number of automated activity logs, including logs of compilations of subroutines, of changes to the CTD, and of simulation runs. A second auxiliary program named MICRODOC documents individual household microfiles by reading the variable directory on the file, the variable definitions from the CTD, and the run history contained in the run log.

The automated documentation system is excellent for maintaining current documentation of parameters and their default values, but it still relies on manual effort to keep the text documentation current. The ASPE maintenance contracts have always included a documentation task, but this task frequently gets squeezed by the press of policy simulation work. We expect that there will always be a portion of the documentation of any microsimulation model that is not subject to automation, and that maintaining the timeliness of the documentation will continue to require constant effort by the individuals involved and the necessary commitment of resources by the sponsoring institutions.

Table Generation

TRIM2 has approached the problem of flexible table generation not by incorporating that capability into TRIM2 but by making it easy to export data for analysis in standard statistical packages, particularly Statistical Analysis System (SAS) and Table Producing Language (TPL). The XPORT module provides great flexibility in defining the filing unit to use as the unit of observation on the analysis file and in specifying the variables to be included. Files can be written in character or binary format. XPORT produces TPL codebooks or SAS INPUT statements and variable labels to make it easy to use the file in those packages.

Good Programming Techniques

Major emphasis was placed on good, structured-programming techniques. A standard style designed to be highly readable was adopted for FORTRAN code in TRIM2. Each subroutine has a standard prologue section of comments describing the purpose, input, and output of the subroutine. As mentioned earlier, portions of these prologues are automatically incorporated in the documentation of the simulation modules. This emphasis on programming style and techniques has made TRIM2 a much easier model to understand, maintain, modify, and extend.

POLICY ANALYSIS IN THE 1980s: WHAT HAS TRIM2 DONE FOR US LATELY?

The implementation of the TRIM2 structure coincided roughly with the 1980 election in which President Carter was defeated by Ronald Reagan. President Reagan's administration came into office in 1981 with an agenda to reduce the size of the federal government.

The passage of both the Economic Recovery Tax Act of 1981 (ERTA), which reduced federal income tax revenues considerably, and the Omnibus Budget Reconciliation Act of 1981 (OBRA), which reduced domestic outlays by a much lower amount, were successes for the administration but left the government with a large structural deficit. This deficit had two important effects on microsimulation modeling. First, it reduced the importance of distributional issues in policy discussions and shifted the focus almost entirely to budgetary consequences. Second, it dramatically decreased the amount of research and development funds available to agencies. Because of this latter effect, government managers more frequently asked what TRIM had done for them lately before approving research expenditures on the model. Effectively, the age of software development had ended, and model developments during the 1980s have been most frequently directed by immediate policy needs.

In addition, because many policy proposals in the post-ERTA/OBRA period were aimed at reducing outlays, government analysts turned to using program data, rather than national Census data, to estimate the impact of proposed legislation. Models based on these program data were developed and run in-house. Correspondingly, the need and demand for generalized microsimulation models, such as TRIM2 and MATH, by federal policy offices decreased significantly. Although many government analysts retained an interest in using these generalized models, declining research budgets combined with these shifting policy concerns to restrict the funds available for developmental work on TRIM2 and MATH.

Furthermore, another major change occurred outside of the executive branch when, in 1983, Alice Rivlin left the directorship of the CBO. The new management team there was less interested in promoting the organization's role in analyzing the distributional consequences of various policies through microsimulation. And the CBO, like the executive branch, was undergoing a budgetary crunch that reduced its ability to fund work outside the organization. The immediate consequence was to limit the number and scope of CBO distributional analyses using large-scale microsimulation models.

By 1983 only two government policy offices, HHS/ASPE and the Food and Nutrition Service (FNS) in the Department of Agriculture, were sponsoring large microsimulation development projects. HHS/ASPE continued to support the maintenance and development of TRIM2, and FNS continued to support the MATH model. Other organizations, such as the Congressional Research Service and the Ford Foundation, funded the models for specific-purpose estimates but provided no ongoing support to maintain the models.

In some respects, the emergence of TRIM2 at The Urban Institute could not have been better timed. TRIM2 offered a number of advantages over TRIM, principally its greater efficiency in processing and storing data, its more straightforward documentation, and its greater ease of use, development, and modification. The efficiencies translated into cost savings that could be used either to reduce the bottom-line costs of a simulation project or to allow the development of more precise simulations for the same cost. The reorganized documentation improved the ease with which the TRIM2 technology could be transferred to new analysts and programmers. TRIM2 runs could be set up more easily and quickly, and programming modifications and development were vastly simplified.

Analysts at ASPE chose to take advantage of the cost savings by maintaining the real cost of the microsimulation maintenance contracts to the government and concentrating the resources on the substantive development of the model. These substantive changes were intended to anticipate policy issues during the early 1980s. In the period from 1981 to 1985, under two successive ASPE microsimulation contracts, the welfare portions of the TRIM2 model were redesigned to accommodate monthly data so as to better approximate program rules. A complex algorithm, based on both individual responses from the CPS and labor force data from the Department of Labor, was developed to distribute earnings across the year in support of these monthly simulations. New and more intricate participation functions were also implemented, and a major expansion of the federal income tax module was begun. The existing state income tax module, which had been developed by MPR for use in MATH, was completely rewritten using actual tax forms from each state. Property tax and sales tax modules were added to the model. These extensive developments were completed largely without the pressure for quick-turnaround results, and consequently were tightly structured and well documented.

The passage of ERTA and OBRA in 1981, however, created concern among analysts and observers outside the executive branch that the Reagan administration was not devoting sufficient attention to the distributional consequences of its proposals. As a result, private foundations showed increased interest in funding projects to examine the distribution of income and benefits across the population. CBO analysts also became interested in learning to run and alter the TRIM2 model themselves, partially as a way to maintain their ability to use microsimulation modeling without depending on outside contractors or depleting scarce research monies. The straightforward documentation of the TRIM2 model allowed the technology to be transferred to CBO staff in a way that TRIM could not have been.

These activities allowed The Urban Institute to improve considerably the substantive core of TRIM2, both by revising existing modules and implementing new ones. The SSI module, which simulates the principal welfare program for elderly and disabled persons, was completely redesigned under funding from CBO and two private foundations. Other private grants funded the development of in-kind benefit modules for the school breakfast and lunch programs for the Women, Infants, and Children (WIC) feeding program, and for Medicare and Medicaid. Perhaps most significantly, CBO analysts began directly running the TRIM2 model to simulate the effects of changes in welfare programs. These simulation results were often used in congressionally initiated reports.[21] There was generally great pressure to get the estimates completed on these projects, and thus insufficient time and resources to adequately document the modules or to go back and restructure modules that had been coded on an ad hoc basis.

Nevertheless, these efforts helped preserve the demand and need for microsimulation models generally and TRIM2 in particular. The CBO analyses helped keep microsimulation modeling visible as a useful tool in the Washington, D.C., policy community while the privately funded projects, which were widely reported in the media, kept general income distributional issues alive in the public debate. At the same time, analysts at HHS/ASPE continued to direct and design improvements in TRIM2 to maintain their preparedness to produce administration responses on a variety of issues. The need for such responses in two areas arose suddenly in the period from late 1985 through early 1987. These policy applications are discussed next.

RECENT USES OF TRIM2: TWO CASE STUDIES

There are clearly periods of inactivity in the application of micro-simulation results to the policy process. These periods, as previously discussed here, allow time for the model to be further developed, documented, and updated, presumably in preparation for a period when the simulation results will once again be required in the policy process. Of course, the model is not of much practical use if it is always under development and its results are never applied to real policy issues. The real test of its long-term utility is whether it actually contributes to policy discussions when they arise.

If, during the development periods, analysts have guessed correctly in anticipating future policy issues and can convince policymakers to fund development, the model results can be immediately useful when an urgent issue arises. If analysts have either guessed incorrectly or are unable to convince their superiors to fund development and a policy issue arises for which the model is unprepared, analysts and programmers are thrown into a period of intensive development akin to the environment in which RIM and KGB were developed. But this latter kind of process can still be successful if the model has been well constructed and adequately maintained, thus providing a framework in which quick-turnaround revisions can be easily implemented and in which efforts can be concentrated on the critical area and not dissipated on "housekeeping" tasks. Two major recent and successful policy applications of the TRIM2 model illustrate examples of each situation: in the first, analysts accurately predicted the rise of a policy issue and were supported by their superiors; and in the second, analysts could not convince their superiors to fund model development on an issue that became important.

TRIM2 and Tax Reform

In 1982, analysts at HHS/ASPE asked The Urban Institute to begin a major project to revise the previously mentioned federal income tax simulation module in TRIM2, known as FEDTAX. The initial purpose of these revisions was to study the distributional consequences of tax expenditures, a large and varied group of items that were excluded or deducted from income for purposes of income taxation, thus reducing federal tax revenues.[22] The initial complex task under this development project was to use data on the Statistics of Income (SOI) file from the Internal Revenue Service to impute both capital gains and itemized deductions to the CPS file, so as to allow the simulation of detailed changes in the treatment of these two groups of tax expenditures. Two complex imputation models were developed from the 1979 SOI files. The itemized deduction imputations included the simultaneous imputation of nine separate categories of deductions to the file and imputed "shadow" deductions to nonitemizers to allow for the simulation of a shift in what was then called the "zero bracket amount" and is now known as the standard deduction.[23]

As the tax expenditure project progressed, however, President Reagan began to seriously consider a major tax reform initiative to be undertaken during his second term. Several significant tax reform proposals had been introduced in Congress, most notably those by Representative Jack F. Kemp and Senator William V. Roth and those by Senator Bill Bradley and Representative Richard A. Gephardt. The general goal of each of these proposals was to reduce personal tax rates by expanding the definition of taxable income so as to leave revenues roughly the same. It appeared likely that the administration's proposal would contain similar expansions in the income definitions.

As discussions of the tax proposals proceeded in both Congress and the administration, the TRIM2 tax expenditure project was expanded at the request of ASPE analysts. New tasks included the imputation of employer-provided benefits, principally health insurance, the estimation of individual retirement account (IRA) contributions, a frequent target for elimination, and the modeling of child care expenses, a possible target for expansion.

When the administration floated its "Treasury I" proposal for public discussion in the fall of 1984, development of FEDTAX in TRIM2 was accelerated considerably. Within a relatively short period, FEDTAX was able to simulate Treasury I and compare its effects to current law. Since HHS/ASPE analysts were interested in both the income distributional consequences of the tax revision and in the incentives for family formation contained in the bills, new and complex sets of algorithms were developed to examine tax burdens by income quantile and by types of families, focusing on the presence of two parents, multiple earners, and young children.

As the tax debate continued, the administration brought forth a new proposal, dubbed "Treasury II," in May 1985. This became the bill that was formally sent to Congress by the president. In November 1985, the House Ways and Means Committee passed its own version of tax reform, which distinguished itself from Treasury II largely in tax rates for higher income taxpayers, in the treatment of child care expenses, and in the treatment of certain deductions and sheltered income, such as mortgage interest on second homes and employer-provided health insurance benefits.

Because of the development work that had been begun in 1982, TRIM2 was able to simulate the subtle differences in these two bills on relatively short notice. In December 1985, about one month after the Ways and Means Committee action, HHS was able to provide the Treasury Department with its assessment of the distributional consequences of both Treasury II and the Ways and Means bills and compare them to current tax law.[24] As the tax reform process continued with the passage of a unique Senate bill in May 1986 and the enactment of a House/Senate compromise bill in October 1986, TRIM2 simulations were able to provide HHS/ASPE analysts with detailed and timely information on the consequences of each bill.

This marked a considerable success for both HHS/ASPE and Urban Institute analysts and for the applicability of the substantive core of TRIM2. Of course, the rapid pace of the model development process as both the House and Senate considered new provisions left the FEDTAX module of TRIM2 with a large number of superfluous subroutines. These have only recently been cleared from the model's code. But the foresight of HHS/ASPE analysts in directing the tax module development two years before tax reform became a major national issue illustrates how successful maintenance and development of microsimulation models can inform policy discussions as decisions are being made.

TRIM2 and Welfare Reform

Tax reform had barely cooled as an issue in March 1987 when Representative Harold E. Ford of Tennessee, the chairman of the House Ways and Means Subcommittee on Public Assistance, and other representatives introduced a set of sweeping changes to the Aid to Families with Dependent Children Program, the nation's most visible welfare program. The Ford bill expanded AFDC eligibility considerably through several key provisions that extended coverage to two-parent families and created a complex national minimum benefit. Furthermore, the rates at which the federal government would match state expenditures were altered significantly, and a new set of work incentives was proposed.

Because the Ford bill was largely aimed at expanding the eligible population, it was not possible to estimate its effects by using the internal government model based on AFDC program data.[25] Most of the changes in the bill could, however, be simulated by the TRIM2 AFDC module.

Unfortunately, the AFDC module had not been seriously examined for three years (when it was used for a CBO project), and many planned revisions had been postponed in favor of the tax reform development. Analysts at ASPE had been nervous about this but could not obtain the additional resources necessary to pursue both tax and welfare model development. Although the TRIM2 AFDC module contained recent state rules and benefit parameters, initial attempts to simulate the Ford bill showed that in key areas, such as the mandate of the two-parent program and the increased earnings-related deductions, the TRIM2 results were not plausible. Furthermore, since Representative Ford was pushing his bill through the subcommittee quickly (a revised version of it passed the subcommittee in April 1987) and Senator Daniel P. Moynihan was working on his own version of welfare reform, it was not clear that revisions to TRIM2 could be made in sufficient time.

In essence, policymakers in the executive branch had been caught off guard. After the passage of the 1981 OBRA legislation, when the size of the AFDC program was reduced, welfare reform was thought to be a relatively remote possibility, and the planned revisions in the AFDC model were given a lower priority schedule. HHS/ASPE and Urban Institute TRIM2 analysts had been placed in a difficult situation by those priorities. In 1987, TRIM2 was not ready for welfare reform. At first, it seemed like a miniature version of the problems confronted by HHS/ASPE analysts when the Carter administration began its 1977 welfare effort: it appeared that TRIM2 might not be useful in periods of critical need for welfare policy.

HHS/ASPE analysts decided to pursue a two-pronged strategy, hoping that one of these would provide the administration with timely and reliable estimates on which to base its position on the Ford bill. First, HHS/ASPE asked The Urban Institute to update and revise the AFDC module quickly, and commissioned a study through the maintenance contract to validate the historical accuracy of the TRIM2 AFDC results (Kormendi and Meguire, 1988). Second, ASPE asked a second contractor, ICF, to use its own microsimulation model to estimate the impact of the Ford bill. The ICF model, known as HITSM (Household Income Transfer Simulation Model), had been developed more recently than TRIM2, and its AFDC simulation was keyed to program data on such characteristics as the number of earners and number of two-parent families. In addition, it was capable of running on a more recent CPS than TRIM2 (1985 versus 1984).

The HITSM estimates were produced relatively quickly, and the aggregate estimates it yielded seemed reasonable. But the model was relatively new and not well known, and its results had not been subjected to the kind of detailed public scrutiny that had been directed at TRIM2 (and MATH) results over the previous decade. There was some question about the internal consistency of the estimated cost and unit effects and concern that holding to program targets made the model too rigid when confronted with significant program expansions that might alter the recipient behavior implicit in current program data. Furthermore, CBO analysts were using TRIM2 to produce the formal congressional estimates of the Ford bill. Given the institutional credibility of CBO and the familiarity of congressional staff and analysts with TRIM2, it may have been difficult for the HITSM estimates to gain credibility in the policy debate, even if they were reasonable. Within the administration, analysts became concerned that HITSM was too untested to rely upon for formal estimates.

The dilemma was in part resolved by the personal problems of Representative Ford, who resigned as chairman of the Subcommittee on Public Assistance in May 1987, and in part by the delay in the formal introduction of Senator Moynihan's bill as the senator's staff deliberated over the precise formulation of key provisions.[26] These events slowed the progress of the bill through the Ways and Means Committee and deferred the need to simulate a new bill introduced in the Senate.

As a by-product of the congressional delays, The Urban Institute had a small amount of time to correct deficiencies in the TRIM2 AFDC simulation. The changes were implemented quickly, in a matter of a few weeks, a situation made possible only by the structure of TRIM2. The child care expense imputations were updated. A more sophisticated participation function that controlled for the number of earners and the number of two-parent families was implemented. The definition of eligibility in the simulation of the unemployed parents segment of the program was expanded to include an option more consistent with the behavior of various states. And several minor corrections were made to benefit and other eligibility parameters.

In May 1987, shortly after Representative Ford stepped down as subcommittee chairman, ASPE analysts were able to begin using the TRIM2 estimates internally for the "simulatable" provisions of the Ford bill. And, when the Moynihan bill was introduced in July 1987, its major provisions altered the income tax code rather than the AFDC laws, and TRIM2 was able to simulate the relevant portions for ASPE analysts. At that point, welfare reform stalled. In 1988, Congress took up the issue again and enacted the Family Support Act of 1988 which was signed by President Reagan in October. In the period from 1987 to 1989, TRIM2 was improved significantly, and the model now includes all of the 1988 AFDC provisions.

The 1987 welfare reform process shows how microsimulation modeling can work even when analysts are caught unaware by some new policy initiative. If the TRIM2 AFDC module had not been updated and maintained in the period after 1984, when it was not being used extensively, it would not have been possible to correct its early problems so quickly. Furthermore, a less flexible and well-constructed model, such as RIM or TRIM, would have been difficult to modify in such a short period of time. And a new model built from scratch like KGB would likely have taken longer to implement and validate and would have confronted a skeptical policy community. Thus, although the microsimulation of the welfare reform proposals of 1987 was often rushed, it did show how the maintenance and development of the simulation software can be critical in the ability of the policy community to respond to legislative initiatives.

SOFTWARE SUPPORT FOR POLICY ANALYSIS IN THE 1990s

The nearly two decades over which the TRIM family of models has been used have seen enormous changes in computer systems. The primary benefits received by the TRIM family from these changes have been the much cheaper computer resources, the removal of core memory constraints due to the availability of vast amounts of virtual memory, and the increased speed and reliability of computers, disks, and tape drives. TRIM2 is also benefiting from the improved features of FORTRAN 77 and from the use of computer-based word processing for documentation.

Many of the changes over this period, however, have not affected TRIM2. TRIM2 remains a batch system using a venerable third generation programming language and operating only on IBM mainframes. It makes no use of database management software or fourth-generation languages, much less of artificial intelligence. The TRIM2 parameter input system is more user friendly than the original TRIM system, but user control of TRIM2 continues to be firmly in the punched-card tradition and does not take advantage of the highly interactive, user-friendly interfaces common to current PC-based software.

Thus TRIM2 is a 1970s-vintage system that nonetheless continues to very satisfactorily meet the major microsimulation needs of its government sponsors. There certainly is not the pressing need for a new generation of the model, as was the case when both TRIM and TRIM2 were developed, but it seems appropriate now to ask what changes might be made to TRIM2 to enable it better to support policy analysis in the near future.[27]

There are three areas in which improvements to TRIM2 would be useful: continued improvement in ease of use, making the model more available for nongovernment projects, and making it more accessible to analysts. These improvements are subject to the constraints that the model must continue to be fully functional on the government sponsors' IBM mainframes, that the current level of detail and complexity of the substantive simulations be maintained, and that the transition must be smooth so that current functionality is not disrupted.

Ease of Use through Interactive Job Set-up

TRIM2 runs are set up and submitted in essentially the same manner as in the original TRIM model 15 years ago. A set of JCL (job control language) and parameter specifications is assembled using an interactive text editor and then is submitted as a batch run. Errors are often made in this step, so the printed run output is examined, corrections are made, and the job is resubmitted. This may occur a number of times before a run executes successfully.

The original design of TRIM2 envisioned interactive job set-up and error correction. The user would employ a menu-based system on a CRT (cathode ray tube) terminal to select the desired input file, simulation modules, and parameter values for the run. Parameters would be checked as they are entered, so that errors could be corrected immediately. The user would have on-line access to the module and parameter documentation and to the catalog of data files to assist in setting up the run.

The primary reason this feature was not developed was that it is difficult and/or expensive to develop interactive programs on IBM mainframes. In contrast to this, most minicomputers and PCs are designed for interactive processing. One possibility that will be explored in the near future is to have at least the job set-up portion of

TRIM2 operate on The Urban Institute's VAX minicomputers or on 386-based PCs, with the idea that jobs would be set up interactively on the mini- or microcomputer and submitted to the IBM mainframe for execution.

Improving the Accessibility of TRIM2 for Nongovernment Projects

The use of TRIM2 for work supported by foundation grants or other nongovernment funding sources has been hampered by the expense of operating TRIM2 on a commercial IBM time-sharing system. This problem would be alleviated, for The Urban Institute at least, if TRIM2 could run on the Institute's VAX 11/780 minicomputer, or even on a 386 PC.

This issue, like that of ease of use, suggests the need for possible changes in the hardware and software used for TRIM2. The TRIM family of models has operated on IBM mainframe computers since the early 1970s. An overriding constraint on future developments is that the model must continue to run on the IBM mainframes available to the government sponsors of TRIM2. A large IBM mainframe is in fact an excellent choice for running the simulation jobs. TRIM2 comes nowhere near straining the capabilities of a large IBM mainframe. Tape handling is generally reliable, and arrangements can usually be made for someone to mount tapes at night and on weekends. Some large jobs may not run during the day, but two or three jobs can be completed in an evening of work during the pressure of a policy debate.

A large Digital Equipment Corporation VAX-Cluster computer center could also provide this level of service while providing an excellent facility for interactive programs. However, such a system is not now available to researchers at The Urban Institute or generally to the government sponsors of microsimulation research. The Institute's VAX 11/780 is certainly capable of running a system as large as TRIM2, but a large run might take most of the night, and, as stated, arrangements would need to be made for mounting the tapes. Smaller runs that involve only a subset of the households on the CPS, potential AFDC families for instance, would be practical on the 11/780.

It would be possible to run TRIM2 on a 386 PC, again gaining an excellent interactive programming capability, but turnaround time would be even slower and the data-handling problems even larger. Given the need for a comprehensive and highly detailed model, the 386 PC does not now appear to be a practical alternative for actually running TRIM2 simulations. However, if the amount of storage required for the data files could be decreased dramatically by using additional file compression techniques, then the PC would become a more attractive alternative.

The direction of development that we foresee is toward a TRIM2 system that is both portable and "distributed." A "distributed" system is one in which processing and data storage involve more than one computer. The model would be portable across IBM mainframes, VAX minicomputers, and 386 PCs. The VAX and PC would be used for interactive job set-up, with the actual simulations run on the IBM mainframe. The VAX would also be used for smaller simulations for nongovernment projects. This scheme has the obvious problems of portability of the program code across machines, of maintaining the consistency of the model and of the parameter database across installations, and of communicating the run specifications from the job set-up computer to the job execution computer. All of these problems are surmountable, but we need to evaluate whether it is worth the effort.

The heavy investment in the current model and the requirement of a smooth transition dictate that FORTRAN continue to be the primary programming language for the next generation of TRIM. To keep open the possibility of portability, TRIM2 programmers have tried to avoid using IBM extensions to standard FORTRAN, but it does appear that a significant effort will be required to make the code fully portable. The last two generations of the TRIM family have supplemented FORTRAN with other languages, as needed, for special functions not easily handled in FORTRAN. These have included assembly language routines for efficient I/O handling and for character string manipulation in FORTRAN IV. In the interest of portability, it may be possible to use C as the supplementary language. One problem with C is that not all the IBM mainframes on which TRIM2 is installed do not have C compilers. It is likely that the assembly routines would not be rewritten on the IBM but would be replaced with C or assembly language routines on the VAX and 386 PC.

Making the Results of TRIM2 Simulations More Easily Available to Policy Analysts and Policymakers

The access of analysts and decisionmakers to model results is of course one of the central issues with any microsimulation model used for policy analysis. Three general types of actors are involved in microsimulation for policy analysis. Policymakers, usually in the legislative or executive branches of government, formulate policy questions. Policy analysts translate those questions into simulation specifications. Programmers run the model using those specifications and pass the results back to the policy analysts. The policy analysts study the simulation results and write policy reports for the policymakers. In the TRIM2 experience, the policy analysts have been stationed in government agencies and at The Urban Institute, but the programmers have worked almost exclusively at The Urban Institute.

In practice, however, this neat scheme is often blurred. With the TRIM2 model, programmers participate actively in the process of specifying the simulations based on the policy questions and, to a lesser extent, in interpreting simulation results. In other organizations that use microsimulation, the reverse occurs, with the policy analysts participating actively in running the simulations and writing the computer code.

The ideal staffing structure would be to eliminate as many intermediate steps as possible and to have the policy analysts participate in the actual simulation process as much as possible. Even with the additional ease of use provided by interactive job set-up, the complexity of the model will limit the ability of any analyst not thoroughly familiar with the model to use the model effectively. And even with the extensive parameterization of the model, most simulation projects require some modification of the model itself, further limiting the participation of a nonspecialist.

It is important to remember that the policy demands placed on TRIM2 simulations require it to be both comprehensive and detailed, and therefore necessarily complex. There is certainly a place for simplified, easy to use models that are directly run by analysts and policymakers. However, this is not the role of TRIM2, and it would be a mistake to reduce its complexity to facilitate use by nonspecialists.

The simulation results that are presented to analysts and policymakers consist primarily of printed tables that are designed for easy comprehension and that include sufficient documentation of the particular run for assumptions to be understood. In addition, TRIM2 files are designed to facilitate the export of data for tabulation and analysis using other software packages. In recent years, printed output has been supplemented by output on floppy disk for input to Lotus 1-2-3 for direct analysis by the government policy analysts. The trend toward more TRIM2 output of this kind is expected to increase over the next few years.

TRIM2 designers have also contemplated the possibility of developing a programming language specifically for microsimulation modeling. Such a language could improve the ease of use of the model by programmers who develop and maintain it, the ease of understanding the code by both programmers and analysts, and the ability of analysts to work directly with the model. The language would simplify accessing both parameters and microfile variables, would provide constructs for operations like defining and processing a filing unit and summing income, and would allow flexible tabulation of simulated data. Developing such a language would be a major undertaking, for which funding is not currently available. It is also not clear that the level of demand for microsimulation modeling would justify such an effort.

In contemplating the future, we feel that the question of continued institutional commitment to maintaining, using, and further developing the TRIM2 framework is a critical one. A commitment from a funding source such as HHS/ASPE or USDA/FNS (U.S. Department of Agriculture, Food and Nutrition Service) to maintain the code and update the parameters is obviously essential to the continued usefulness of the model. An institutional commitment would also be necessary to support any major development effort. In the long run, however, the most important element may be a commitment by policymakers to actually use the model for policy analysis, even if this requires a significant development effort to further improve the model's applicability. Indeed, unless policy analysts at a supporting institution understand the model reasonably well and use it, directly or indirectly, for policy analysis, it will become difficult to justify financial support for maintenance and development of microsimulation systems such as TRIM2.

Notes

1. See, for example, the excellent descriptions and critiques of 13 micromodels contained in the conference volume edited by Haveman and Hollenbeck (1980).

2. Social Security, which is exclusively federal, is by far the largest of any of the programs. Many state and local programs were and are supported in some way by federal resources, either in the form of matching grants (as is currently the case with the Aid to Families with Dependent Children Program) or through the direct payment of benefits (as is currently the case with the Food Stamp Program).

3. See Miller and Herriott (1977), p. 1.

4. Developments of the Micro Analysis of Transfers to Households (MATH) model,

for example, have been directed in recent years by the interests of its principal funder, the U.S. Department of Agriculture's Food and Nutrition Service. MATH thus has a far more complex simulation of the Food Stamp Program than comparable models such as TRIM2. TRIM2, on the other hand, has been used extensively by several funders to calculate detailed after-tax incomes, and thus has more complex simulations of federal and state income taxes.

5. Moeller (1972), p. 9.

6. Ibid., pp. 7–16.

7. The name of HEW was changed to the Department of Health and Human Services (HHS) in 1978 when President Jimmy Carter created a separate cabinet-level Department of Education. Hereafter, to minimize confusion, we will use HHS to identify the Department during all periods.

8. LeMat, Bergsman, and Miller (1971), p. 1.

9. Moeller (1972), pp. 17–18.

10. For a good summary of the events surrounding this development, see Fallows (1981a), pp. 16–23.

11. HHS/ASPE has had many staff members who have supported the concept of microsimulation over the last decade and a half. Among early analysts who created the TRIM maintenance concept were Joan Turek-Brezina, Jane Lee, Charles Seagrave, and Kenneth Touloumes. The former two remain with the agency today. These analysts were joined later by Eugene Moyer, William Prosser, Daniel Weinberg and, more recently, Reuben Snipper.

12. The terms *master routine* and *simulation module* are used interchangeably throughout this chapter.

13. "Spaghetti code" is a common term in programming referring to computer code which contains many jumps in logic and cannot be easily followed.

14. See U.S. Department of Health, Education and Welfare (1976).

15. MATH is a trademark of Mathematica Policy Research.

16. See U.S. Congress (1977a, b).

17. The Treasury Department's version of TRIM/MATH lacked a wide in-house institutional support base, however, and by the late 1970s was not being seriously maintained.

18. Much of this discussion is taken from Fallows (1981b), which, in turn, was based on Betson, Greenberg, and Kasten (1980).

19. The KGB experience raises an interesting question. If KGB is viewed as a "throwaway" model that is to be used for a few years for a limited set of policy questions, rather than as an enduring framework for microsimulation, then KGB must be viewed as a success. Its primary problem may have been that it pushed against the limits of what a short-term throwaway model can be expected to do. We feel certain that TRIM as it existed in 1977 could not have been modified adequately in the five-week period over which KGB was developed. We are equally certain that an economist and two experienced TRIM2 programmers working intensively over five weeks *could* have developed the necessary simulation modules using TRIM2 as it exists today. This leads to the question of whether there is still a role for "throwaway" models focused on short-term policy analyses when there exists a generalized and efficient software framework such as TRIM2.

20. For a more complete discussion of the efficiency gains from the new file structure, see chapter 4 in Webb et al. (1982 and later).

21. See, for example, U.S. Congress (1985).

22. Notable tax expenditures in 1982 included income from government transfer programs, such as Social Security, AFDC, and SSI, 60 percent of capital gains, and a host of itemized deductions such as health insurance expenditures, state and local taxes, and both mortgage and nonmortgage interest payments.

23. Final results of the TRIM2 tax expenditure simulations were analyzed and published by a senior HHS/ASPE analyst in a prominent journal (see Weinberg, 1987).

24. The Treasury Department and the Joint Committee on Taxation (JCT) each had its own model, similar in nature, based on Internal Revenue Service data. The official estimates came from those models, but the TRIM2 results were reconciled as closely as possible to those official estimates. The disadvantages of the Treasury and JCT models were that they did not include nonfilers in their database and were also unable to disaggregate tax units into different kinds of families by demographic group and gross income, including nontaxable income such as Social Security benefits, whereas TRIM2 could do this quite easily.

25. The reason for this is straightforward. The database used for this model included only current participants and could therefore not capture newly eligible families.

26. Senator Daniel P. Moynihan's staff had circulated several draft versions of a bill beginning in fall 1986, but a final bill was not introduced until July 1987.

27. In the longer run, into the 1990s, the development of microsimulation models may be dramatically affected by a new National Academy of Sciences study being funded jointly by HHS/ASPE and the U.S. Department of Agriculture's Food and Nutrition Service. The NAS report, due to be completed in 1990, will examine the history and impacts of microsimulation modeling and recommend a course for future development.

References

Beebout, Harold, and Peggy Bonina. 1973. "TRIM: A Microsimulation Model For Evaluating Transfer Income Policies." Working Paper 971-04. Washington, D.C.: Urban Institute.

Betson, David, David Greenberg, and Richard Kasten. 1980. "A Microsimulation Model for Analyzing Alternative Welfare Reform Proposals: An Application to the Program for Better Jobs and Income." In *Microeconomic Simulation Models for Public Policy Analysis*, edited by Robert Haveman and Kevin Hollenbeck. New York: Academic Press.

Fallows, Susan. 1981a. *Acceptance of an Innovation: Development and Implementation of Microsimulation Models for Social Welfare Policy Making in U.S. Federal Agencies.* Irvine: Public Policy Research Organization of the University of California at Irvine.

Fallows, Susan. 1981b. *The Politics of an Innovation: Use of Microsimulation Models for Partisan Analysis.* Irvine: Public Policy Research Organization of the University of California at Irvine.

Haveman, Robert, and Kevin Hollenbeck, eds. 1980. *Microeconomic Simulation Models for Public Policy Analysis*. New York: Academic Press.

Kormendi, Roger, and Philip Meguire. 1988. "Dynamic Validation of the TRIM Welfare Simulation Model." Paper prepared for the U.S. Department of Health and Human Services, Office of the Assistant Secretary for Planning and Evaluation. Ann Arbor: School of Business Administration, University of Michigan.

leMat, Mary Frances, Anne B. Bergsman, and Herbert J. Miller. 1971. *Evaluation of the TRIM Model*. Washington, D.C.: Hendrickson Corporation.

McClung, Nelson. 1970. "Estimates of Income Transfer Effects." In *The President's Commission on Income Maintenance Programs: Technical Studies*. Washington, D.C.: U.S. Government Printing Office.

Miller, Herman P. and Roger A. Herriott. 1977. *Microsimulation: A Technique for Measuring the Impact of Federal Income Assistance Programs*. Durham, N.C.: Institute of Policy Science and Public Affairs, Duke University.

Moeller, John F. Sept. 20, 1972. "Development of a Microsimulation Model for Evaluating Economic Implications of Income Transfer and Tax Policies." Paper prepared for the Conference on the Computer in Economic and Social Measurement, sponsored by the National Bureau of Economic Research, State College, Pennsylvania.

U.S. Congressional Budget Office. 1977a. *Poverty Status of Families under Alternative Definitions of Income*. Washington, D.C.: U.S. Government Printing Office.

U.S. Congressional Budget Office. 1977b. *Welfare Reform: Issues, Objectives, and Approaches*. Washington, D.C.: U.S. Government Printing Office.

U.S. Congress (99th Congress, 1st session). Committee on Ways and Means. 1985. *Children in Poverty*. Washington, D.C.: U.S. Government Printing Office.

U.S. Department of Health, Education & Welfare. 1976. *The Income Supplement Plan: The 1974 HEW Welfare Replacement Proposal*. Washington, D.C.: HEW.

Webb, Randall. 1979. "Toward a New Generation of TRIM: Efficient Data Structure and Supporting Features." Working Paper 1281-02. Washington, D.C.: Urban Institute.

Webb, Randall, Ann Bergsman, Clara Hager, Douglas Murray, and Eric Simon. [1982, 1983, 1984] 1986. "TRIM2 Reference Manual: The Framework for Microsimulation." Working Paper 3069-01. Washington, D.C.: Urban Institute.

Weinberg, Daniel H. 1987. "The Distributional Implications of Tax Expenditures and Comprehensive Income Taxation." *National Tax Journal* 40(2)(June):237–53.

Wilensky, Gail R. 1970. "An Income Transfer Computational Model." In *The President's Commission on Income Maintenance Programs: Technical Studies.* Washington, D.C.: U.S. Government Printing Office.

Chapter Three

MICROSIMULATION AS A POLICY INPUT: EXPERIENCE AT HEALTH AND WELFARE CANADA

Richard J. Morrison

When a policy analyst examines an income transfer system, the underlying question driving the analysis is likely to be a variant of that fundamental query of political economy, "Who gets what?" To be sure, there may be a variety of relevant "whos": for instance, the federal government, provincial governments, households, or perhaps "Ontario female-headed, single-parent families with preschool children." And there may be a variety of relevant "whats": for instance, a new government benefit, a tax increase, an altered tax credit, or a liberalized access to an existing tax deduction. Or again, the focus may include aspects of "when" and "how." But, at the core, the analyst will regularly wish to ascertain the impacts of a given system of transfer programs on specific actors or on larger populations. This chapter describes two technologies, MAPSIT and SIMTAB, used by Canada's Department of National Health and Welfare (hereafter Health and Welfare Canada) to calculate such impacts. Because of this descriptive focus, relatively little attention is given to the broader literature on microsimulation in policy analysis. Instead, the references provided here can serve as entry points to that literature.[1]

Sometimes the thrust of the question, "Who gets what?" is descriptive, concentrating on the present system of tax and benefit programs: What are the characteristics of poor, elderly unattached individuals? What is the share of total personal income taxes paid by families with children? What fraction of two-earner families with preschool children pays reduced taxes as a result of the deductibility of child care expenses? What is the amount of the tax expenditure from specified deductions for a family in situation "X"? To answer these questions, the analyst must identify the relevant systems of tax and benefit programs and then ascertain how those systems affect the relevant individuals or populations.

At other times the thrust of the question is more analytic, perhaps dealing with the probable impacts of changing the present system:

How would the disposable income for a family in situation "Y" change if a specific deduction were replaced by a new tax credit? How much of an additional dollar of earnings would the family be able to retain, once all the resulting benefit reductions and additional taxes payable are considered? Would any families currently in poverty have their disposable incomes increased by more than $100 per year? What fraction of families with two or more children under the age of 18 would benefit from this change? What fraction of two-earner units would see no changes in their disposable incomes? What would be the size of the monetary impact on provincial governments over the next fiscal year? To answer this analytic question, the analyst must describe the present and proposed program systems and how those systems affect the families that interact with them.

Whether the thrust is descriptive or analytic, policymakers quickly recognize that simple back-of-the-envelope calculations cannot give acceptable answers to most of the questions. Instead, sophisticated computer simulations are necessary. This necessity arises both because there are too many interrelated questions and because there is a requirement for consistency across the several answers. The need for computer simulations is also due to the complexity of the relevant programs and systems. Even for a single family, there may be many relevant family characteristics and hundreds of relevant program parameters. Then, too, there is the often complex and linked logic of the administration of the several tax and transfer programs, whereby changes in one program will often have secondary and even tertiary impacts on a family via other taxes and benefits. Given not only the responsiveness required to function in an active policy development environment but also the reliability required in what may sometimes be an adversary process, as well as the internal consistency required to address complex sets of related questions, computer models are necessary.

Although computer modeling serves as a tool to help the policymaker manage the complexity inherent in transfer systems, the complexity itself remains. Thus, the models themselves are necessarily complex. Unless considerable care is taken, they quickly become large and intractable, as well as difficult to maintain. Because models typically contain large numbers of assumptions, many of them implicit, different models of the same system can lead to different conclusions. Reconciliations across models may be problematic at best. Further, because the models are complex, they are too time-consuming to build anew for each new problem, even considering their advantages in speed and internal consistency relative to hand calculations. In short, the use of the computer, by itself, does not resolve the problem of simulating complex tax/transfer systems in a reliable and responsive fashion.

Fortunately, the problem of consistency across models contains, within itself, the germ of its own resolution. Rather than building models anew each time, or perhaps adapting previous models to new demands, it is possible to create software that addresses the construction of models from a higher level of abstraction. That is, one can build higher level software systems that are specifically designed to facilitate the development of powerful, consistent models of tax/transfer systems and of the impacts of changes to them.

This is the approach that Health and Welfare Canada has taken. Two model building packages, MAPSIT and SIMTAB, assist analysts in building and applying models quickly. MAPSIT and SIMTAB automate many of the repetitive aspects of model building and support the drive for consistency across models. In essence, by exploiting commonalities across models, they free analysts from many of the mechanical tasks in modeling and allow them to concentrate more on matters of substance. The result is policy impact derivations that are faster and internally more consistent.

This chapter focuses mainly, then, on describing the MAPSIT and SIMTAB modeling packages and on illustrating how they contribute to sound policy development. Illustrative Canadian applications show how the models are used individually, and how they serve to complement each other. Finally, because the development of *forecasts* of cost and clientele impacts is such an integral part of microsimulation practice in support of policy development, a short appendix treats the special problems of "aging" cross-sectional data so that simulations can more easily address the present or future, rather than the past.

MAPSIT

For purposes of the present discussion, the description of MAPSIT precedes that of SIMTAB because it is simpler to begin with a technology that addresses single families than with one that treats a large population.

Microsimulation as Example Generation

MAPSIT's primary focus is that of "example generation along a continuum of incomes." More specifically, the analyst typically builds MAPSIT models to simulate the workings of transfer systems as they affect individual families, but with the calculations carried out over the entire continuum of the family's earnings.

For descriptive analyses, the analyst usually treats a single transfer system; the calculations focus on the derivation of all transfers to and from the family, and on the calculation of the family's disposable income. For analytically oriented models, the analyst usually models two separate systems over the continuum. The calculations generally model all of the transfers for an existing system and some "proposed" system. The essence of the analysis lies in the derivation of the key differences in transfers and disposable incomes between the systems. Each of the three main properties of this approach—the focus on individual families, the focus on systems of transfer programs, and the focus on the income continuum—deserves elaboration.

First, it is critical that analysts be able to simulate impacts affecting individual families, because, in the final analysis, programs and systems have their direct impacts on these individual families. Because individual families form the basis of our social structures, policies and programs will be judged to succeed or to fail largely based on their impacts on individual families, not in terms of their impacts on some grand averages. For questions of equity and work incentives, it is individual families who are the natural units of analysis.

Second, analysts must be able to simulate the impacts of *systems* of taxes and benefits, because the effects of individual programs may be either accentuated or attenuated by other programs in the system. Because programs are linked through a variety of administrative devices—for example, categorical eligibility, benefits from one program being treated as income by other programs, and deductions allowed in some programs for taxes or premiums paid to other programs—any meaningful characterization of the impact of a program, or of a change in a program, must consider the entire transfer system; it must consider the composite effect on the family of the direct and indirect impacts arising from any of the programs affecting the family. Similarly, questions of equity and work incentives inherently require consideration of the properties of whole transfer systems rather than of individual programs.

Third, analysts must be able to simulate impacts along an entire continuum of income, to address many of the questions that arise naturally. At what income level does a benefit begin to decline? When does a tax begin to be payable? When do a program's benefits fall to zero? When does a family begin to pay as much in taxes as it receives in benefits? How many income levels are there at which a small increase in income leads to a large drop in disposable income? Just how big are the drops and where do they occur? What are the family's work incentives as measured by true marginal tax rates, cumulative marginal tax rates, or average tax rates on income above some base level? Analyses that restrict themselves to a specific grid of income values may miss important interactions that occur between those grid points. Finally, an analysis conducted along a continuum of earnings lends itself naturally to meaningful graphic presentations.

These same requirements and their importance emerged clearly in a U.S. context some time ago (see, for example, Storey, 1973; Aaron, 1973; and Lurie, 1975; and the references they cite).

The recognition of the three requirements is not limited to the theoretical. To the contrary, these concerns affect the way in which policy development is practiced. Although hardly providing a comprehensive description, a few examples can suggest this broad spectrum of application. Allen (1972) developed the Cumulative Tax Rate Model to render more efficient the calculation of the tax rates implicit in *systems* of tax/benefit programs. Moynihan (1973) highlighted the role that MAPSIT-like analyses played in the collapse of the Nixon Family Assistance Plan during hearings in the U.S. Senate. Lewis (1983) analyzed the incentive structures for the consumer and two levels of government regarding the choice among alternative forms of child care. Murray (1984) placed heavy emphasis on the incentives that program systems provide to families in regard to family structure.

The MAPSIT Package

MAPSIT (Modular Analysis Package for Systems of Income Transfers) is an integrated software package that assists an analyst in simulating the effects of systems of tax and benefit programs on individual families over an income continuum. Although the package is much too complex to explain in detail here, the following points capture its major characteristics:

TREATMENT OF THE WHOLE CONTINUUM

MAPSIT provides the analyst with a precise, but natural, language for describing the logic of individual transfer programs and their interaction in transfer systems.

The distinguishing feature of this language is its ability to manipulate piecewise linear relationships or functions rather than scalar variables. Thus, for example, one of MAPSIT's operations enables the analyst to add together two or more piecewise linear relationships to produce a "resultant" relationship; using such an operation, the analyst might add together the relationships representing flows to and from the family (all given as functions of the breadwinner's earnings) to produce the relationship between the family's earnings and its disposable income.

TOTAL CONTROL OF THE SUBJECT FAMILY

The availability of a language, rather than a specific model, means that the analyst can model the situation for any given family. The analyst completely controls the family characteristics of interest, and the desired combination of actual or hypothetical programs. The analyst is thus free to model systems in any desired level of detail and can choose precisely those assumptions and characteristics most appropriate to the issue at hand.

A FULL MODELING PACKAGE

The major components of the MAPSIT package consist of (1) an editor module for building models that are sequences of instructions in the modeling language, sequences that serve to describe the logic of the relevant transfer programs or systems; (2) a computation module to calculate the numeric consequences of the models so constructed, deriving all of the relevant dependent variables as functions of the chosen independent variable; and (3) a report generation module to present the numeric results in a variety of graphic and tabular formats that have proven useful as policy inputs.

POWER STEMMING FROM DERIVATION OF INFLECTIONS

Because of MAPSIT's ability to derive "turning points," that is, the X and Y values that would appear as inflection points if the relationships were graphed, many desirable results fall out of the analyses automatically. For example, program break-evens and tax thresholds are directly available. Marginal tax rates are also readily available, since they correspond to the slopes of the relationships. Tables or plots of relationships, and sums or differences among relationships, displayed as functions of the independent variable, are available as well for the asking.

TAX/TRANSFER LIBRARY

Health and Welfare Canada maintains a substantial library of sub-models containing reasonable approximations of most major federal and provincial tax and benefit programs. The library facilitates the construction of new models, because an analyst needs only a single MAPSIT operation to link the model being constructed to any chosen submodel from the library. Some MAPSIT models consist largely of links to elements in the library.

INDEPENDENCE FROM DATABASES

Because the focus of MAPSIT simulations rests with determining the impacts of transfer systems on individual families, the analyst is not constrained by the availability of an appropriate survey or administrative database; MAPSIT does not use databases. Instead, the analyst models the logic and selects the parameters appropriate for whatever families and transfer systems are most relevant for the analysis. MAPSIT derives automatically the associated numerical implications and presents the results.

INTERNAL AND EXTERNAL SUPPORT

Substantial supporting material, including a 400-plus page *Reference Manual* (Morrison et al., 1986), ensures that users receive the support necessary for complex projects. Further support is available directly from on-line help messages, from the MAPSIT library, and indirectly from the extensive collection of models that serve as starting points for many new analyses. Considerably more detail on MAPSIT, its theoretical underpinnings, and its usage in both Canadian and U.S. policy applications is available in Lewis and Morrison's *Income Transfer Analysis* (1987).

A Descriptive Example

Although the preceding software-oriented description of MAPSIT's features serves as a useful starting point for understanding its use as a policy development tool, a more pragmatic appreciation of MAP-SIT's utility requires more substantive illustrations. This section uses an uncomplicated MAPSIT application to demonstrate such descriptive analysis.

As of the 1978 tax year, the "child benefit system" of benefits to families with children in Canada had two main components, Family Allowances and, in the income tax system, an exemption for children under 16 years of age. Family Allowances in 1978 were, generally speaking, taxable demogrants of $25.68 per child per month (i.e., $308.16 per year) paid to the mothers of children aged 0 through 17 years, and taxable in the hands of whichever parent claimed a personal exemption for the child, usually the higher earner. (In Canada, much more than in the United States, the income tax system is administered on an individual, rather than family, basis.) The personal exemption, $460, was usually claimed by the parent in the higher tax bracket, and served to reduce the taxable income of that parent and thus the income tax payable. In all Canadian provinces and territories, the provincial/territorial definition of taxable income is similar or identical to the one used for federal income taxes.

MAPSIT analyses were used to derive, across provinces and a variety of family structures, the "net child benefit" accruing to the family as a result of these two provisions. Broadly speaking, the net child benefit began as the gross amount of Family Allowances received, and then, as the higher income earner began to pay taxes, gradually rose as that taxpayer moved into higher and higher tax brackets. The general upward slope of the net child benefit results directly from the exemption at that time being somewhat larger than the taxable amount of Family Allowances received for the child. Concern was expressed that the increase in the value of the net child benefit along the income spectrum displayed inadequate attention to the needs of lower income families.

The focus of the MAPSIT analyses lay with describing the workings of the then-current system to the relevant policymakers. The thrust was twofold: first, to convey the increase of net child benefits with income, and second, to characterize the dependence of the pattern in regard to the source of income, family size and structure, and province of residence.

Part of figure 3.1, included in the next section, depicts the value of the net child benefit for a two-parent, two-child family in Ontario in 1978; some minor details have been suppressed to keep the presentation from becoming overly technical. In the figure, the main difference between this 1978 relationship and the upward trend just described is a "hump" about $100 high extending from about $9,000 of earnings to $25,000 and then tapering off to zero. This feature arises from a temporary provision in the income tax system that gave an extra $50 per child tax reduction to middle-income families.

Figure 3.1   THE CHILD BENEFIT SYSTEM

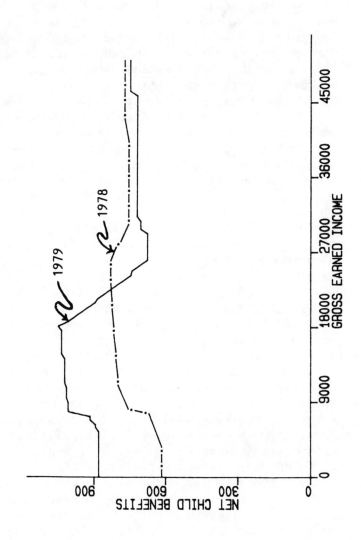

COMPARATIVE CHILD BENEFITS: 1978 & 1979

A More Analytic Example

During 1978 the Canadian government introduced legislation that altered the child benefit system. Family Allowances, which were indexed to the consumer price index to protect their purchasing power, were rolled back to $20 per child per month. Further, a new component, the child tax credit, was added to the income tax system. The credit had a guarantee equal to $200 per year for each child for whom the family received Family Allowances. There was an exemption of the first $18,000 of net family income, beyond which each additional dollar of annual net family income reduced the credit by 5¢. Because the credit was refundable, even families with no tax liability received the full benefit of the guarantee.

The 1979 child benefit system thus had three components. The personal exemption for the children remained unchanged except for the indexing that maintained its real value. The Family Allowances program, which provided benefits to both high- and low-income families, had been cut back. However, the system now included a new program, the refundable child tax credit, that gave benefits primarily to low- and middle-income families. The design of the credit ensured that both its guarantee and break-even increased with family size.

Figure 3.1, a plot produced by MAPSIT, compares, for an illustrative two-parent, two-child family in Ontario, the benefits received in 1978 and in 1979. The benefits were received either as direct payments or as reductions in taxes payable, including the extra $50 per child tax reduction for middle-income families before (1978) and after (1979) the change to the system. Low- and middle-income families enjoyed increases in their child benefits. Higher income families experienced a decrease in the total value of child benefits. Although benefits under the new (1979) system did not always decrease with increasing income, the overall slope became distinctly negative, with higher income families receiving a strictly lower benefit than comparably structured low-income families.

Figure 3.2 begins to be more interesting. It shows the values of the three components of the 1987 child benefit system. On the bottom is the after-tax value of Family Allowances; this value is generally declining because, as the marginal tax rate increases, a progressively larger proportion of the benefit is paid back in income taxes. The second component of the system, the value of the child exemption, looks a bit different. Near the lower end of the income spectrum, the exemption is of no value to an individual who has so little income

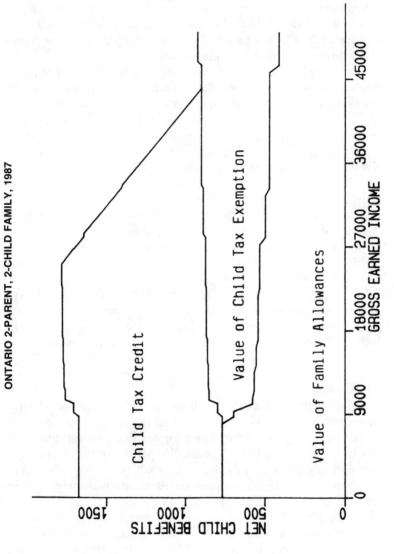

Figure 3.2   CHILD BENEFIT SYSTEM COMPONENTS

ONTARIO 2-PARENT, 2-CHILD FAMILY, 1987

that no tax would be payable even without the exemption. Once the filer becomes liable for income tax, the exemption becomes more valuable in proportion to the relevant marginal tax rate. The third component of the system, the child tax credit, is the most clearly progressive. Low-income families receive the full value of the guarantee per child, while higher income families receive nothing. The upper envelope of the figure, then, represents the value to the family of all three components taken together.

To this point the level of actual "analysis" does not appear particularly difficult. However, the demands of a compact example have masked a good deal of complexity that analysts using MAPSIT handled, as a matter of course, during the policy development phase. A few examples will suffice to give the flavor of these complications.

As the first illustrative complication, Family Allowances are not always a fixed amount per month per child. In Alberta, the amount per child depends on the child's age. In Quebec, there is a separate provincial Family Allowance benefit; both the federal and provincial benefit levels per child depend on the number of children in the family. The federal benefit further depends on the age of the child. Moreover, depending on the filing structure of the family and the specific allowances claimed, portions of the provincial benefit may have to be paid back to the government in whole or in part.

In a second complication, the impact of the child benefit system differs qualitatively for one-parent families because an "equivalent to married" exemption can be claimed for one of the children in the family. This exemption is considerably larger than the normal personal exemption for a child. In essence, the child exemption is irrelevant for the first child in a single-parent family, but not for the other children.

A third difficulty is that the situation is also more complicated for two-earner families. Because, as stated previously, the Canadian income tax system is administered primarily on an individual basis, one has to consider the optimal filing structure for the family, one that will minimize its total tax liability. That is, one must ascertain which parent should claim personal exemptions for which children. This problem is aggravated because provincial tax credits may also depend on the filing structure that the family adopts.

Other simplifications involve assumptions such as the family's sources of income, the income of the children themselves, the family's rent or property tax payments, and the levels of child care expenses or voluntary (deductible) contributions to registered savings plans.

MAPSIT in Its Educational Role

Although MAPSIT analyses are used primarily by those organizations actually developing policy, their application extends further. The following examples demonstrate MAPSIT's role as an educational device.

During the parliamentary debate on the introduction of the child tax credit, *Hansard*, the Canadian equivalent of the *Congressional Record*, used plots similar to those in figures 3.1 and 3.2 to illustrate the workings of the proposed credit and system (*Hansard*, October 31, 1978). The inclusion of graphics in *Hansard* is extremely rare. Subsequently, consultations with the provinces about the implementation of the proposed changes used sets of tables and plots illustrating the impacts on a variety of family types. The analyses incorporated, of course, the provinces' specific configurations of Family Allowances, provincial income taxes, and provincial tax credits, as well as all of the federal tax and benefit programs common across provinces. Finally, when the changes were introduced to the public, through articles and inclusions in federal Family Allowance mailings, illustrative outputs comparable to those regularly produced in MAPSIT were used to explain the changes to those affected (Health and Welfare Canada, 1978).

In sum then, MAPSIT is a powerful tool for descriptions and analyses of existing and hypothetical transfer programs and transfer systems. By addressing programs and systems as they affect individual families across the income spectrum, the package enables sharply focused analyses of how the programs and program changes achieve or fail to achieve various policy objectives. MAPSIT's strength is greatest in areas such as causality (e.g., explaining *why* the plots of the several benefits and incomes have the shapes that they do), equity, and work incentives, areas that often pose considerable difficulties for other analytic techniques.

SIMTAB

Although the analyst addresses the same policy issues with SIMTAB as with MAPSIT, the perspective is very different. Whereas a MAPSIT model addresses a single family, a SIMTAB model examines an entire population.

Microsimulation for Cost and Clientele Estimation

SIMTAB's primary focus is that of distributional impact analysis. The analyst models systems of transfer programs as they affect individuals, but from a different perspective. Now, instead of carrying out the modeling across an income continuum, the analyst carries it out across the relevant population of Canadian families. Instead of seeking to understand the impacts of the system on a single family per se, the analyst seeks to calculate its impacts on each of the individual families comprising the database and then to aggregate these results across populations of interest.

SIMTAB thus reflects microsimulation in the sense of simulating impacts at the individual or microlevel, but with the units then being aggregated to address questions that are primarily macro or distributional. It shares much of the underlying philosophy, although few of the specific techniques, of the TRIM family of models in the United States. In this sense it is a Canadian variant of the tradition developed by Harold Beebout, Nelson McClung, Guy Orcutt, Alice Rivlin, and others. Sulvetta (1976) and Harris (1978) provide historical background on this U.S. evolution. Randall Webb et al. (1982 and later) describe the TRIM2 package that was developed, maintained, and applied by The Urban Institute.

In contrast to MAPSIT models, for which databases are irrelevant, a SIMTAB model seeks to ascertain system impacts on a population that is characterized by a database. That is, the analyst begins with a database of records, each containing a number of variables. The variables correspond to the characteristics of a family sampled in the survey that produced the database.

For example, the variables give the number of parents, the numbers of children in different age groups, and the education, occupations, and work histories of the family head and spouse. They provide the immigration status, housing tenure, province of residence, and size of place of residence. They indicate the incomes of each of the family members from each of a variety of sources. Finally, each record contains a variable corresponding to the sampling ratio used for that type of family in the survey. That is, this "weight" variable tells how many families in Canada the record represents. A record thus describes a number of families in Canada. Collectively, the records, some 40,000 of them, represent the population of Canadian families fairly well. The appendix to this chapter provides additional detail on the nature of the databases used for SIMTAB models.

The strength of microsimulation analysis as a policy input lies in its capacity to construct new variables from those already in the database. For example, knowing the family structure and numbers of children, the analyst can calculate the dollar amount of the personal exemptions claimable in the tax system, perhaps as an input to some tax expenditure analysis. Calculating income taxes payable with and without the presence of the exemptions, one can ascertain the value of the exemptions to the family. The analyst may ascertain the families' eligibilities for various benefit programs, or their obligations to pay taxes or premiums, and may calculate the amounts of the transfers to or from the families.

But another type of variable creation is also important. The analyst can create discrete-valued "control" variables to serve as row, column, or page headings for the analytic outputs. For example, it may be useful in an analysis to have families categorized as (1) unattached individuals, (2) couples with no children at home, (3) couples with such children, and (4) one-parent families, with this classificatory variable constructed from information available in the database.

The analyst uses SIMTAB models to simulate the effects of tax and benefit programs for each of the records in the database. Then, weighting the records by the numbers of families they represent, the analyst constructs the specific distributions or cross-tabulations of interest. For descriptive models the analyst usually focuses on the existing tax/transfer system. One may, for example, wish to generate a cross-tabulation of the dollar value of the poverty gap by income level and age of family head, controlling for family type. In the case of analytic models, the tables may well focus on contrasts between the existing system and some proposed system. The analyst may wish, for example, to count the number of families who would benefit by more than $100 a year from a switch to some proposed system, perhaps categorizing the families by number of preschool children and province of residence.

SIMTAB models share with MAPSIT a focus on individual families and on systems of transfer programs. Then, taking advantage of the weight variable, they permit the analyst to sum items such as the number of families losing disposable income as a result of a policy change, or the number of single-parent families who have a marginal tax rate that exceeds 50 percent. Similarly the analyst could count the numbers of dollars of various benefits going to "target" families or calculate the average benefits received by such families. Because one can calculate the reactions of all the other tax/transfer programs to a change in one program, one can easily deal with net effects rather than just gross effects. For example, the analyst can measure the effective, or net, impact of a given taxable benefit, being careful to incorporate into the analysis how the receipt of that benefit may increase taxes payable or decrease the amounts of other benefits that the family receives.

The strength of microsimulation analysis thus lies in its flexibility. The analyst is not forced to perform post hoc manipulations of some existing aggregates or semiaggregate data. Instead, the analysis can present directly what is really wanted regarding both tabulated and control variables. Subject to the limitations of the database (e.g., the availability of relevant input variables and adequate data density), the analyst can exert complete control over the system being modeled and the appropriate level of detail for the modeling. Exerting control over the family unit and income definitions, as well as over the algorithms for all of the transfer programs and their interactions, the analyst can stay as close as desired to first principles. The models then offer considerable surface validity, in addition to being more straightforward to validate. In essence, compared to the kinds of semiaggregate techniques used previously, such microsimulation models are very much "glass boxes" rather than "black boxes."

The SIMTAB Package

SIMTAB's name reflects its two major purposes: the *SI*Mulation of transfer systems and policy impacts, and the *TAB*ulation of those impacts. It enables policy actors to estimate the probable impacts of policy proposals, both in terms of total program costs or savings and in terms of distributional impacts. Because the analyst can simulate the impact for each family in the database and then aggregate across the weighted records, it is possible to estimate total costs and clientele, or changes in them. Because the analyst has complete control over the basis for any aggregation, these totals can be broken out by any variables and in any level of detail appropriate to the underlying database. Like MAPSIT, the SIMTAB package is much too complex to explain in detail here, but the following brief summaries outline its major features:

SIMTAB AS A MODELING PACKAGE

First, there is the relationship between SIMTAB and its associated analytic models. SIMTAB is not a model, but a modeling package within which one builds models. The main body of SIMTAB "knows how to perform" several tasks that greatly facilitate microsimulation analyses: (1) Given the name and location of a database, SIMTAB can access and display detailed directories of its variables, including presentations of categorical variables for which different values indicate different classifications (e.g., 1 = Head is male, 2 = Head is female). (2) Given the database, SIMTAB knows how to read it, extract desired variables from its compressed format, and make these variables available to the user's model. (3) SIMTAB can link with the analyst's model, passing database records to it and calling on it to create the variables whose derivation is defined in the model. (4) Using the original database variables, or the new variables created by the model, SIMTAB can create nearly any cross-tabulation specified by the analyst, tabulating records or variables by any combination of control variables available. The usual onhancements are also available: (a) the nesting of control variables, (b) the computation of averages, (c) the inclusion of row/column percentages, (d) the transmission of results to disk files, paper, or both, (e) the ability to select for analysis a subset of the database, (f) a choice between weighted and unweighted tables, and (g) the provision of extensive labeling.

HIGH-LEVEL LANGUAGE

SIMTAB models are written in FORTRAN. Technically, they are subroutines that SIMTAB calls to perform the transformations and to create new variables. The use of a high-level language gives the analyst a great deal of power. Since FORTRAN is a compiled language, the calculations are relatively inexpensive. A typical analysis using all 40,000 records and involving perhaps 150,000 invocations of the income tax subroutine costs roughly $100 U.S. at commercial overnight rates.

HEAVY PARAMETERIZATION

A typical SIMTAB model is highly parameterized, and is thus well suited for sensitivity analyses or the manipulation of program parameters. Using this approach, the analyst can easily alter a program guarantee, a tax rate, the taxability of an income source, or an age requirement for participation in a program. Heavy attention is given to the precise documentation of the parameter configuration used in any given run. Extensive, detailed documentation is printed out as an inherent part of the SIMTAB output. Without such documentation, analysts might be unclear as to the specific set of parameters used in a particular run. This type of uncertainty would, of course, render any conclusions drawn from the run much less useful.

STRUCTURE

A SIMTAB model is composed of three main portions. The first portion, executed once before the processing of the database begins, allows the analyst to perform all of the setup activities necessary for the analysis (e.g., declaring global variables, reading in all of the parameters, and documenting them). The second portion, usually the most complex, contains the analyst's transformations. It is executed once for each case in the database and generates the variables needed for the output tabulations. Normally these are the taxes and transfers for the base system and an option system, plus the relevant difference and categorical control variables. A third portion, executed once after all of the records have been processed, permits the analyst to print out any specialized tables compiled in the model itself (as opposed to cross-tabulations that SIMTAB compiles for the analyst).

LIBRARIES

A crucial portion of the SIMTAB environment is a set of two libraries of subroutines that the analyst can use in building models. One library contains subroutines that model the logic of tax and benefit programs. Taking advantage of the heavy parameterization built into these subroutines, the analyst can include major transfer programs, conveniently controlling hundreds of the programs' parameters, with only a few CALL statements in the model, and a few prompts in the control file. The second library contains utility subroutines to perform a variety of the "overhead" tasks associated with modeling. For example, with a single CALL statement, the analyst can read in a matrix of parameters, document a vector or matrix of parameters, break a continuous variable into categories, or perform a look-up in a piecewise linear function. Other subroutines assist the analyst in the crucial task of validating models to ensure that they are doing exactly what the analyst intended.

CONTROL FILES

A specific SIMTAB analysis is driven by a control file that tells SIMTAB which database, which model, and which parameters to use, and also which tabulations to produce. Thus, to conduct an analysis, the analyst builds a model, constructs the relevant parameter files, and then defines a control file that coordinates them. Once a model has been validated, the analyst can use it to analyze large numbers of policy options in a short space of time. More than 10 distinct policy options have been "run" in a single night, with extensive distributional outputs produced for each option.

It will be obvious to policy analysts experienced in microsimulation that the SIMTAB and TRIM2 approaches have much in common in terms of their general view of microsimulation analysis. At the same time, the specific implementations are quite distinct, the packages having evolved to meet different day-to-day needs. For example, where an analyst using TRIM2 specifies the "run" via a set of parameters that defines the sequence of simulation modules, options, and the data (e.g., tax rates) to be used, an analyst using SIMTAB specifies a run via a control file that identifies a single SIMTAB model, the relevant representative database, the names of the files containing the needed program parameters, and the sets of cross-tabulations desired as output from the run.

Whereas, in TRIM2, the analyst focuses on the sequencing and coordination of preexisting modules, the SIMTAB analyst directly writes or adapts FORTRAN statements that may or may not call on elements of the SIMTAB subroutine libraries. Whereas the TRIM2 analyst uses a sophisticated supervisor to coordinate simulations and tabulations across multiple databases and intermediate results files, the SIMTAB analyst specifies a run that is essentially self-contained; in a single pass through a single database, SIMTAB simulates a base tax/transfer system, an option system, and the relevant difference variables, produces the desired items from a menu of available "hardwired" outputs, and compiles and prints the desired sets of cross-tabulations; such cross-tabulations consist of user-selected tabulation variables tabulated across user-selected categorical variables, possibly nested several levels deep.

Whereas TRIM2 results are regularly catalogued and saved in a database for subsequent reanalysis, typical SIMTAB usage does not warrant such retention, in part because of SIMTAB's flexibility in specifying extensive tabulations in the initial run, and in part because of the proportion of policy options that are purely exploratory or are needed strictly for sensitivity analyses.

SIMTAB Descriptive Analyses

Most of the SIMTAB descriptive analyses are straightforward. The analyst begins by building a model that creates any relevant transfers that are missing from the database being used. The model also derives any other variable that may be needed (e.g., a variable to be counted or a discrete-valued classificatory variable). The analyst then creates a "control" file that provides run identification information, tells SIMTAB what database and model to use, and specifies the tabulations that should be produced. SIMTAB does the rest. A few examples illustrate the kinds of descriptive analysis possible using this approach.

SIMTAB models have been used to provide a comparative description of families in poverty. Families were divided into three categories: "poor" (i.e., with incomes falling below Statistics Canada's low income cutoffs), "near poor" (i.e., up to 20 percent above those cutoffs), and "nonpoor" (i.e., more than 20 percent above the cutoffs). The cutoffs themselves are functions of family size and size of place of residence.

The families were also categorized by various features of interest— for example, province, major source of income, presence of children, age and sex of family head, and tenure. Tabulations then described the numbers of families possessing various combinations of these characteristics. Row and column percentages in the tables yielded the distribution and incidence figures for poverty as measured by this definition. One aspect of the analysis compared the characteristics of the poor families with those of their near-poor and nonpoor counterparts.

A second aspect of the analysis added to its value. SIMTAB generated tables with the several federal transfer benefits set individually to zero. Clearly, with any given benefit set to zero, fewer families would have incomes exceeding the low-income cutoffs. For each federal benefit, the number of new families falling below the cutoffs owing to the absence of benefits from that program served as a measure, at the margin and with respect to the rest of the system, of the benefit's efficacy in helping to reduce poverty as measured by the cutoffs.

Since the distributional information was also available, the programs' efficacies for specific subpopulations could also be investigated. In addition, using an analysis in which *all* of the federal benefits were set to zero, one could examine the role of total federal benefits in alleviating poverty.

In a second example, another largely descriptive analysis, generally similar to the one just described, was developed to focus on the elderly population. Instead of the "primary" classification of families being by relation to the low-income cutoffs, the family head's age was used. Families were classed as "elderly" (i.e., with a head 65 years of age or older), "near-elderly" (i.e., with a head 60 to 64), or "nonelderly." Cross-tabulations of this variable with others such as major source of income, level of income, income quintile, province, and size of place of residence gave a picture of the situation for elderly and near-elderly families as compared to their younger counterparts.

Finally, to conclude this brief set of examples for descriptive applications, SIMTAB has served to generate other descriptive analyses focused on the characteristics of families potentially eligible to receive benefits from particular benefit programs. For some of these programs, comparisons with program data provide a good characterization of "take-up," permitting administrators to gauge the numbers of families or individuals that are eligible for benefits but who choose not to avail themselves of this eligibility. Similar descriptive analyses for taxpaying populations provide, when compared against aggregated taxation data, a basis for judging the effectiveness of SIMTAB's tax estimation subroutines and parameters.

Analytic Simulations with SIMTAB

Although the ability to conduct descriptive analyses using SIMTAB is valuable to the policy analyst, it is secondary. SIMTAB's major thrust lies with generating analytic, policy-oriented microsimulations. In other words, although the tabulation abilities of SIMTAB are important, it is the simulation capabilities, the power to transform existing variables, to create new ones, and to make comparisons, that are most relevant to the analyst.

Generally speaking, analytically oriented models are used to compare two transfer systems. One of the systems is almost always the current, or "base," system, with transfers to and from all of its programs modeling tax and benefit programs currently in place. The other system modeled is the "option" system. Although much of the option system may be identical to the base system, some of it will differ—perhaps a parameter is changed, or the logic of an existing program may be altered, or, again, a new program may be added to the current system or an existing one removed.

Whatever the nature of the difference between the present and option systems, the analyst can model the two of them in parallel. Using statements in FORTRAN, and making use of the library of subroutines, the analyst instructs the model to calculate the relevant transfers in the two systems. The categorical variables needed as control variables are also calculated, along with summary variables such as measures of disposable income.

Now the real power of microsimulation comes into play. Because the variables from both systems are available simultaneously, the analyst can create for each case whatever difference variables are relevant. For example, one may want to know the size of the increase or decrease in federal income taxes payable as a result of shifting from the present system to the option system. One may want to know whether a family gains or loses as a result of the shift, its status being measured by the sign of the change in disposable income. One may wish to calculate the increase or decrease in the family's poverty gap.

With all of the desired variables—transfer, comparative, and control—computed for the records in the database, the analyst calls on the tabulation facilities in SIMTAB to perform the appropriate aggregations, case by case, as the database records are processed. For example, the analyst can ascertain the number of families who would cease to be poor were some policy proposal to be implemented. Or the analyst can find out the net cost to the federal government of additional benefits payable under the option system. Or, again, the analyst can aggregate transfers across the cases to discover what proportion of a new benefit is available to the target families and what proportion is "eaten up," directly or indirectly, by additional income taxes or reductions in the benefits of other programs in the system. In sum, whatever the analyst can create a variable to measure, it can then be tabulated in total or by populations of interest. Once again, a few examples, this time analytic in nature, will illustrate the potential inherent in this approach.

First, suppose the analyst wishes to measure the value of a particular tax expenditure (e.g., the revenues lost to the federal government owing to the presence of a personal exemption in the income tax system). Using SIMTAB, the analyst simply models the tax calculation twice, once with the present exemption and once with the exemption set to zero. SIMTAB's heavily parameterized tax calculation subroutines make this easy to do.

When the model is executed, the tax payable variable is calculated for the two systems and the difference taken. Then the analyst can aggregate over whatever populations are relevant to assess the distribution of the tax expenditure. The sum over all the populations gives a static estimate of the total size of the tax expenditure corresponding to the existence of the exemption. As a bonus, the secondary impacts on provincial income taxes, or on other benefit programs, are also available for the asking.

Second, SIMTAB has been used extensively to consider possible changes to the child benefit system. One of the changes implemented was a one-time increase in the value of the child tax credit's guarantee per child. SIMTAB analyses permitted estimates not only of the cost of the increase but of its distribution across populations such as one-parent families, and the differential impact by sex of recipient. Again, a variety of related analyses was performed (e.g., calculation of the average impact per family and per child across provinces).

Third, analysts have used SIMTAB extensively to estimate the consequences of actual and hypothetical changes to programs affecting elderly families in Canada. For example, the Guaranteed Income Supplement is an income-tested benefit potentially available to individuals aged 65 or over. From time to time, increases in the program guarantee, above the automatic indexing for price increases, are undertaken. SIMTAB models estimate the costs of such program enrichment, along with the associated increases in program clientele. Breakouts are provided by province, sex, and income level of recipient, and type of family unit. Other calculations indicate the reduction in the poverty gap for specific groups of elderly units and the number of units who move beyond the low-income cutoffs as a result of the changes.

Finally, to conclude this set of analytic applications, the analyst can also use SIMTAB to investigate the probable effects of introducing completely new programs. One set of SIMTAB analyses investigated the distributional impacts that would result from any of a set of programs to help subsidize housing costs for target populations. The model built for this investigation permitted several different types of subsidy programs, all of them highly parameterized.

SIMTAB as a Policy Tool

SIMTAB's success as an instrument for policy development is linked to its flexibility and speed. The flexibility of its transformations stems from the use of a high-level computer language; any logic that the analyst can describe in FORTRAN can then be executed by SIMTAB. Fortunately, much of the variable creation and alteration activity is not especially complex in terms of the programming required. Users remain policy analysts foremost and do not need to possess the full range of programming skills more appropriate to a computer scientist.

SIMTAB's capacity for speed and responsiveness, so necessary in an active policy environment, comes from several sources. First, the tabulation facilities that are part of SIMTAB cover most of the commonly needed output formats; often one can take an existing model and use it as is, changing only the control file that describes the particular tabulations desired as analytic outputs. One especially valuable output form is that of disk files that can then be downloaded

to microcomputers and manipulated via spreadsheets. Second, because models are built in a heavily parameterized form, new analyses
are often possible using existing models with only the parameters
changed. Thus, the analyst can examine multiple options in a single
day. Third, because models are built to be fairly general, often one
can make small alterations in an existing model to achieve one's
goals. Fourth, even when new models have to be developed, the use
of subroutine libraries for transfer programs and recurring tasks speeds
that development.

As with MAPSIT, part of SIMTAB's impact has been an increasing
sophistication on the part of those using its outputs. Whereas before
it was sufficient to ask simply what the cost of a given program
change would be, now there is a regular demand to know the impacts
on particular populations, to count the winner and loser families
associated with the change, as well as the sizes of the gains and
losses, and to look at the prospective changes from the perspective
of different actors: the subpopulations of families directly affected,
the federal government, and the several provincial governments.
SIMTAB allows these demands to be met and offers the added advantage of an internal consistency across answers, a consistency that
cannot be matched using hasty, semi-aggregate analyses, no matter
how sophisticated they may be.

MAPSIT AND SIMTAB TOGETHER

The example generator, MAPSIT, and the distributional impact estimator, SIMTAB, are designed to be used individually, and sometimes a policy analysis will use only one or the other. However, for
certain kinds of analyses, it is desirable or even necessary to use the
two packages together. As experience with the two microsimulation
packages has grown, most analyses have begun to use both of them.
A brief example will illustrate this potential for symbiosis.

During the development of the child tax credit, several MAPSIT
models showed the impacts on individual families. Indeed, the analysis of "worst-case" families, those with structures most likely to
turn them into losers under the new system, played a key role in the
development of the specific parameter values for the child tax credit.
For the most part, these parameters involved the guarantee per child,
the exemption after which benefits began to be taxed back, the rate
at which the benefit is reduced as the family receives additional

income beyond the exemption, and the choice of the income base for the credit.

Because several of the MAPSIT analyses used worst-case examples, their results were interpreted by some as suggesting that the winner/loser ratios developed from cost/clientele estimates might be overly optimistic. Consequently, additional MAPSIT analyses were conducted using more representative family structures and assumptions. Then, applying known income density functions for these families, analysts used MAPSIT as a crude cost and clientele estimator. The strongly improved winner/loser ratios resulting from these analyses were consistent with the original SIMTAB cost/clientele results and afforded a better appreciation of the differences between the worst-case and typical-case situations. In another aspect of choosing parameters for the child tax credit, MAPSIT and SIMTAB analyses were used alternately to converge on a parameter configuration that protected low-income families, maximized the ratio of winner to loser families, and kept the overall costs of the program changes within the target figure. The MAPSIT analyses indicated what was happening to the typical- and worst-case families in each province; these results suggested the directions for changes to the guarantee and the exemption. SIMTAB analyses then addressed the aggregate financial requirements of the proposed shifts in parameters and measured the impact on the overall ratio of winners to losers, as well as the ratios for special-interest populations such as single-parent families.

Together then, MAPSIT and SIMTAB proved effective in situations where neither of them could have solved the problems efficiently in isolation. It is in this sense that the two technologies are complementary rather than competing.

SUMMARY

MAPSIT, an example generator, and SIMTAB, a cost/clientele estimator of distributional impacts, are two microsimulation packages developed by Health and Welfare Canada. Taking advantage of commonalities across microsimulation models, they automate many of the repetitive aspects of modeling to render the analyses cheaper, faster, and more sophisticated. Extensive libraries of "pieces of models" enhance these gains in power, economy, and responsiveness. Both independently and together they are central to quantitative assessments of policy initiatives.

However, for all their usage and utility, neither MAPSIT nor SIM-TAB is regarded as the final word in its domain. Both packages have evolved considerably from their initial specifications. Experience in using them has increased the sophistication of policymakers with respect to the kinds of outputs that are considered useful and achievable; often it has indicated both the feasibility and desirability of further generalizations. Moreover, on the basis of experience to date, neither technology has reached its limits. Indeed, the growing complexity of transfer systems, the increasing sophistication of the policy-oriented clients using the analyses, and the constant pressure for responsiveness suggest that the evolution will continue.

THE SIMTAB DATA AGING MODEL

This appendix outlines briefly the approach that Health and Welfare Canada has used to adjust its databases to ensure that analysts building policy-oriented models can focus on the substance of the policies rather than the mechanics of projecting estimates into the future.

For most of its SIMTAB analyses, Health and Welfare uses as its database the public-use version of the Survey of Consumer Finances (SCF). This database contains about 40,000 records in the census family version most relevant for many policy simulations. Each record contains about 100 variables describing a family in terms of its membership and the characteristics of its members (e.g., education, age, immigration status, and labor force attachment), and gives the income of the family from several sources, with a few additional variables for the amounts received by individual members.

Despite its status as the best database for microsimulation, the SCF poses several difficulties for an analyst interested in estimating the impacts of alternative policy options. These include difficulties with missing incomes, insufficiently disaggregated variables, missing variables, incomes current to the year preceding the survey rather than the year of the intended forecast, and historically accurate but outdated distributions on variables such as size of family and labor force participation.

One initially appealing reaction to the difficulties just described would be to try to simulate policy impacts for the income year represented in the source (unaged) database and then make ad hoc adjustments to the estimates thus derived. This approach may work for a few isolated analyses, but if one makes a diet of it, problems of internal consistency across analyses would quickly become serious obstacles to credible, responsive policy development. Equally important, analysts would end up spending significant effort in deriving appropriate adjustment factors for particular program/subpopulation combinations. These factors and their interpretations, rather than the substance of the analyses, would then quickly become the major foci of attention.

Health and Welfare Canada has chosen an alternative approach. When a new database first becomes available, considerable attention is devoted to "aging" it to the current year and to the one after that. A complex SIMTAB model carries out a variety of adjustments to the database (i.e., transformations of its variables). The output of this model is not, however, cross-tabulations, but a new, aged database.

Indeed, the Data Aging Model (DAM), as it is called, is Health and Welfare's most complex SIMTAB model, running to about 150 pages of FORTRAN source code plus thousands of numerical parameters, and requiring a technical specifications document of some 350 pages. In essence, considerable effort is devoted to getting the aging done right, "once and for all," so that attention thereafter can rest entirely with the policy substance of analyses.

The essence of the data aging approach can best be illustrated via a brief review of the major problems encountered with respect to the "raw" data, and the model's adjustments in response to them. In broadest summary, the major problems and their treatments in the Data Aging Model are as follows:

Missing Incomes

Statistics Canada provides income reconciliations (on a National Accounts basis) that show significant fractions of income from certain sources to be missing. For example, only about 70 percent of Social Assistance (welfare) benefits are reported to the SCF, and only about 80 percent of unemployment insurance benefits. To address the missing incomes, the Data Aging Model assigns to some families who did not report income from given sources "appropriate" amounts of income, using as its guide both program data and data from families who did report income from the source. The imputation algorithms further make assignments that respect the correlation patterns for the receipt of incomes from multiple sources.

Income Allocation

Many of the income items are given only for the family as a whole. However, because Canadian income taxes are administered largely on an individual basis, the analyst needs to know the specific amounts received by specific individuals in the family. The Data Aging Model has a number of algorithms that use the records' partial income totals by family member to maximum advantage to elicit the amounts of each type of income received by each family member. A major simplifying assumption is that all income not belonging to the head or spouse belongs to the oldest child.

Dated/Inappropriate Transfers

Detail on other income sources is insufficient for many policy purposes. For example, benefits from two federal programs, Old Age Security (a demogrant) and the Guaranteed Income Supplement (an income-tested program), are reported as a single item. In addition, source database variables for transfers may reflect program structures or parameters that are no longer appropriate. Where possible, variables that correspond to transfer program amounts are simulated using families' characteristics. This approach permits the use of up-to-date program parameters and logic. Further, such simulation is often necessary for the workings of the models, particularly when program parameters vary under the policy options examined. Calculating the benefit similarly for the base and option systems helps to ensure that impact measures based on differences are meaningful. It also facilitates a consistent treatment of program "take-up" issues where families in both the base and option systems may not claim benefits to which they are entitled.

Missing Variables

Certain variables necessary for the realistic simulation of transfer programs (e.g., the amounts of deductions necessary for the calculation of federal and provincial income taxes) are missing entirely from the SCF. Where the missing variables are critical to policy simulations, they can often be synthesized using statistical matching or distributional information available from other data sources.

Dated Incomes

The income data are roughly two years old when the SCF is first made available. However, policymakers are generally interested in estimates appropriate for the present year and on into the future. The Data Aging Model inflates each dollar-denominated variable by its own growth rate, with some of the growth factors further broken out by characteristics of the recipient.

Demographic Adjustments

Similarly, the demographics naturally reflect the survey period rather than the current distribution of the population by factors such as province, age, family size, and labor force participation. The Data Aging Model employs a "static aging" technique whereby the case weights of the individual records are adjusted so that the marginal distributions for the resultant database match official Statistics Canada projections for several key variables simultaneously. Examination of the multiplicative factors derived and used for adjusting the original record weights reveals a tight distribution about a rate corresponding to total population growth. Health and Welfare Canada has concluded from this finding that the adjustments that it applies to the SCF record weights are not creating significant distortions of the database. Thus, analysts can be fairly confident that policy conclusions drawn from the SIMTAB analyses are not artifacts of the demographic adjustments.

Advantages of the Data Aging Approach

Overall, although the data aging approach requires a substantial initial investment, it exhibits several advantages sufficiently important to render that investment worthwhile. These advantages include:

DEPTH

The explicit concentration of attention on the database encourages a more integrated approach to adjustments than would occur with multiple ad hoc mechanisms adopted under the time pressures usually associated with individual substantive analyses. With a formal, data aging effort it is appropriate to involve more people and to bring more sets of expertise to bear, thus yielding a higher quality product. There is greater opportunity to document the techniques used because of economies of scale. This permits more openness to what has been done and facilitates the ability of other analysts to make improvements to the aging techniques.

RESPONSIVENESS

Substantive models can then be considerably more simple because they do not have to include transformations to age the database or the resulting estimates. This characteristic facilitates responsiveness via quicker model construction and simplifies the task of model validation.

CROSS-MODEL RECONCILIATION

If different analysts using the same database to address the same problem area should happen to get different answers, they can concentrate their attention on the substance of the models, confident that the differences do not arise from different data adjustment assumptions.

In sum, the data aging model approach, although not without its costs, contributes sufficiently to the responsiveness, accuracy, and interpretability of microsimulation results to justify the effort.

Note

1. The opinions presented in this paper are those of the author and are not necessarily shared by Health and Welfare Canada or the government of Canada.

References

Aaron, Henry J. 1973. *Why Is Welfare So Hard to Reform?* Washington, D.C.: Brookings Institution.

Allen, Jodie T. 1972. "The Cumulative Tax Rate Model." Working Paper 505-2. Washington, D.C.: Urban Institute.

Hansard. Oct. 31, 1978. Ottawa, Ont.: Queen's Printer.

Harris, Robert. 1978. *Microanalytic Simulation Models of Public Welfare Policies.* Washington, D.C.: Urban Institute.

Health and Welfare Canada. Dec. 1978. "Family Allowances Cheque Insert (National)." Ottawa, Ont.: Health and Welfare Canada.

Lewis, Gordon H. 1983. "The Day Care Tangle: Unexpected Outcomes When Programs Interact." *Journal of Policy Analysis and Management* 2(4): 531–47.

Lewis, Gordon H., and Richard J. Morrison. 1987. *Income Transfer Analysis.* Washington, D.C.: Urban Institute Press.

Lurie, Irene, ed. 1975. *Integrating Income Maintenance Programs.* New York: Academic Press.

Morrison, Richard J., William J. Bradley, R.K.P. Ellis, et al. 1986. *MAPSIT Reference Manual, Version 5.* Ottawa, Ont.: Health and Welfare Canada.

Moynihan, Daniel P. 1973. *The Politics of a Guaranteed Income.* New York: Vintage Books.

Murray, Charles. 1984. *Losing Ground: American Social Policy, 1950–1980.* New York: Basic Books.

Storey, James R. Dec. 20, 1973. "Public Transfer Programs: The Incidence of Multiple Benefits and the Issues Raised by Their Receipt." In *Studies in Public Welfare.* Washington, D.C.: Joint Economic Committee, U.S. Congress Subcommittee on Fiscal Policy. Revision of April 10, 1972.

Sulvetta, Margaret. 1976. *An Analyst's Guide to TRIM: The Transfer Income Model.* Washington D.C.: Urban Institute.

Webb, Randall, et al. [1982, 1983, 1984] 1986. "TRIM2 Reference Manual: The Framework for Microsimulation." Working Paper 3069-01. Washington D.C.: Urban Institute.

Chapter Four

THE DEVELOPMENT OF THE DYNAMIC SIMULATION OF INCOME MODEL (DYNASIM)

Sheila R. Zedlewski

In the mid-1960s several factors stimulated the development of microanalytic simulation models. First, the U.S. Congress expressed a need for better quantitative analysis of public welfare policies. Second, microdatabases and the computer capability for handling them, two essential ingredients for microsimulation models, became more widely available. Third, Guy Orcutt's pioneering work, published in 1961, generated interest in the development of microsimulation models as tools for policy analysis (Orcutt, Greenberger, Korbel, and Rivlin, 1961).

A number of static microsimulation models were developed during the 1960s. The most noteworthy of these was the Reforms in Income Maintenance (RIM) model, developed to evaluate alternative welfare reform plans under consideration by President Johnson's Commission on Income Maintenance. As discussed in chapter two, this model later evolved into The Urban Institute's Transfer Income Model (TRIM). TRIM and its descendants have been used extensively for analysis of public welfare programs and the federal and state income tax systems.

In 1969 work began on the development of a full-scale, dynamic, microsimulation model at The Urban Institute.[1] The first version of the Dynamic Simulation of Income Model (DYNASIM), completed six years later, represented an ambitious effort to include a representation of all of the major demographic and economic events, including transfer of wealth and the interrelationship between the macro- and microeconomy. The dynamic model was distinguished from its static counterparts in its attempt to capture behavior so that the implications of demographic and economic trends could be forecast through time.[2] DYNASIM was intended not only for policy analysis but also as a general social science research tool. Expectations were that the model would continue to grow in complexity and in its representation of economic behavior.

DYNASIM's computer software, the Microanalytic Simulation of Households (MASH) system, qualified as state-of-the-art computer technology. It was interactive, its data were stored in virtual memory rather than magnetic tape, and it had an extensive command language of its own. It was elegant and worthy of presentation at any computer association meeting across the country.

In contrast to the original system, the current version of DYNASIM has a more limited substantive focus, and its computer software is rather simple. DYNASIM2 was designed with a focus on policy applications that require long-run behavioral projections of demographic and labor force behavior. Its software reflects a conscious attempt to minimize the computer costs required by long-run dynamic forecasts, making the technology more practical, and thus, more broadly used. The current computer software is straightforward. Population data are stored on magnetic tape, and processing is sequential.

This chapter reviews the evolution of the DYNASIM2 model at The Urban Institute. It compares the current model with its predecessor, with a particular focus on how policy applications have directed DYNASIM2 development since 1976. The chapter concludes with a discussion of the future possibilities for the DYNASIM2 model.

DEVELOPMENT OF THE ORIGINAL DYNASIM MODEL

The development of DYNASIM[3] was the first attempt to build a fully dynamic microsimulation model that incorporated simulations of all the key elements of individual and family behavior. DYNASIM starts with a representative sample of individuals and families in the United States. Simulation units (families and persons within families) evolve from year to year, experiencing divorces and marriages, births, deaths, employment, unemployment, and so forth. Each year's simulation provides a new set of family and person characteristics, which become the foundation for simulating the next year's demographic and economic events. Moreover, each year's forecasted population can be analyzed as a synthetic sample of the U.S. population representative of some future year.

The original model consisted of three program sectors: the micropass sector, the marriage union program sector, and the macromodel program sector (figure 4.1). The micropass sector contained a sequenced set of program modules, each containing the description of

Figure 4.1   STRUCTURE OF DYNASIM

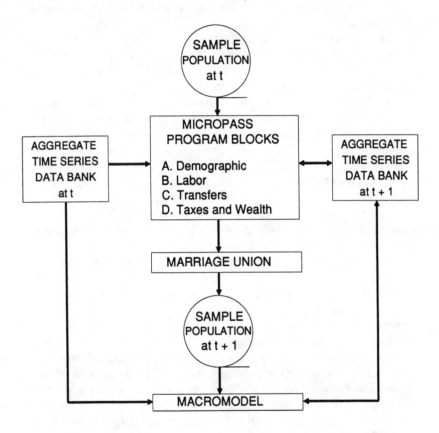

Source: Orcutt et al. (1976)

an operating characteristic plus accounting identities, necessary summations, and provisions for random draws in accordance with specified probabilities. The marriage union sector matched eligible males and females who were selected for a first marriage or a re-marriage in the micropass sector, and it created new families in the sample population. The macroeconomic sector was a time series model that established links between the macroeconomic variables and microanalytic results. Simple feedbacks between the two models were included.

The micropass program sector, the main body of the DYNASIM system, was further divided into five program blocks: the demographic, labor, transfers, tax, and wealth blocks. The demographic program block included operating characteristics to simulate birth, death, first marriage, remarriage, divorce, disability, education, and location. The labor program block contained modules to simulate wage rates, labor force participation, hours in the labor force, and unemployment. The transfers program block contained modules that simulated Social Security benefits and eligibility, other pensions, unemployment compensation, Aid to Families with Dependent Children (AFDC), Supplemental Security Income (SSI), and the Food Stamp Program. The wealth and taxes program block (never actually implemented in the DYNASIM system), consisted of modules to simulate saving, inheritance, and taxes.

Data to support the development of the micropass sector were drawn from diverse sources (see table 4.1). Decennial censuses, Vital Statistics data, Current Population Surveys, and the Panel Study of Income Dynamics (PSID) data were used to develop the DYNASIM operating characteristics. The modules also varied considerably in terms of their degree of complexity. The modules' sophistication ranged, for example, from simple probability matrices developed from published data (for example, location) to more sophisticated, original, behavorial equations (for example, hours in the labor force).

The goals of the original model were ambitious. Orcutt, Caldwell, and Wertheimer (1976) outlined several broad purposes for the DYNASIM model:

1. It was to facilitate the use of microentity-focused research results. That is, DYNASIM was to offer a framework for consolidating and applying past, present, and future research work of many individuals in varied areas of the social sciences. The model was to guide research and enhance its usefulness.
2. It was hoped that the model would have a predictive capability.

If the model's operating characteristics and their linkages were based on theories of real world behavior, it would be possible to analyze and tabulate synthetic population data representative of some future year.

3. It could be used in policy experimentation either by altering the parameters or other specifications of the model. Tax laws, Social Security laws, or income maintenance arrangements could be simulated so that the likely consequences of proposed policy changes could be estimated.

4. It was to be used to explore the interactions of socioeconomic forces to offer guidance to policymakers in coping with natural uncertainties. For example, it could analyze the long-run offccts of declining birth or mortality rates by capturing the interrelationships between these demographic trends and other events simulated in the model.

5. It could be used to generate microunit histories. The ability of the microanalytic model to merge and meld data from many disparate bodies of data could yield an augmented U.S. Census longitudinal file with a richer description of microunits than is possible on the basis of any single survey.

The model was built by a team of researchers, most of whom were located at The Urban Institute and were hired specifically to develop models for the DYNASIM system. One analyst developed the labor sector, two others focused on developing the demographic program block, and another developed the transfers program block. The project also supported a number of outside consultants to develop operating characteristics for DYNASIM; one worked on its macroeconomic model, and another the wealth sector. Table 4.1 indicates the depth and breadth of the research completed during this developmental period.

The software system developed to support the DYNASIM model was also ambitious and sophisticated. It was designed with the expectation that persons active in research and policy explorations involving microanalytic models would act as an "invisible college" actively communicating with each other and the microanalytic model (Sadowsky, 1977). The computer system MASH (Microanalytic Simulation of Households) was designed for an interactive computing environment to facilitate this research sharing. It also had a command language structured to allow research persons to interact directly with the model, its data, and each other. The MASH system included an on-line attribute library, a machine-readable codebook system,

Table 4.1 PROGRAM BLOCKS OPERATIONAL IN THE ORIGINAL DYNASIM MODEL

Program Block	Research Source
A. Demographic	
1. Birth	Parameters estimated from Vital Statistics data.
2. Death	Parameters estimated from three sources. Vital Statistics data from 1933 to 1968 were used to estimate an exponential time trend by age, race, and sex. Data from 1940, 1950, and 1960 Censuses were used to capture marital status differentials in mortality. Data from 1960 Matched Records Study were used to estimate differentials by education.
3. First marriage	Based on analyses of merged 1960–70 Census database to estimate race, sex, age, period, and cohort differentials. The March 1971 Current Population Survey (CPS) was used to estimate the "social-structural" regression coefficients.
4. Remarriage	Probabilities calculated from published tabulations of 1967 Survey of Economic Opportunity.
5. Divorce	Marriage duration, period, and cohort parameter estimates based on 1949–71 Vital Statistics data. Regression coefficients to estimate social–structural effects were estimated from 1968 to 1972 Panel Study of Income Dynamics (PSID).
7. Work disability	Regression coefficients to predict entries into and exits out of disability status based on 1969–72 data from PSID.
8. Education	Enrollment and grade completion probabilities based on analysis of 1960 and 1970 Census data, 1972 CPS, and secondary analysis of other studies completed in 1967 and 1969.
9. Location	Probabilities for moving and migration based on published tabulations from 1971 CPS.
B. Labor	
1. Wage rate	Separate regression equations for six demographic groups using 1968–73 data from PSID. Includes separate equations to estimate relative wage rate and an autoregressive error term.
2. Labor force participation	Probability tables estimated from pooled data from 1968 to 1973 from PSID. Lagged participation was included as an explanatory variable.
3. Hours	Separate regression equations for eight demographic groups using 1968–73 PSID. Includes separate equations to estimate hours and autoregressive error term.

4. Unemployment | Unemployment probabilities from cross-tabulation of pooled data from PSID. Unemployment rates estimated using regression analysis of PSID data, with one equation capturing cross-section differences and another the autoregressive error term.

C. Transfers
1. Social Security | Model estimated presimulation earnings histories based on data from 1 percent Sample Longitudinal Employee-Employer Data File, and calculated retirement benefits based on pre- and postsimulation earnings histories.

2. Other pensions | Regression equations to predict receipt of a pension and amount of pension estimated from 1969 to 1972 PSID data.

3. Unemployment Compensation | Model based on simplified set of Unemployment Compensation rules weighted by region of the country.

4. Aid to Families with Dependent Children (AFDC) | Regional representation of AFDC program drawn from Boland's 1973 work.

5. Supplemental Security Income (SSI) | Simplified representation of federal program rules and state supplementation collapsed by region.

6. Food Stamp Program | Simple representation of federal program rules.

D. Wealth and Taxes[1]
1. Saving | Predictions of ratios of saving and dissaving to income based on regression analysis of 1962 Survey of Financial Characteristics of Consumers (SFCC) and 1963 Survey of Changes in Family Finances (SCFF).

2. Inheritance | Data from several sources were used to model transmission of wealth at death, including regression analyses of 1962 estate tax files and 1969 estate tax returns in Washington, D.C. Inheritance from outside family based on regression analysis of 1963 SCFF.

3. Taxes | Based on main features of 1972 statutes.

[1]This program block was specified but never implemented in the DYNASIM system.

and on-line dictionaries for each system user. MASH's population data were handled by a software virtual memory simulator, allowing nonsequential access to each person and family in the file. The development of the DYNASIM model and its software may have been the largest effort ever undertaken for the sole purpose of developing a social science research and policy tool. The agencies and foundations that funded it took a chance that the model would ultimately be successful and useful in policy analysis. Although at times they became frustrated with the lags in development, they were generally supportive and optimistic that the model would have a long-run payoff. These organizations included the U.S. Office of Economic Opportunity, the U.S. Department of Health, Education & Welfare (HEW), the National Science Foundation, the U.S. Treasury Department, and the Ford Foundation.

POLICY APPLICATIONS OF THE DYNASIM MODEL

Early applications of the DYNASIM model were essentially explorations of its properties and demonstrations of its potential. Several of these are described in Orcutt, Caldwell and Wertheimer (1976). For example, demographic experiments were conducted, the monte carlo error for small sample sizes was measured, and the consequences of equalizing women's earnings with men's were examined. These demonstrations typically used small samples (from 1,000 to 4,000 persons), and, if forecasting was an element of the analysis, the forecast period never exceeded 10 years.

Shortly after the model was completed, analysts used the DYNASIM model to analyze the interrelationships between demographic and macroeconomic trends and the AFDC and Unemployment Insurance programs (Wertheimer and Zedlewski, 1978; Zedlewski, 1977). These efforts to demonstrate DYNASIM's usefulness for more practical policy analyses were unsuccessful in the sense that they did not generate much interest in using the DYNASIM technology for the analysis of welfare policies. At the time, the DYNASIM model was limited to running on fairly small samples, and its initial file (the 1970 Census Public Use Sample) was six years out of date. In contrast, persons interested in analysis of income maintenance programs wanted to use the most up-to-date data possible and sample sizes large enough to support detailed distributional and even state analyses. Moreover, the TRIM model had already established itself as a useful tool for evaluating welfare program reform or tracking program trends over time.

During the mid-1970s Social Security was also an issue of top policy concern. The Old Age, Survivors and Disability Insurance (OASDI) trust fund was in serious financial trouble, and Congress had to face the fact that the automatic cost-of-living mechanism established in 1972 resulted in benefits far in excess of what was intended. Inflationary growth in earnings had to be decoupled from the inflationary adjustments in the benefit formula.

Analysts at the Office of the Secretary in HEW, supporters of the DYNASIM development, recognized that the model could be used to simulate the effects of alternative benefit formulae and indexing schemes on the level and distribution of Social Security benefits. They awarded The Urban Institute a grant to develop long-run projections of earnings histories for this purpose. This was the first time that DYNASIM was called upon to assist government staff in making public policy decisions. DYNASIM was used to simulate 40-year earnings histories for a cohort of persons in their early twenties in 1960 (Hendricks, Holden, and Johnson, 1976).

These files were used in a number of related policy analyses. HEW published a paper on redistribution within the Social Security system, reflecting the work completed by the Office of the Secretary prior to the passage of the 1977 Social Security Amendments (Thompson, 1976). The simulated earnings histories were also used to analyze proposals to eliminate dependence as a factor in entitlement to spouse's benefits in a study mandated by the Social Security Amendments of 1977 (U. S. Department of Health, Education & Welfare, 1979). In a related study, Gordon (1978) used these data to explore the treatment of women and one-earner and two-earner families under five alternative Social Security systems.

EVENTS LEADING TO DYNASIM2

These applications of the DYNASIM model clearly demonstrated its usefulness in the analysis of retirement and aging issues. The unique characteristic of the DYNASIM model was its ability to simulate individual biographies and to use these biographies to simulate alternative Social Security and pension benefit schemes. At the same time, concern about retirement income issues was intensifying. There was growing recognition that our aging society would place unique demands on our retirement income systems. With the growth in private pensions in the 1970s and the increasing federal regulatory role in this area (ERISA, the Employee Retirement Income Security Act, was passed in 1974), a need for a model that could project the effects of different rules governing private pensions also became obvious.

Subsequently, James Schulz at Brandeis University, a member of DYNASIM's original advisory board, was awarded a grant from the National Science Foundation to develop a policy-oriented private pension model for the DYNASIM system. This required that Schulz and analysts at The Urban Institute add a number of additional operating characteristics to the DYNASIM system. Simulation of private pensions required not only projections of labor force histories but also projections of job turnover, industry attachment, and pension coverage on each job. Schulz's pension benefit model was very detailed and based on an analysis of the diversity in pension plan characteristics in the United States. The model represented a wide variety of benefit formulae, various types of Social Security integration schemes, early and late retirement provisions, and so on (Schulz, 1979). Schulz's Pension Simulation Model (PENSIM) was completed in 1979. Because of its complexity, PENSIM was not fully integrated with DYNASIM. Instead, it used the simulated earnings history files from the DYNASIM system, and calculated Social Security and pension benefits outside of the model. Schulz made several presentations of his model's results (see, for example, Schulz, 1982) and stimulated more interest in using dynamic models for pension analyses.

Although these first DYNASIM applications established its usefulness in the retirement policy area, they also pointed out a number of shortcomings in the DYNASIM system. One was that large sample sizes (almost always required for policy analysis necessitating detailed distributional analysis) placed great strains on the MASH software. The virtual memory simulator and its disk space requirements had definite physical limitations. Moreover, the elapsed time required to process a large number of persons in an interactive time-sharing environment was excessive. It could take from 4 to 12 hours to complete a single year's projection. Needless to say the computer runs were also extremely costly.

Scrutiny of DYNASIM's early projections also demonstrated some of its substantive shortcomings. The simulated earnings history files were carefully validated by comparing the DYNASIM results over the 1967–72 period with actual histories reported in the Panel Study of Income Dynamics (PSID) data (Holden and Hendricks, 1976). These comparisons showed that the labor force model did not accurately capture individual differences in labor force attachment over a long period, and it produced too much variation in individual earnings from one year to the next.

Work moved along a number of fronts to capitalize on the DYNASIM model's potential to make a unique contribution in the retirement policy area and to correct the problems inherent in the original model. However, the funding climate had changed considerably by this time and financial support to correct the faults of the original DYNASIM system was not easily obtained. There were no longer any general backers of the DYNASIM model. Research money was tight, and many of the original DYNASIM supporters were frustrated because the DYNASIM system had substantial weaknesses. Instead, individual researchers had to "sell" DYNASIM's capability as a useful part of a specific policy analysis, arguing that some development was necessary to achieve the desired goal.

Three separate and unrelated government contracts eventually made the second version of DYNASIM possible. In 1979 The Urban Institute was awarded a contract from the Department of Labor to evaluate the change in the Age Discrimination in Employment Act (ADEA), which increased the mandatory retirement age from 65 to 70. This contract included an analysis of the impact of mandatory age limits on retirement behavior and a simulation of the long-range effects of the ADEA legislation, and presented a prime opportunity to develop a specialized retirement model for the DYNASIM system. At the same time, another group at the U.S. Department of Labor became interested in bringing Schulz's PENSIM model in-house. They became convinced that a new DYNASIM software system would be required to do this—one that was portable to a government computer and inexpensive to run. Finally, the Institute was awarded a contract from the Congressional Budget Office to develop a version of DYNASIM for them that would be suitable for general retirement policy analysis. The original CBO contract provided for updating many of the demographic operating characteristics, the development of a more complete policy-relevant social security model, and the integration of Schulz's PENSIM model with DYNASIM. The contract was later extended to include a complete reestimation of DYNASIM's Labor Program Sector, as CBO analysts soon realized the seriousness of the original labor model's shortcomings.

DEVELOPMENT OF THE DYNASIM2 MODEL

These three contracts basically made possible the development of DYNASIM2, which was designed with a primary focus on long-range retirement income issues. The system includes elements of the original DYNASIM model, Schulz's PENSIM model, a number of additional operating characteristics, and other system features that are geared specifically toward simulating long-range forecasts of earnings and fertility histories. DYNASIM2 is an eclectic microsimulation model, combining elements of both dynamic and static microsimulation.

Figure 4.2 shows the current configuration of the DYNASIM2 system at The Urban Institute. The model is divided into three sectors— the Family and Earnings History (FEH) model, the Jobs and Benefits History (JBH) model, and the Cross-Sectional Imputation Model (CSIM). The FEH model most closely resembles the original DYNASIM model. It is fully dynamic and simulates demographic and labor force behavior on an annual basis. The model simulates birth, death, first marriage, remarriage, divorce, work disabilities, education, labor force participation, hours in the labor force, wage rates, unemployment, and location. The major output of the FEH model is a file that contains longitudinal demographic and labor force histories for each person in a sample of the U. S. population, as well as a snapshot of the characteristics of that population representative of the final year of simulation. Any of the variables simulated by the FEH model can be saved in what is called a microtime series stored on each person's record. Typically, histories for fertility, marriage (including information that permits linkages between former husbands and wives), labor force participation, and earnings are stored as microtime series.

This FEH output file is the input for the second sector of the DYNASIM2 system, the Jobs and Benefits History model. JBH simulates job change, industry attachment, pension coverage, Social Security, private pension benefits, and retirement age. In contrast to the FEH model, an entire history of these events is simulated for each person in the sample at one time. The JBH model essentially incorporates all of the features of Schulz's PENSIM model, with the addition of a detailed model of the Social Security system, modules to simulate government pensions, and a behavioral retirement model. The third sector of the DYNASIM2 system is a static, cross-section model that imputes additional characteristics to the projection file and calculates various taxes and transfers. Currently, the model in-

Figure 4.2   STRUCTURE OF DYNASIM2

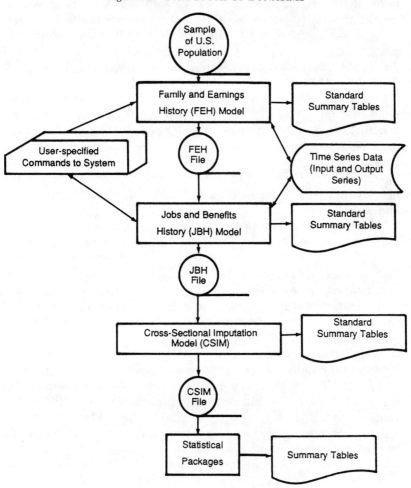

cludes imputations for health, institutionalization, home ownership, financial assets, and Supplemental Security Income.

The current program sectors in DYNASIM2 and research basis for each module are outlined in table 4.2. As is evident from this table, a few of the DYNASIM2 modules are simple updates of the original DYNASIM operating characteristics, some are complete reestimations of the originals, and others were added to meet the goal of providing a fairly complete retirement representation of the retirement income system. DYNASIM2 is documented in a number of places (Johnson, Wertheimer, and Zedlewski, 1983; Johnson and Zedlewski, 1982; Wertheimer, Zedlewski, Anderson and Moore, 1986; Zedlewski, 1984a).

Besides its departure from the fully dynamic microanalytic modeling concept, DYNASIM2 includes another feature that represents a significant departure from the original Orcutt design. The model includes a vast array of time series adjustment factors that allow a user to force the model's aggregate predictions to line up to external forecasts. The adjustment factors are fairly detailed, permitting the user to align most demographic and economic events by age, race, and sex.

There are several purposes for these adjustment factors. One is that the user can be assured that the model's aggregate predictions over a historic period accurately track actual events. The other is that the user can line up the model's aggregate predictions to other demographic or macroeconomic forecasts. This second purpose is useful both for ensuring broader acceptance of the model's projected individual histories and for simulating alternative demographic and economic paths. A variety of demographic and macroeconomic projections have gained acceptance over time. For example, the U.S. Bureau of the Census regularly forecasts three paths for future mortality rates. These, in turn, are used by the Office of the Actuary in the Social Security Administration to project different paths for the OASDI trust fund. A typical application of the DYNASIM2 model will force the aggregate outcomes of its death operating characteristic to match one of the Census forecasts.

The time series adjustment factors also replaced the macroeconomic model that was an integral part of the original DYNASIM system. In DYNASIM2 external forecasts of the aggregate rate of employment, unemployment, real growth, and real interest rates are used to guide the results of the microeconomic operating characteristics. Thus, DYNASIM2's underlying behavioral equations pick up the social–structural effects of the demographic and economic events simulated, but the aggregate results are typically aligned to external forecasts.

Another important distinction between DYNASIM2 and DYNA-SIM is its software. DYNASIM2's computer system is fairly portable (given the complexity of the model). The model is written mostly in FORTRAN, and it processes the population data sequentially in a binary integer format. It was designed for a mainframe computer with batch processing. The software does include some of the original features of the MASH system, such as an on-line time series dictionary and a machine-readable codebook. It also has a simplified command structure that allows the user to tell the model how to proceed.

The DYNASIM2 software is capable of processing large data files much more inexpensively than its predecessor. DYNASIM2 typically starts with an initial file of 60,000 persons. As the number of persons increases with each projection year, so does the number of data elements stored for each person on the file. As mentioned, the model can record microtime series for any event chosen by the user, and, typically, individual histories of earnings, marital status, fertility, labor force participation, and retirement benefits are saved on the output files. A population simulated to the year 2030, for example, consists of 77,800 persons with about 500 individual pieces of information saved for each person. Processing costs, of course, increase during the simulation period, but never to the point that they make long-run simulations prohibitive. For example, the number of central processing unit (CPU) minutes an FEH run takes per year increases from 7 minutes for projections in the 1980s to 11 minutes by 2030. Contrary to DYNASIM, the DYNASIM2 system has also proven to be fairly portable. It has been installed on several government computers, and parts of the system have been installed on The Urban Institute's VAX microcomputer.[4]

POLICY APPLICATIONS OF DYNASIM2

Table 4.3 summarizes some of the applications of the DYNASIM and DYNASIM2 models. The current DYNASIM2 structure supports analysis of policies that require projections of individual life histories. Although the model is not limited to these types of applications, almost all of its applications have been in the retirement or aging area.

For example, the model has proved useful in analyzing the long-

Table 4.2 PROGRAM BLOCKS OPERATIONAL IN THE DYNASIM2 MODEL

Program Block	Research Source
	FAMILY AND EARNINGS HISTORY MODEL
A. Demographic	
1. Birth	Original DYNASIM model, updated to recent Vital Statistics data.
2. Death	Vital Statistics data from 1933 to 1976 were used to update the exponential time trend (McKay, 1979); otherwise, same as original DYNASIM model, adjusted to match recent mortality rates.
3. First marriage	Social–structural differences based on reanalyses of March 1971 Current Population Survey (CPS). Internal alignment of constant term added so that marriages follow trends by race, age, and sex shown in Vital Statistics data through current year.
4. Remarriage	Probabilities calculated from recent published Census tabulations.
5. Divorce	Cohort parameter estimates taken from work by Preston and McDonald (1979). Marriage duration prediction adopted from work by Weed (1980) and analysis of Vital Statistics data. Social–structural effects on divorce rates were adapted from Cherlin (1977).
7. Work disability	Original DYNASIM model.
8. Education	Original DYNASIM model with parameters adjusted to match recent Census data.
9. Location	Original DYNASIM model with parameters adjusted to match recent Census data.
B. Labor	
1. Wage rate	Separate regression equations for 16 demographic groups using 1968–81 data from Panel Study of Income Dynamics (PSID). Includes separate equations to estimate relative wage rate and transitory and permanent components of the error terms.
2. Labor force participation	Separate probit equations for 16 demographic groups estimated from pooled 1968–81 PSID data. Separate estimates of transitory and permanent error components for each group.
3. Hours	Separate regression equations entrants into labor force and for eight demographic groups of stayers using 1968–77 PSID. Includes equations to estimate hours and error term equations that take into account both serial correlation of the residuals and the correlation between hours and wage rates to improve prediction of annual earnings.
4. Unemployment	Original DYNASIM model.

THE JOBS AND BENEFITS HISTORY MODEL

C. Jobs

1. Job change — Probabilities by sex, education, and industry estimated from January 1973 CPS, updated to reflect recent U.S. Bureau of Labor Statistics data by industry.

2. Industry movement — Probabilities by sex and industry estimated from January 1973 CPS, updated to reflect recent Bureau of Labor Statistics (BLS) data by industry.

3. Social Security coverage — Assignment depends on employment sector and recent administrative data.

4. Pension coverage — Probabilities by industry, sex, and hours of work, based on cross-tabulation of March 1983 CPS.

D. Transfers

1. Social Security — Policy-oriented model that includes detailed representation of all the Social Security benefit rules, including retirement, dependent, survivors, and disability benefits. Requires matched earnings history file for presimulation earnings histories.

2. Private pensions — Policy-oriented model developed by Schulz (1979) using 1974 and 1979 BLS Surveys of Defined Benefit Plans, updated to reflect coverage trends and legislation through 1988 and recent BLS data.

3. Government pensions — Federal government plan and prototypical state government pension plans based on analyses of current plan rules.

4. IRAs and KEOGHs — Participation imputed on the basis of equations estimated from 1979 and 1983 Current Population Surveys, and updated to reflect legislation through 1988.

CROSS-SECTIONAL IMPUTATION MODEL

E. Wealth

1. Assets — Income from financial assets assigned to older families based on tobit regression model estimated using 1984 Survey of Consumer Finances.

2. Home ownership — Probit function estimated using 1984 Survey of Consumer Finances.

F. Health

1. Health — Ordered probit model assigns older persons to one of four health categories: no activities of daily living (ADLs), 1–2 ADLs, 3–4 ADLs, and 5 or more ADLs based on analyses of data from 1984 Supplement on Aging and 1984 Long-Term Care Survey.

2. Institutionalization — Probability of institutionalization based on combined sample from 1984 Supplement on Aging and 1984 Long-Term Care Survey.

G. Means-tested transfers

1. Supplemental Security Income — Representation of federal program rules and state supplementation.

Table 4.3 APPLICATIONS OF THE DYNASIM MODEL: 1977–87

Reference	Application
	DYNASIM
Hendricks, Holden, and Johnson (1976)	Create a file of simulated family and earnings histories through the year 2000 for analysis of Social Security and private pension issues (grant from U.S. Department of Health, Education & Welfare (HEW).
Thompson (1976)	Examination of intracohort redistribution in Social Security retirement program.
Zedlewski (1977)	Estimation of impact of macroeconomic conditions on Unemployment Insurance program.
Wertheimer and Zedlewski (1978)	Simulation of Aid to Families with Dependent Children (AFDC) Program from 1975 to 1985 under different combinations of demographic and economic assumptions (grant from HEW).
U.S. Department of Health, Education & Welfare (1979)	The Social Security Amendments of 1977 mandated a study of the ways in which the Social Security system could be adjusted to respond to the changing roles of men and women. Simulated lifetime histories of changes in earnings and marital status were used to calculate Social Security benefit amounts in the year 2000 under present law, earnings sharing, and a double-decker system.
Gordon (1978)	Exploration of the treatment of women, one-earner, and two-earner families under five alternative Social Security systems (grant from private foundation).
Wertheimer and Zedlewski (1978)	Several conditional forecasts of socioeconomic status of the U.S. elderly population (grant from U.S. Administration on Aging).
	DYNASIM2
Storey et al. (1981)	Estimation of long-term effects of mandatory retirement through the year 2000 as part of large study to evaluate effects of 1978 ADEA Amendments (U.S. Department of Labor, 1979–81).
Moore and Wertheimer (1982)	Forecast effects of six different patterns of teenage childbearing on welfare costs in 1990 (grant from National Institute on Child Health and Development).
Zedlewski (1984a)	Forecast private pension system to the year 2020 under different assumptions about pension coverage, portability, and cost-of-living adjustments of pension benefits (grant from U.S. Department of Health and Human Services to Brookings Institution).

Michel, Storey, and Zedlewski (1983)   Estimation of long-range effects of 1983 Social Security Amendments (product of the Changing Domestic Priorities project to examine shifts in social policies funded by consortium of foundations and corporations).

Zedlewski (1984b)   Evaluation of earnings sharing alternative to the Social Security system (commissioned by women's advocacy groups interested in social security reform for women and funded by several private foundations).

Congressional Budget Office (1986)   Evaluation of earnings sharing concept as mandated by U.S. Congress in Social Security Amendments of 1983.

Zedlewski (1988)   Estimation of long-range effects of private pension rule changes included in Tax Act of 1986, and several other alternatives to pension coverage, vesting, and portability (Rockefeller Foundation and National Senior Citizens Law Center).

Zedlewski, Barnes, Burt, McBride, and Meyer (1989)   Estimation of needs of elderly in 21st century under different assumptions about future mortality rates and health characteristics (grant from Administration on Aging).

run effects of the 1983 Social Security Amendments and in evaluating an earnings-sharing alternative to the current Social Security system. This later application is particularly interesting for demonstrating the power of this type of model. DYNASIM2 simulates individual histories for each person in the population, including keeping track of changes in family structure over time. Earnings sharing requires that retirement benefits be based on one-half of a couple's Social Security wages for each year of marriage plus the entire amount of a person's own credits during the period that he or she was not married. Moreover, when a spouse dies, the survivor "inherits" the credits that were earned by the spouse during the period that they were married. Thus, in order to calculate a Social Security benefit under earnings sharing, the life histories of all previous spouses must be referenced. DYNASIM2 allows the tracking of each spouse's history because it stores a unique address for each person on the file, in addition to addresses for every person ever in the family.

The DYNASIM2 type of technology was required to evaluate the distributional consequences of earnings sharing because the earnings history records of the Social Security Administration (SSA) do not include marriage records. DYNASIM2 was used at The Urban Institute to evaluate the effects of an earnings sharing system to the year 2030 (Zedlewski, 1984b). Similar analyses were completed by the Social Security Administration using a similar model (U. S. Department of Health and Human Services, 1985), and the Congressional Budget Office used their version of DYNASIM2 to examine the earnings sharing issue for Congress (Congressional Budget Office, 1986).

The ability to reference family histories is useful in another type of application. Projecting the magnitude of the long-term care needs of the future elderly population has become the topic of a number of recent studies. The probability of requiring long-term care in an institutional setting is significantly lower when an older person has a spouse or child who is able to care for them at home. The lower birth rates and higher divorce rates that have characterized the baby-boom generation may lead to a dearth of family caregivers for baby boomers in their old age, thereby increasing their need for institutional care.

DYNASIM's capability was recently used for this type of application (Zedlewski, Barnes, Burt, McBride, and Meyer, 1989). The goal of the entire project, funded by the Administration on Aging, was to project the future needs of the elderly population in various areas, given alternative assumptions regarding their future mortality and disability rates. Effects on long-term care needs, as well as the potential demand for social services and the interrelationships between these types of services were considered.

This application took advantage of a number of the unique features of a microanalytic model. As mentioned, alternative mortality and health scenarios were projected to the year 2030. There is considerable disagreement over potential future increases in longevity for Americans. The Social Security Administration's "middle-of-the-road" assumptions project that future improvements in mortality rates will be more moderate than they have been in the past 20 years or so, based on the argument that advances in medical treatment for diseases affecting the elderly are likely to slow down. Others argue that the SSA's "pessimistic"[5] assumptions that project historical declines in mortality rates are more realistic. Another uncertainty surrounds the issue of how healthy the older population might be. Increases in longevity do not necessarily imply that the rate of disability among older Americans will remain constant (Manton, 1986; Ycas, 1987). Thus the DYNASIM2 projections of the elderly population also varied the future rates of disability among older Americans.[6]

The DYNASIM2 model was used to show what each of three mortality/disability scenarios will imply for future needs of the elderly population. The results showed a range of possible outcomes—from low mortality and disability rates to high mortality and high disability rates. The effects of the different assumptions on other demographic and economic outcomes were simulated, and the implications for future health, income, and social service needs of the elderly were explored.

FUTURE POSSIBILITIES

There seems to be a resurgence of interest in dynamic microsimulation modeling, presumably attributable primarily to the computing advances realized during the 1980s. Computing power, both from efficiency and cost standpoints, has increased tremendously, making the development, implementation, and use of these models much more practical. The wider accessibility and affordability of dynamic models means that more analysts are considering questions that require life-cycle-type analyses and applications that require long-range future projections.

Cheap and efficient computer power means not only that simulations can run quickly and cheaply, but also that operating characteristics can be developed quickly. Large public-use databases can easily be processed with standard software. Statistical analysis of these data and estimation of fairly sophisticated behavioral modules have been simplified considerably. Models such as DYNASIM2 need to be continually updated. As noted, it took years to develop the original DYNASIM model, partly because of slow and expensive computers and the fact that analysts often had to write their own statistical routines. Statistical packages such as SPSS were just becoming available. Often analysts had to sacrifice analytical content to get a reasonable model estimated within existing computer limitations. In contrast, operating characteristics can now be estimated on personal computers or microcomputers using essentially free computer time, and sophisticated software packages are widely available.

As mentioned earlier, one of the goals of the DYNASIM development was that it should serve as a receptacle for the best behavioral equations developed by social scientists across the country. To date it has proven to be very difficult to adapt good research results to the DYNASIM model. The best research models typically include variables that are not simulated, and sometimes their structure is too complicated to incorporate directly into a simulation model. Only in rare circumstances have analysts been able to adapt external behavioral research to the DYNASIM2 model (see table 4.2). Increased computing power should make it possible to achieve this goal in the future. It is no longer very expensive to reestimate a model so that it is compatible with the simulation system, and analytical datasets are often easily transportable, making in-house adaptations possible.

The revolution in computing also means that implementation and validation of new modules is considerably easier. In fact, in the foreseeable future modules could easily be tested on a PC, using a subset of a large population data file as input. Then, fully tested modules could be swapped into the mainframe version of the DYNASIM2 system. The entire DYNASIM2 model might also be run on a PC. Today the only limitations seem to be that PCs still cannot store the large amounts of microdata generated by the model, in addition to the significant time required to process a 60,000-person population file. Steven Caldwell of Cornell University has already developed a version of the DYNASIM2 family and earnings history model for an IBM PC.

Advances in computing power also have made model validation much easier. Multiple runs that test the sensitivity of results to variations in random numbers or other parameters are feasible. More extensive validation of model results should mean that there will be further acceptance of this type of research tool. Analysts and policymakers need to be able to understand and explain where the model's results are "coming from" before the results can be useful in the policy arena.

In short, recent advances in computing power and software availability are likely to ensure that microanalytic models such as DYNASIM2 will continue to be developed and expanded. But, of course, successful future model development will also require adequate research funding, trained microsimulators, and appropriate data. If interest in dynamic models does expand as they become more practical, then funding will naturally follow. This should, in turn, facilitate the training of microsimulators.

However, the lack of recent, appropriate input data presents a particular challenge for applications in the retirement and aging area. A critical input to the DYNASIM2 system or to any other life-history projection model is a representative data file rich in demographic and economic detail, preferably with some historical information already recorded. DYNASIM2 creates a history of earnings for each individual as it proceeds. However, since the Social Security system counts earnings for all years from 1951 or age 21, whichever is later, the model requires at least some presimulation earnings information for all persons retiring before the year 2008. (At that point, the entire benefit computation period falls within the simulation period.) Currently, DYNASIM2 uses the 1973 Exact Match file for applications in the retirement and aging area. The 1973 file was a match of the 1973 Current Population Survey, actual Social Security Earnings Records, and Internal Revenue Service 1972 tax return information. A less successful attempt was made to produce a similar file for 1978, and this file never became publicly available. Unfortunately current legal privacy constraints prohibit the production of a new Exact Match file. Thus, analysts will probably have to rely on alternative statistical procedures that impute presimulation earnings to Census files.

In conclusion, while the DYNASIM project at The Urban Institute may have only been partially successful in meeting its developers' original, ambitious goals to date, it may simply be that DYNASIM was an idea ahead of its time. But one can now say with confidence that the time is ripe to develop efficient, inexpensive models that can be used broadly throughout the research community. Current computing power means that the research work of many individuals in varied areas of the social sciences could be adapted to enhance the current basic structure of the model. Moreover, a more complete economic model, one that includes all facets of micro-behavior as well as a model of the macroeconomy, is now feasible. The current DYNASIM2 model could be enhanced, for example, to include more life-cycle transitions, more specific geographic detail, and a macroeconomic model. In many respects, the computer technology of the 1960s and even the 1970s lagged far behind what was needed for a model to achieve its original goals.

ADDENDUM: OTHER MICROANALYTIC MODELS

This chapter's discussion focused only on the development of the DYNASIM2 model at The Urban Institute. There have also been a number of other developments of microanalytic models, a quick review of which may help readers gain a fuller picture of dynamic model development. Guy Orcutt and James Smith, leader and member of the original DYNASIM team at The Urban Institute, respectively, developed a dynamic model called the Microanalytic Simulation System (MASS) that essentially included all of the original DYNA-SIM operating characteristics (Smith, Franklin, and Orcutt, 1977). MASS was written in PL1 for a university computer and was capable of processing large amounts of data inexpensively. Thus, this model was completed prior to The Urban Institute's DYNASIM2. Orcutt and Smith have further developed MASS and have applied it in a number of policy areas, but particularly in the area of the intergenerational transmission of wealth (Smith and Orcutt, 1980). Smith has also been working on further developments of this model (Smith, 1986).

The MASS system was further developed for the Social Security Administration (McKay, 1979). The SSA used this model in 1985 to simulate earnings sharing proposals (U. S. Department of Health and Human Services, 1985). Although analysts incorporated some different versions of operating characteristics than those used in the DYNASIM2 system, the SSA's simulation results were remarkably similar to those produced in the DYNASIM2 earnings sharing analysis. Both projects, however, used the same aggregate forecast assumptions.

As mentioned earlier, the Congressional Budget Office was one of the chief supporters of the development of DYNASIM2, and they have an in-house version of the model. They have made a few changes in their version of DYNASIM2, but it still closely resembles DYNASIM2 at The Urban Institute.

As mentioned, Steven Caldwell has recently developed a version of DYNASIM for an IBM PC computer. This model, called the Cornell Simulation Model (CORSIM), essentially incorporates operating characteristics analogous to those included in DYNASIM2's FEH model.

In a totally separate effort, ICF developed its own microanalytic model, the Pension and Retirement Income Simulation Model (PRISM). This model has been used extensively for studies evaluating the private pension system, and, more recently, it has been used to project long-term health care costs. It is described by Kennell and Sheils in the chapter following.

Notes

1. See Orcutt, Caldwell, and Wertheimer (1976) for a general history of the development of dynamic microsimulation models through 1973 and Smith (1986) for a review of developments subsequent to 1974.

2. TRIM provides for population aging through a reweighting scheme that permits a user to make assumptions regarding changes in population size, unemployment rates, or real growth. This aging technique works satisfactorily for short-run projections, but it cannot capture the important long-run interactions among changing economic and demographic events.

3. The original DYNASIM model is fully documented in Orcutt, Caldwell, and Wertheimer (1976), and its computer software, MASH, is documented in Sadowsky (1977).

4. The major hurdle in transferring from an IBM installation to the VAX was the conversion of the various inputs to the model—the micropopulations, and the on-line dictionary files.

5. That is, pessimistic so far as the OASDHI Trust Funds are concerned.

6. A health model for the elderly population was recently developed for DYNASIM2. An ordered probit model to predict the degree number of limitations in activities of daily living (ADL's), indicative of the degree of disability among the elderly, was estimated using data from the 1984 National Health Interview Survey and the 1984 Long-Term Care Survey. This model is described in Hacker and McBride (1989).

References

Cherlin, Andrew. Aug. 1977. "The Effect of Children on Marital Dissolution." *Demography*, 14(3).

Congressional Budget Office. Jan. 1986. *Earnings Sharing Options for the Social Security System*. Washington, D.C.: Congressional Budget Office.

Gordon, Nancy M. 1978. "The Treatment of Women in the Public Pension Systems of Five Countries." Working Paper 5069-1. Washington, D.C.: Urban Institute.

Hacker, R. Scott and Timothy McBride. July 1989. "Dynamic Simulation of Income Model (DYNASIM), Volume III: The Cross-Sectional Imputation Model (CSIM)." Urban Institute Working Paper 3646-01. Washington, D.C.: Urban Institute.

Hendricks, G., R. Holden, and J. Johnson. 1976. "A File of Simulated Family and Earnings Histories through the Year 2000: Contents and Documentation." Working Paper 985-3. Washington, D.C.: Urban Institute.

Holden, Russell, and Gary Hendricks. June 1976. "Simulation of Job Changes and Movements between the Government and Private Sectors." Working Paper 985-2. Washington, D.C.: Urban Institute.

Johnson, Jan, Richard Wertheimer, and Sheila Zedlewski. Nov. 1983. "The Dynamic Simulation of Income Model (DYNASIM), Volume I: The Family and Earnings History Model." Urban Institute Project report to the Congressional Budget Office. Washington, D.C.

Johnson, Jan, and Sheila Zedlewski. Dec. 1982. "The Dynamic Simulation of Income Model (DYNASIM), Volume II: The Jobs and Benefits History Model." Urban Institute Project Report to the Congressional Budget Office. Washington, D.C.

Manton, Kenneth. 1986. "Past and Future Life Expectancy Increases at Later Ages: Their Implications for the Linkage of Chronic Morbidity, Disability, and Mortality." *Journal of Gerontology* 41(5).

McKay, Cindy. Sept. 1979. "Micro Analytical Simulation System Technical Documentation," Volume I. Washington, D.C.: The Hendrickson Corporation.

Michel, Richard, James Storey, and Sheila R. Zedlewski. Dec. 1983. "Saving Social Security: The Short- and Long-Run Effects of the 1983 Amendments." Changing Domestic Priorities Discussion Paper. Washington, D.C.: Urban Institute.

Moore, Kristin, and Richard Wertheimer. 1982. "Teenage Childbearing: Public Sector Costs." Final Report to the National Institute of Child Health and Human Development. Washington, D.C.: Urban Institute.

Orcutt, Guy, Steven Caldwell, and Richard Wertheimer. 1976 "Policy Exploration through Microanalytic Simulation." Washington, D.C.: Urban Institute.

Orcutt, Guy, M. Greenberger, J. Korbel, and A. Rivlin. 1961. *Microanalysis of Socioeconomic Systems: A Simulation Study.* New York: Harper and Row.

Preston, Samuel and John McDonald. Feb. 1979. "The Incidence of Divorce within Cohorts of American Marriages Contracted Since the Civil War." *Demography*, 16(1).

Sadowsky, George. 1977. "MASH: A Computer System for Microanalytic Simulation for Policy Exploration." Washington, D.C.: Urban Institute.

Schulz, James. 1979. "The Economic Impact of Private Pensions on Retirement Income." Final Report to the National Science Foundation, Washington, D.C.

Schulz, James. 1982. "Problems of American Pensions: Microsimulation Policy Analysis." *Journal of Institutional and Theoretical Economics*, no. 138.

Smith, James. 1986. "Microanalytic Simulation and Social Policy." In *Microanalytic Simulation Models to Support Social and Financial Policy*, edited by G. Orcutt, J. Mertz, and H. Quinke. New York: Elsevier-North Holland Science Publishing.

Smith, J.D., S.D. Franklin, and G.H. Orcutt. 1977. "The Intergenerational Transmission of Wealth: A Simulation Experiment." In *The Distribution of Economic Well-Being*, edited by T.F. Juster. Studies in Income and Wealth, National Bureau of Research, No. 4. Cambridge, Mass: Ballinger Publishing.

Smith, James, and Guy Orcutt. 1980. "The Intergenerational Transmission of Wealth: Does Family Size Matter?" In *Modeling the Distribution and Intergenerational Transmission of Wealth*, edited by J. D. Smith. Chicago: University of Chicago Press.

Storey, James, et al., 1981. "The Effects of Raising the Age Limit for Mandatory Retirement in the Age Discrimination in Employment Act." Mandatory Retirement Study Final Report. Washington, D.C.: Urban Institute.

Thompson, Larry. 1976. "Intracohort Redistribution in the Social Security Retirement Program." In *1976 Proceedings of the Business and Economics Statistics Section of the American Statistical Association.* Washington, D.C.: The American Statistical Association.

U.S. Department of Health, Education, and Welfare. Feb. 1979. *The Changing Roles of Mean and Women.* Washington, D.C.

U.S. Department of Health and Human Services. Jan. 1985. *Report on Earnings Sharing Implementation Study.* Washington, D.C.

Weed, James. 1980. "National Estimates of Marriage Dissolution and Survivorship," Series 3, No. 19. Washington, D.C.: U.S. Department of Health and Human Services, National Center for Health Statistics.

Wertheimer, Richard, and Sheila R. Zedlewski. 1978. "The Impact of Demographic Change on the Distribution of Earned Income and the

AFDC Program: 1975–1985. In *The Economic Consequences of Slowing Population Growth*, edited by Thomas Espenshade and William Serow. New York: Academic Press.

Wertheimer, Richard, Sheila R. Zedlewski, J. Anderson, and K. Moore. 1986. "DYNASIM in Comparison with Other Microsimulation Models." In *Microanalytic Simulation Models to Support Social and Financial Policy*, edited by G. Orcutt, J. Mertz, and H. Quinke. New York: Elsevier-North Holland Science Publishers.

Ycas, Martynas. Feb. 1987. "Recent Trends in Health near the Age of Retirement: New Findings from the Health Interview Survey ." *Social Security Bulletin* 50(2): 5–30.

Zedlewski, Sheila. Feb. 1988. "Effects of Reduction in the Hours of Work Pension Participation Requirement." Urban Institute Working Paper 3066-01. Washington, D.C.: Urban Institute.

Zedlewski, Sheila. 1984a. "The Private Pension System to the Year 2020." In *Retirement and Economic Behavior*, edited by Henry Aaron and Gary Burtless. Washington, D.C.: Brookings Institution.

Zedlewski, Sheila. Dec. 1984b. "The Distributional Consequences of an Earnings Sharing Proposal." Research Report 3344. Washington, D.C.: Urban Institute.

Zedlewski, Sheila. 1977. "Distributional Impact of Two Macroeconomic Scenarios and a Negative Income Tax Program." Urban Institute Working Paper 5075-5. Washington, D.C.: The Urban Institute.

Zedlewski, Sheila, Robert Barnes, Martha Burt, Timothy McBride, and Jack Meyer. 1989. "The Needs of the Elderly in the 21st Century." Urban Institute Project Report to the Administration on Aging. Washington, D.C.: Urban Institute.

Chapter Five

PRISM: DYNAMIC SIMULATION OF PENSION AND RETIREMENT INCOME

David L. Kennell and John F. Sheils

During the next 30 years the number of elderly persons in the United States will increase by over 50 percent. Although over the past 30 years there have been dramatic improvements in the economic status of the elderly, their economic status in the future is uncertain. Key decisions about private pension regulation, Social Security policy, and tax incentives for retirement savings all hinge on the likely economic status of the future elderly.

The Pension and Retirement Income Simulation Model (PRISM) was developed to simulate the economic status of the elderly during the period from 1980 to 2020. As a dynamic simulation model, PRISM was designed to incorporate the range of factors that would effect the income of the elderly, including changes in retirement income programs like Social Security, private pensions, and individual retirement accounts, changes in labor force participation rates, and changes in key economic variables. This chapter examines the PRISM model, its key assumptions, how it differs from the DYNASIM model, and some illustrative results from the model.

OVERVIEW OF PRISM METHODOLOGY

The ICF Pension and Retirement Income Simulation Model (PRISM) simulates the distribution of retirement income from both public and private sources for elderly families through the year 2025. PRISM models income from Social Security, private and public employee retirement plans, individual retirement accounts (IRAs), earnings, assets, and the Supplemental Security Income (SSI) program, as well as estimates taxes paid in retirement. The model also simulates utilization and financing of long-term care by the elderly in future years.[1]

PRISM simulates the distribution of income from public and private sources among households of various socioeconomic groups for a sample of individuals age 25 and older in 1979 obtained from the ICF Pension/Social Security Database. These data are an exact match of the May 1979 Pension Supplement of the Current Population Survey (CPS) with Social Security Administration earnings history data for 1951 through 1977. The model's simulations of retirement income are based upon the characteristics of individuals in 1979, their family and work histories prior to 1979, and simulations of the future workforce experience of these individuals. The model allows analysts to estimate the distribution of retirement income under current policy and to analyze the impact that changes in Social Security policy or employer pension regulation may have on various segments of the retired population.

The model is also designed to estimate the utilization and financing of long-term care services by elderly of various socioeconomic groups in future years. In a joint effort with the Brookings Institution, ICF modified the PRISM model to estimate utilization of various long-term care services including institutional (i.e., nursing home) and noninstitutional (i.e., home health, caregiver, etc.) care for a representative sample of individuals through the year 2025. The Brookings/ICF Long-Term Care Financing Model also estimates total long-term care expenditures and the amounts paid for long-term care services by various public and private sources including Medicare, Medicaid, and out-of-pocket payments. The model permits analysts to model the impact of alternative public policies concerning long-term care financing. Also, the model allows analysts to study how changes in retirement income policy will affect individuals' capacity to pay for long-term care services in future years.

PRISM is a dynamic microsimulation model that simulates the distribution of retirement income for a representative sample of the population. For each individual in the model, PRISM uses probabilities estimated primarily from recent Census data to simulate each individual's earnings, periods of employment, and family structure between 1979 and the date of retirement. ICF has integrated PRISM with the ICF Macroeconomic-Demographic Model of the U.S. Retirement Income System to ensure that its estimates of labor force participation and earnings are consistent with the projected aggregate growth of the economy.[2]

Using the simulated work histories, the model calculates the Social Security benefits and IRA accumulations for each individual, as well as SSI benefits and earnings from employment once the individual reaches retirement age. When individuals are simulated to enter a pension covered job, the model assigns them to an actual pension plan selected from a representative sample of private and public retirement plan sponsors. When these individuals meet the plans' eligibility standards, PRISM calculates their benefits using the plans' actual benefit provisions. The model also estimates the amount of individuals' assets in retirement based upon the distribution of assets reported in the 1983 Survey of Consumer Finances data. Separate amounts are estimated for financial assets and home equity. Individuals are assumed to receive an annual income from nonhousing assets equal to about 8 percent of their financial assets.

The model then simulates elderly individuals' utilization of home health and nursing home services and estimates sources of financing for these types of care. The Brookings/ICF Long-Term Care Financing Model portion of PRISM estimates payments for long-term care services by service, including Medicare, Medicaid, private insurance, and household out-of-pocket expenses. The model also simulates the use of household financial assets, assets to finance long-term care, and the impact of these on income the elderly receive from assets. This is a particularly important feature for studies of poverty among the elderly, because many nursing home residents and their spouses are often driven into poverty as their income-producing assets are exhausted to pay for nursing home care.

As shown in figure 5.1, the PRISM model has four basic components: the ICF Simulation Databases, the ICF Work History Model, the ICF Retirement Income Simulation Model, and the Brookings/ICF Long-Term Care Financing Model. Each of these is described in the paragraphs that follow.

The ICF simulation databases constitute the first component. ICF has developed two major databases for use in PRISM. The ICF Pension/Social Security Database contains detailed pension coverage, labor force, and income information for a large, representative sample of the population. This database is useful for analyses of pension and Social Security benefits because it provides information on current and historical pension plan participation and a history of coverage and covered earnings under the Social Security system for each individual in the database.

ICF developed this database by linking together information provided in the Special Pension Supplement to the May 1979 Current Population Survey with actual Social Security Administration (SSA) data on covered earnings of a subset of the individuals included in the May 1979 survey. (The May 1979 CPS is a survey of a represen-

Figure 5.1   FLOW DIAGRAM OF PENSION AND RETIREMENT INCOME SIMULATION
MODEL (PRISM)

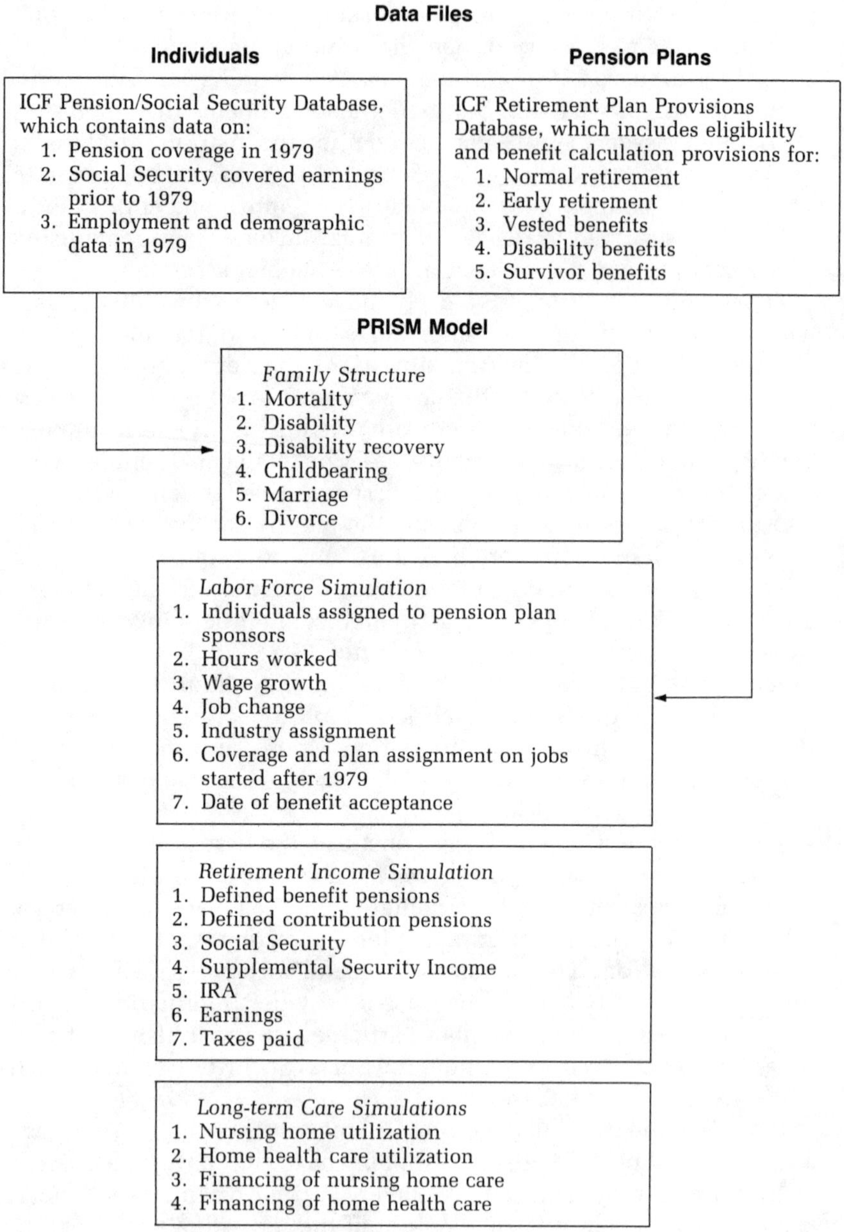

Data Files

Individuals   **Pension Plans**

ICF Pension/Social Security Database,   ICF Retirement Plan Provisions
which contains data on: Database, which includes eligibility
  1. Pension coverage in 1979   and benefit calculation provisions for:
  2. Social Security covered earnings   1. Normal retirement
     prior to 1979   2. Early retirement
  3. Employment and demographic   3. Vested benefits
     data in 1979   4. Disability benefits
                                                                      5. Survivor benefits

PRISM Model

Family Structure
  1. Mortality
  2. Disability
  3. Disability recovery
  4. Childbearing
  5. Marriage
  6. Divorce

Labor Force Simulation
  1. Individuals assigned to pension plan
     sponsors
  2. Hours worked
  3. Wage growth
  4. Job change
  5. Industry assignment
  6. Coverage and plan assignment on jobs
     started after 1979
  7. Date of benefit acceptance

Retirement Income Simulation
  1. Defined benefit pensions
  2. Defined contribution pensions
  3. Social Security
  4. Supplemental Security Income
  5. IRA
  6. Earnings
  7. Taxes paid

Long-term Care Simulations
  1. Nursing home utilization
  2. Home health care utilization
  3. Financing of nursing home care
  4. Financing of home health care

tative sample of the U.S. population conducted by the Bureau of the Census, which contains detailed information on the coverage of working individuals by private and public pension plans and other economic and demographic information.)

About one-half of the individuals interviewed in the May 1979 CPS pension supplement were also surveyed by the Bureau of the Census in March 1978 and March 1979. Consequently, as shown in figure 5.2, for approximately 28,000 individuals, we were able to include additional earnings and employment information for each year between 1977 and 1979.

As shown in figure 5.2, the employment and pension coverage information from the CPS surveys was also matched with SSA information on the taxable earnings and Social Security coverage of each of these individuals during the 1937–77 period. This match of SSA data with that of CPS was made possible by an earlier study conducted by the Bureau of the Census and the SSA that matched the March 1978 CPS with SSA data on individuals' actual earnings histories prior to 1978. Because many of those interviewed in the May 1979 CPS were also interviewed in March 1978, the linkage of SSA data with the May CPS was straightforward. As a result, as shown in figure 5.2, for a representative sample of over 28,000 adults, the ICF Pension/Social Security Database contains: (1) pension information for 1979, (2) employment data for 1977–79, (3) income data for 1977 and 1978, (4) quarters of Social Security coverage credited annually for 1937–77, (5) annual covered taxable earnings for 1951–77, and (6) family structure and background data for 1977–79.

The data were also organized into family units so that the distribution of pension coverage among married couples could be analyzed. This was a straightforward procedure, because the CPS provides information on each member of the surveyed households and on how individuals within a household are related to each other through marriage or kinship.

The individual records from the ICF Pension/Social Security Database provide the population data used in the ICF work history and retirement income simulation models. For a particular group of the population or for the entire population, a sample of actual records is selected for use in the simulation.

The ICF Retirement Plan Provisions Database, the other major database for use in PRISM, contains detailed eligibility and benefit formula information for a representative sample of 325 public and private retirement plan sponsors. These data include benefit and eligibility information current as of January 1984. The representative

Figure 5.2 DATA SOURCES USED TO CREATE THE ICF PENSION/SOCIAL SECURITY DATABASE

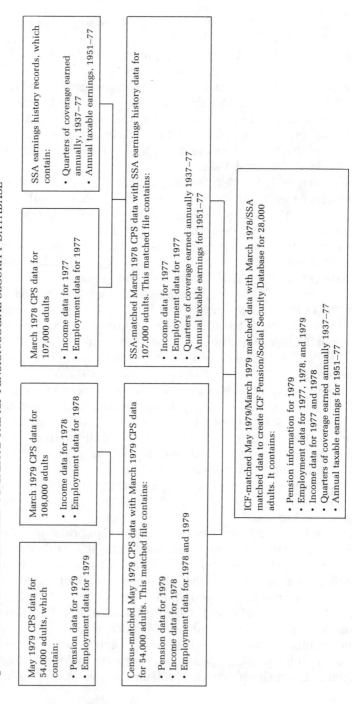

plan sponsors include both single and multiemployer plan sponsors from all industries, including the public sector. The database contains information on the defined benefit and/or defined contribution plans that each of these sponsors maintains for hourly and/or salaried employees. Because the database contains data on the primary and supplemental plans of each of the 325 sponsors, these data include 475 separate pension plans.[3]

The ICF Work History Model is the second major component of PRISM. It uses dynamic simulation techniques to generate work, wage, and family histories for individuals selected from the ICF Pension/Social Security Database. It can be divided into two parts: *family structure simulation*, which simulates mortality, disability, childbearing, marriage, and divorce, and *labor force simulation*, which simulates the labor force experience of each individual. The model assigns covered individuals to one of the plan sponsors in the ICF Retirement Plan Provisions Database and simulates the decision to accept pensions and Social Security. This model has been linked to the ICF Macroeconomic-Demographic Model so that it produces consistent, long-run estimates of labor force participation and earnings in its simulations.

The ICF Retirement Income Simulation Model is the third component of PRISM. It calculates before- and after-tax benefits at retirement from the plans in which each individual has participated. This model also calculates Social Security benefits and benefits from IRA accounts established by individuals. Finally, the model calculates benefits for low-income individuals from the Supplemental Security Income program.

The Brookings/ICF Long-Term Care Financing Model is the fourth component of the model. It simulates movements into and out of nursing homes and utilization of health care services provided in the home (noninstitutional services). The model estimates total charges for nursing home services and the amounts paid by various sources including Medicare, Medicaid, and out-of-pocket payments from cash income and financial assets. The model also estimates sources of payment for noninstitutional services including Medicare, Medicaid, private out-of-pocket, and other sources.

The first version of PRISM was developed in 1980 for the Office of Pension and Welfare Benefit Programs at the U.S. Department of Labor and the President's Commission on Pension Policy. Since 1980, PRISM has undergone substantial revisions and enhancements designed to improve its capacity to model Social Security and pension policy. The model has been used by a number of public and private organizations to analyze a wide range of retirement policies including: changes in Social Security, pension incomes under alternative revisions to the Employee Retirement Income Security Act (ERISA) (e.g., five-year vesting, limitations on Social Security integration, and so on), taxation of pension accruals, and retiree health coverage provided through pension plans.

COMPARISON OF PRISM AND DYNASIM

PRISM was designed to simulate the ways in which Social Security, pensions, earnings, IRAs, SSI, and taxes will together shape the distribution of retirement income, and, hence, the sources of financing for long-term care. The model permits simulations of changes in Social Security benefit provisions, modifications in federal pension regulations, alternative economic assumptions, and alternative policies on financing of long-term care.

Like The Urban Institute's DYNASIM model, PRISM uses dynamic simulation techniques to "age" a representative sample of individuals to future years by simulating year-to-year changes in age, marital status, employment status, and other socioeconomic variables. For each individual in the sample, the models produce a life history of employment and family structure data that is used to estimate incomes in retirement from Social Security, pensions, SSI, and other sources.[4] These life history simulations are crucial to analyses of Social Security and pension income programs, which typically calculate benefit amounts based upon an individual's lifetime earnings while covered under these retirement income programs.

Although PRISM and DYNASIM are similar in concept, there are significant differences in the data and methodologies they employ, as described by Haveman and Lacker (1984). First, they point out that PRISM is a streamlined model that primarily simulates events pertaining to accumulation of retirement income, whereas DYNASIM is a more general population model that simulates a broader range of events (for instance, education of children, etc.).

Second, the models use different population samples. PRISM uses the Pension Supplement to the May 1979 Current Population Survey, which is matched with Social Security earnings history data for 1951 through 1977 for each individual surveyed. DYNASIM uses the March 1973 Current Population Survey, which was matched with Social Security Summary Earnings Record (SER) data for each individual.

Third, the two models use different techniques to simulate incomes from pensions. PRISM simulates pension income by: linking an individual's periods of covered employment with a sample of actual retirement plan sponsors and using the actual benefit provisions of these plans to calculate retirement benefits, including those provided through supplemental plans. DYNASIM uses a series of random processes to assign covered individuals' pension plan provisions such as participation and vesting standards, formula type, and benefit accrual rates. In developing PRISM, we chose to assign individuals to a sample of plan sponsors to capture the important interrelationships between the benefit provisions and other plan provisions. For example, by matching to a sample of actual plans, the simulations reflect that some plans may be structured with generous vesting provisions while providing low benefit accruals. This approach also reflects that some plans provide generous benefit levels but require longer periods to vest. Also, because individuals are actually linked with a specific plan sponsor, we are able to simulate an individual's benefits under both the sponsor's primary plan and any supplemental plan the employer may provide.

Fourth, PRISM is constrained to replicate exogenous specifications of employment and population trends, whereas DYNASIM generally develops these estimates endogenously. PRISM is designed to develop life history simulations for individual observations while in the aggregate replicating macroeconomic projections of employment levels by age, sex, and industry, and demographic projections by age, sex, and marital status. DYNASIM can and has been calibrated to replicate exogenous totals. However, the PRISM system automatically develops calibration factors during each year of the simulation, whereas in DYNASIM these calibration factors are developed outside the model and entered as inputs.

A fifth difference between the models is that PRISM includes a simulation of long-term care utilization and financing. This was added to PRISM after Haveman and Lacker's 1984 review of the two models. PRISM's Brookings/ICF Long-Term Care Financing Model permits simulations of alternative means of financing long-term care services and provides estimates of the impact this will have on various payors (Medicare, Medicaid, family out-of-pocket, etc.) in future years. It also permits simulations of how the asset stocks of the elderly are drawn down as these resources are used to pay for long-term care services. Because income from assets is one of the most important sources of income for the elderly, simulation of the impact of long-term care on asset stocks is a crucial factor in modeling the incomes of tomorrow's elderly.

PRISM MODEL ASSUMPTIONS

To simulate the future workforce experience and retirement incomes of individuals, PRISM requires a large number of assumptions concerning the likelihood of future events for each individual, such as the likelihood an individual will continue to work, whether he or she will become divorced or marry, and whether he or she will contribute to an IRA. The key assumptions are discussed in the paragraphs following.

Demographic Assumptions

PRISM simulates mortality, disability, childbearing, and changes in marital status. During each simulation year individuals are simulated to die, become disabled, recover from disability, bear children, and become married or divorced. The current version of the model uses a variety of assumptions to make these estimates, most of which are consistent with the Alternative II-B assumptions used in the 1986 report of the Trustees of the Federal Old Age and Survivors Insurance and Disability Insurance Trust Funds (hereafter, "1986 Trustee's Report"). The major suppositions are as follows:

Mortality. PRISM uses the Alternative II-B mortality assumptions used in the 1986 Trustee's Report. Mortality rates vary by age, sex, disability status, and number of years since becoming disabled. Mortality rates vary during each simulation year to reflect projected improvements in mortality made by the Social Security Actuary.

Disability. For persons under 65, PRISM uses the rates of disability developed by the Social Security Actuary for 1986. These rates vary by age and sex and are assumed to remain unchanged over time.

Recovery From Disability. PRISM uses rates of disability recovery developed by the Social Security Actuary for 1979–80. These rates vary by age, sex, and number of years since becoming disabled. These are the most recent rates available and are assumed to remain unchanged over time.

Childbearing. Fertility rates in the model are based upon an ICF analysis of recent Bureau of the Census data on women who gave birth to children during the 1976–80 period. These fertility rates vary by age, marital status, employment status, and number of children. In the model, these rates are constrained to match the Alternative II-B assumptions of fertility in the 1986 Trustee's Report. These rates assume a moderate growth in childbearing through 2010.

Marital Status. All probabilities concerning marriage and divorce are obtained from monthly Vital Statistics data developed by the National Center for Health Statistics. The aggregate rates match the Alternative II-B projections in the 1984 Trustee's Report. Divorce rates vary by the age of husband and wife. Marriage rates vary by age, sex, and marital status (i.e., never married, divorced, or widowed) of the individual. In the model, individuals selected to become married are joined with a member of the opposite sex based upon data on the distribution of newly married individuals by age of husband and wife reported in Vital Statistics data. The marriage and divorce rates are assumed to remain constant in the future.

Labor Force and Economic Assumptions

PRISM simulates each individual's employment history from 1979 (the date of the May 1979 CPS survey) through the date of retirement. During each simulation year, the model simulates wage rates, hours worked, job change, and industry of employment. The simulations were constrained to match November 1985 Bureau of Labor Statistics (BLS) projections of employment and industry composition and the Alternative II-B assumptions from the 1986 Trustee's Report of average wage rates in future years. The major suppositions are as follows:

EMPLOYMENT LEVELS OVER TIME

PRISM was constrained to simulate aggregate levels of employment consistent with BLS forecasts of labor force participation rates for 1985–2000. Labor force participation rates after 2000 are assumed to remain constant for each age/sex group. These forecasts include: (1) trends in employment for men and women of various age groups, (2) projections of economic growth and (3) trends in the age of retirement. We used unemployment rates from the 1986 Trustee's Report for the years 1986–2020. Actual participation rates and unemployment rates were used for 1979–85.

IMPACT OF SOCIAL SECURITY AMENDMENTS ON LABOR FORCE PARTICIPATION

The Social Security Amendments of 1983 provided incentives for the elderly to stay in the labor force longer. These provisions included the eventual increase in the normal retirement age to 67, an increase in the early retirement penalty, an increase in the delayed retirement credit, and a decrease in the reduction of benefits for earnings over the test amount. Independent evaluation of these provisions has yielded several estimates of their effects.

We assumed that labor force participation rates among individuals aged 62 through 67 will tend to increase starting in the year 2000 as the normal retirement age is gradually increased. Consequently, we adjusted the BLS forecasts of employment for individuals aged 62 through 67 to reflect these changes in labor force participation.

IMPACT OF ELIMINATION OF MANDATORY RETIREMENT AT AGE 70

Prior to 1987, employers could legally require workers to retire when they reached age 70. Legislation passed in 1986 made such regulations illegal for most employers. The potential consequences of this legislation are: The U.S. Department of Labor has estimated an additional 200,000 workers over 65 in the labor force by the year 2000; and Edward Lazear (1979) predicted that those approaching mandatory retirement will gain, while employers and younger workers will lose as a result of this policy. We modified the BLS labor force participation rates for persons aged 70 and over, which assume no change in mandatory retirement law, to increase employment by 200,000 persons by year 2000 based on the Department of Labor estimates.

EMPLOYMENT BY SOCIOECONOMIC GROUP

Given the levels of labor force participation for different age/sex groups, the model simulates the number of hours each individual will work during each simulation year based upon an analysis of Bureau of the Census data on employment patterns during the period 1976–80. For each individual, the decision to work and the number of hours worked in a year varies by age, sex, hours worked in each of the three previous years, marital status, presence of children at various ages, pension receipt status, and Social Security benefit receipt status.

INFLATION

Consumer prices are assumed to increase at the rate specified under the Alternative II-B assumptions in the 1986 Trustee's Report.

INTEREST RATES

We assumed that assets in all defined contribution plans and individual retirement accounts (IRAs) earn interest at an average annual rate of 7.0 percent. This is the average annual interest rate assumed in the Alternative II-B assumptions for 1986–2000 in the 1986 Trustee's Report.

WAGE GROWTH

Aggregate changes in wage levels are assumed to increase at the rate assumed in the Alternative II-B assumptions of the 1986 Trustee's Report (see table 5.1). In general, average wages are assumed to grow by one and a half percentage points in excess of the inflation rate in each year after 1990. Actual wage growth rates are used during the 1979–84 period. Given these aggregate rates, the hourly wage rates for each individual in the model are adjusted during each year based upon an analysis of Bureau of the Census data on patterns of wage growth. Rates of wage growth vary by age, sex, and whether or not the individual changed jobs during the year.

Table 5.1 ASSUMED REAL EARNINGS DIFFERENTIALS

Year	Real Earnings Differential (%)
1984	1.7
1985	0.3
1986	1.5
1987	1.3
1988	1.0
1989	1.9
1990	1.6
1991	1.6
1992	1.7
1993	1.5
1994	1.5
1995–99	1.4
2000–2009	1.6
2010 and later	1.5

Source: Alternative II-B assumptions from 1986 Annual Report of the Board of Trustees of the Federal Old Age and Survivors Insurance and Disability Insurance Trust Funds, April 1986.

JOB CHANGE

The probability that an individual will change jobs is based upon an ICF analysis of Census Bureau data concerning job change patterns during 1979. Job change is modeled as a function of the age, part-time/full-time status, and job tenure of each worker. These probabilities are assumed to remain constant over time.

MATERNITY JOB TERMINATIONS

Women who have children often leave the labor force. In some instances, these women may reenter the labor force and resume working for the same employers they had prior to giving birth. In PRISM, we assumed that a woman who has a child and leaves her job in the same year will become reemployed at the same job, if the woman reenters the labor force within five years of having the child and the woman became employed in the same industry she was in prior to having the child.

INDUSTRY CHANGES

PRISM assigns individuals to an industry of employment when they change jobs or enter the labor force. The industry assigned to these individuals varies by age, full-time/part-time status, and industry of prior job. As shown in table 5.2, the model assumes that over time, a higher proportion work in the services industries, and a lower

Table 5.2 PERCENTAGE DISTRIBUTION OF WORKERS BY INDUSTRY OF EMPLOYMENT ASSUMED IN PRISM FOR SELECTED YEARS

Industry	1980 (%)	1982 (%)	1984 (%)	1990 (%)	1995 and after (%)
Mining	0.89	0.95	0.84	0.78	0.71
Construction	4.53	4.20	4.63	4.41	4.50
Manufacturing	20.78	19.08	18.81	18.10	17.40
Transportation	5.02	5.03	5.31	5.23	5.27
Trade	18.71	19.24	19.41	19.70	19.56
Finance	5.09	5.32	5.46	5.51	5.55
Service	17.55	18.44	18.70	20.05	21.14
State and local	12.96	12.96	12.58	11.99	11.86
Federal	3.28	3.28	3.24	2.93	2.80
Self-employed	9.55	9.85	9.49	9.84	9.98
Agriculture	1.64	1.65	1.53	1.46	1.23
Total	100	100	100	100	100

Source: Based upon unpublished November 1985 Bureau of Labor Statistics assumptions for 1990 and 1995.

proportion work in the manufacturing industry. These industry composition estimates are based upon November 1985 BLS projections for the 1985–95 period. After 1995, industry composition is assumed to remain constant.

Pension Coverage Assumptions

For each job individuals have during the simulation, PRISM determines whether they are covered by a retirement plan and assigns covered workers to actual pension plan sponsors in the ICF Retirement Plan Provisions Database.

PENSION COVERAGE

As workers change jobs or enter the labor force during the simulation, retirement plan coverage is simulated using coverage rates reported for job changers and labor force entrants in the May 1979 CPS. The model is further constrained to replicate coverage rates reported in the May 1983 EBRI/HHS CPS pension supplement. These coverage rates vary by the individual's industry of employment, full-time/part-time worker status, age, and real wage rate. Plan coverage on an industry basis assumed not to change between 1983 and 1988, the latter year referring to when the new nondiscrimination rules introduced in the 1986 Tax Reform Act became effective. The coverage rates for 1979, 1983, and 1989 are presented in table 5.3.

IMPACT OF 1986 TAX REFORM ACT ON PENSION COVERAGE

Internal Revenue Service pension plan nondiscrimination rules that became effective in 1989 stipulate that, in general, no more than 30 percent of a plan sponsor's employees could be excluded. Previously, employers could legally exclude up to 44 percent of their employees from the plan. The Tax Reform Act requires that plans satisfy at least one of the following requirements: (1) the plan benefits at least 70 percent of all nonhighly compensated employees, (2) the plan benefits a percentage of nonhighly compensated employees that is at least 70 percent of the percentage of highly compensated employees benefiting under the plan, or (3) the average benefit percentage for nonhighly compensated employees is at least 70 percent of the average benefit percentage for highly compensated employees. We modeled the impact of this provision by estimating the number of persons in each industry who were not participating in a pension plan even though their employer sponsors a pension plan and they appear to meet the most restrictive age and service criteria allowed

Table 5.3 PENSION COVERAGE ASSUMPTIONS

	Industry Coverage Rate, 1979	Industry Coverage Rate, 1983	Industry Coverage Rate, 1989
Federal government	0.93	0.93	0.93
State and local government	0.88	0.83	0.83
Mining	0.82	0.75	0.79
Manufacturing	0.76	0.70	0.73
Transportation	0.75	0.75	0.77
Finance	0.67	0.67	0.75
Construction	0.43	0.41	0.43
Trade	0.43	0.46	0.51
Services	0.43	0.47	0.52
Agriculture	0.19	0.22	0.22
Self-employed	0.14	0.14	0.14

Sources: Coverage rates for 1979 were derived from an ICF analysis of the May 1979 Current Population Survey. Coverage rates for 1983 were based on an ICF analysis of May 1983 EBRI/HHS CPS Pension Supplement. Coverage rates for 1989 were estimated by ICF by adjusting 1983 coverage rates to reflect the potential impact of the nondiscrimination rules in the Tax Reform Act of 1986.

under ERISA (i.e., age 25 with at least 1,000 hours worked over a period of one year). In the model, the coverage rates for each industry were increased starting in 1989 so that no more than 30 percent of these individuals are not participating in their employer's plan.

PLAN ASSIGNMENT

Individuals are assigned to plan sponsors in the ICF Retirement Plan Provisions Database in proportion to the number of individuals actually covered by that plan sponsor. PRISM assigns individuals to plans of similar industry, firm size, Social Security coverage status, union coverage status, multi/single-employer plan status, and hourly/salaried worker status. In addition, individuals are assigned only to plans that are consistent with the characteristics of the plan reported by the individual in the May 1979 CPS. To do this, the model takes into account the individual's reported participation and vesting status as well as plan contribution requirements and participation in a supplemental plan.

Retirement Decision Assumptions

The model simulates early, normal, and late retirement from both pension plans and Social Security. We assumed the current Social

Security legislation (including the 1983 amendments which increased the age at which unreduced benefits will be available) were in place throughout the simulation. The important assumptions in the retirement decision are summarized in the paragraphs following:

SOCIAL SECURITY BENEFIT ACCEPTANCE

PRISM simulates the age at which individuals start to receive Social Security benefits. These benefit acceptance rates vary by the age and sex of the individual. The rates were derived from Social Security benefit receipt data by age and sex during 1980. PRISM also assumes that eligible individuals 62 years of age or older will automatically accept benefits if they are disabled or unemployed or receiving an employer pension. These assumptions lead to an increase in Social Security early retirement because the number of individuals receiving pensions will increase over time in the simulations.

SOCIAL SECURITY SURVIVOR'S BENEFITS

Individuals are simulated to accept Social Security survivor's benefits in the first year they are eligible.

EMPLOYER PENSION BENEFIT ACCEPTANCE

PRISM determines when an individual is eligible to accept employer pension benefits and then simulates the decision to accept the benefit. Benefit acceptance rates were developed by ICF based upon an analysis of recent Bureau of the Census data on pension benefit recipients.

IMPACT OF ELIMINATING MANDATORY RETIREMENT AT AGE 70

All plans in the ICF pension plan database were modified to eliminate mandatory retirement beginning in 1987.

ACCEPTANCE OF DEFERRED VESTED BENEFITS

Individuals who are vested and leave their job prior to their eligibility for early or normal retirement receive a deferred vested benefit. These benefits are assumed to go into pay status when the individual reaches the plan's normal retirement age.

Employer Pension Plan Assumptions

PRISM simulates the size of the benefit individuals will receive from each pension plan in which they earn a benefit during the simulation. PRISM uses the actual provisions of the plan to which the individual was assigned to determine each individual's eligibility and benefit amount. In general, pension plan provisions are assumed to remain unchanged over time, except in instances where plan rules must be changed to be in compliance with the Retirement Equity Act of 1984 (REA) and the Tax Reform Act of 1986. The following assumptions are used in PRISM:

BENEFIT FORMULAS

The benefit formulas in defined benefit plans are indexed to changes in wages for flat and unit benefit formulas. Defined contribution plan salary bend points are also indexed to wage growth. Final pay defined benefit and all other parts of defined contribution plan formulas are held constant. No changes in participation, vesting, or other plan provisions are assumed except where required by REA or the Tax Reform Act of 1986.

IMPACT OF REA ON PARTICIPATION RULES

REA mandates that starting in 1985, the minimum age requirement for participation will be reduced from 25 to 21 and that service between the ages of 19 and 22 will be considered for determining vesting. Starting in 1985, we modified the provisions of any private plans not already in compliance with these provisions.

IMPACT OF THE TAX REFORM ACT OF 1986 ON VESTING

The Tax Reform Act would require private sector single-employer plans to vest benefits at least as rapidly as under the following two schedules: full vesting upon completion of five years of service, or 20 percent vesting after the completion of three years of service and 20 percent more for each subsequent year.[5] Starting in 1989, we modified the provisions of any private single-employer plans not already in compliance with these provisions.

LIMITS ON SOCIAL SECURITY INTEGRATION

Private sector plans that integrate benefits with Social Security will be required to limit their integration formulas. Although IRS regulations currently place restrictions on how plans may integrate benefits, under current law, some low-wage workers have their pension benefits severely reduced or even completely eliminated through integration. The Tax Reform Act retains and simplifies current IRS regulations on integration. In addition, the act establishes additional restrictions on integration that apply separately to three types of integrated plans, as follows:

For defined benefit *excess* plans, the rate at which benefits are provided for pay up to the integration level of a plan may not be less than 50 percent of the rate at which benefits are provided in excess of that level. In addition, the integration level may not be more than the Social Security wage and benefit base.

For defined benefit *offset* plans, the offset may not reduce a participant's benefits by more than 50 percent.

For defined *contribution* plans, the provisions are similar, except that they apply to the rate of employer contributions. In addition, for defined contribution plans, the rate for pay in excess of the integration level may not exceed the rate for up to that level by more than the OASDI tax rate.

COST-OF-LIVING ADJUSTMENTS FOR PENSIONS

We assumed that benefits for private plan beneficiaries from defined benefit plans will be indexed at half the rate of inflation up to a maximum of 2 percent per year. All early and normal retirement benefits from the Civil Service Retirement Plan are assumed to increase at the annual rates of inflation. State and local government benefits are assumed to increase at the rate of inflation up to a maximum of 4 percent each year. These assumptions are based upon a prior ICF study that analyzed cost of living adjustments over a 10-year period for a representative sample of pension plans. We assumed that none of these plans index vested benefits.

POSTRETIREMENT SURVIVOR'S BENEFIT OPTION

Table 5.4 presents the assumptions used to determine which married individuals choose to elect the postretirement joint and survivors' option. Because REA mandates that starting in 1985 spousal consent is required to waive survivor's benefit coverage, we assumed that

Table 5.4 PROBABILITIES THAT MARRIED INDIVIDUALS WILL CHOOSE TO ELECT THE JOINT AND SURVIVOR'S OPTION, BY SIZE OF BENEFIT

	Probability of choosing Postretirement Joint and Survivor's Option	
Benefit size (1980 dollars)	Before REA (%)	After REA (%)
Less than $3,000	30	50
$3,000 or over	75	85

Source: ICF assumptions.

the rate of joint and survivor's election will increase after the act is implemented. Individuals who accept the postretirement survivor's option are assumed to receive a 50 percent joint and survivor's annuity. This annuity provides a surviving spouse with a benefit equal to half that received by the deceased individual while living.

PRERETIREMENT SURVIVOR'S OPTION

Many plans automatically provide individuals with preretirement survivor's coverage. In these plans, all individuals are assumed to "elect" the preretirement survivor's option. In the other defined benefit plans, the model assumes that 60 percent of married individuals will elect the preretirement survivor's option. Because REA mandates spousal consent for waiver of the survivor's coverage, we assumed that after REA is implemented, 80 percent of all married individuals will elect this option.

VESTED BENEFICIARY SURVIVOR'S BENEFITS

As mandated by REA, preretirement survivor's coverage will be extended to spouses of individuals who receive vested benefits. Thus, the model simulates survivor's benefits for spouses of vested beneficiaries who die between the time they leave the job and the date the benefits would have gone into pay status. In all instances, the survivor's benefit is assumed to be a 50 percent joint and survivor's annuity.

MATERNITY

Under REA, workers who leave a pension plan may return to the job and retain their prior years of service for participation and vesting status, provided the break in service is less than or equal to the greater of five years or the number of years of service prior to the break. Although both men and women may benefit from this provision, it is intended to assist women who leave their job for maternity. Because we modeled reemployment by the same employer in maternity cases only (see the previous subsection titled "Labor Force and Economic Assumptions"), this rule is applied in the model only to women who have children. In addition, due to further REA liberalizations in crediting service for maternity cases, we assumed that working women who have a child receive one year of credited service for the year the child is born, regardless of the number of hours they worked.

PARTICIPATION IN SAVINGS AND THRIFT PLANS

Table 5.5 summarizes the assumptions on participation in supplemental thrift and savings plans for those individuals who are eligible to participate in them.

EMPLOYEE CONTRIBUTIONS

In plans that require employee contributions as a condition for plan participation, the model assumes that individuals contribute the amount required to obtain the maximum employer contribution.

LUMP-SUM PAYMENTS

In the current version of PRISM, individuals who are vested in a defined contribution plan and change jobs are selected to "roll" their lump-sum payment into an IRA on the basis of lump-sum rollover data obtained from an analysis by Larry Atkins of the May 1983 EBRI/HHS CPS Pension Supplement. Current law permits individuals to "'roll over" any lump-sum pension payment into an IRA in order to defer payment of taxes on this income until these benefits are drawn upon as income after reaching age 59." The likelihood of a rollover varies by age, marital status, benefit level, and income. For individuals aged 55 or older, we applied a separate rollover rule, whereby all lump sums over $1,750 will be rolled over into an IRA and saved for retirement.

IMPACT OF TAX REFORM ACT ON ROLLOVERS

The Tax Reform Act would eliminate 10-year averaging, thus increasing individuals' incentives to roll over into an IRA lump-sum distributions received from a pension plan. Individuals aged 59 or

Table 5.5 SAVINGS PLAN PARTICIPATION ASSUMPTIONS

	Employer Match Rate[b]		
Hourly Wage Level[a]	Low (%)	Medium (%)	High (%)
Less than $4	20	25	30
$4–$7	40	50	60
More than $7	60	75	90

Source: ICF assumptions.
a. Earnings level in 1980 dollars.
b. Plans that match $1 of employee contributions with less than 50¢ of employer contributions are low-match plans. Plans that match $1 of employee contributions with 50¢ to 99¢ are medium-match plans. Plans that match $1 of employee contributions with $1 or more of employer contributions are high-match plans.

older are permitted to make a one-time election to use five-year forward averaging for a lump-sum distribution that is not rolled over into an IRA. Also, individuals attaining age 50 prior to January 1, 1986, may also make a one-time election to use five-year averaging for a lump-sum distribution. We assumed that the impact of these provisions would be to increase by 50 percent the proportion of individuals who roll over lump-sum distributions and save these assets for retirements.

LUMP-SUM PAYMENTS AS RETIREMENT INCOME

Individuals are assumed to draw upon their defined contribution lump-sum payments (those not cashed out) in the form of an annuity. This annuity is assumed to start at the earlier of either the age the individual accepted Social Security benefits or the year he or she first started receiving a defined benefit pension, but not earlier than age 55.

Individual Retirement Account Assumptions

PRISM models the accumulation of IRA savings. The assumptions used in this analysis are derived primarily from IRA participation data provided in the May 1983 EBRI/HHS CPS pension supplement. ICF recalibrated the assumptions used in these simulations so that PRISM assumptions are consistent with the 1983 estimates of the number of individuals participating in IRAs and the amount of IRA assets accumulated. The key assumptions in our IRA simulations are summarized next. In addition, we modified the IRA submodel of PRISM to reflect the impact of the 1986 Tax Reform Act on IRA savings.

IRA ADOPTION FOR NON-COVERED WORKERS

Table 5.6 summarizes the assumptions used in modeling the adoption of IRAs by *noncovered* workers. These estimates do not include workers assumed to roll over vested benefits into IRA arrangements. ICF estimated these adoption rates using May 1983 EBRI/HHS CPS pension supplement data on noncovered individuals establishing an IRA during 1982.

IRAs FOR COVERED WORKERS

We developed a separate set of IRA adoption probabilities for individuals *covered* by a pension plan, which apply only to 1982 (shown in table 5.7). These probabilities were estimated using the

Table 5.6 IRA ADOPTION ASSUMPTIONS FOR NONCOVERED WORKERS, BY AGE AND FAMILY EARNINGS LEVEL

Family Earnings Level	Age						
	25–34 (%)	35–39 (%)	40–44 (%)	45–54 (%)	55–59 (%)	60–64 (%)
Less than $15,000	0.24	0.24	0.48	0.48	0.72	0.96
$15,000–24,999	0.96	0.96	1.20	1.44	1.68	2.16
$25,000–29,999	1.20	1.32	1.44	2.40	2.40	3.60
$30,000–34,999	1.80	2.40	3.60	4.20	4.80	6.00
$35,000–49,999	3.60	3.60	4.20	4.80	6.00	8.40
$50,000 or more	6.00	6.00	6.00	6.00	12.00	12.00

Source: ICF estimates, based in part upon May 1983 EBRI/HHS CPS pension supplement data.

Table 5.7 IRA ADOPTION PROBABILITIES FOR COVERED WORKERS IN 1982, BY FAMILY INCOME AND AGE OF WORKER

Family Earnings Level	Age						
	25–34 (%)	35–39 (%)	40–44 (%)	45–54 (%)	55–59 (%)	60–65 (%)
Less than $15,000	4.0	7.0	4.0	9.0	13.0	20.0
$15,000–24,999	8.0	8.0	9.0	17.0	27.0	19.0
$25,000–29,999	9.0	14.0	16.0	23.0	30.0	47.0
$30,000–34,999	16.0	20.0	19.0	28.0	46.0	51.0
$35,000–49,999	16.0	27.0	31.0	43.0	46.0	45.0
$50,000 or more	35.0	43.0	48.0	57.0	70.0	63.0

Source: ICF estimates, based in part upon May 1983 EBRI/HHS CPS pension supplement data.

May 1983 EBRI/HHS CPS pension supplement data on covered workers who established an IRA in 1982. In years after 1982, we assumed that the IRA adoption rates for covered workers would be the same as for noncovered individuals (see table 5.6), except as described next.

IRA CONTRIBUTIONS

Once an individual is selected to adopt an IRA, PRISM simulates his or her decision to contribute to the account for each year after the IRA is established. The model assumes that individuals contribute only if they are employed during the year. All individuals are assumed to contribute in the year the IRA is established. In succeeding years, individuals are randomly selected to contribute to their account based upon the probabilities presented in table 5.8. These probabilities were estimated using May 1983 EBRI/HHS CPS pension supplement data on the number of individuals with IRA accounts who are currently contributing.

IRA CONTRIBUTION AMOUNT

The amount that individuals are assumed to contribute to their IRA in a given year varies with family income, age, sex, and marital status. If an individual is selected to contribute to an IRA the model randomly selects the amount to be contributed based upon the distribution of IRA contributions reported in the May 1983 EBRI/HHS CPS pension supplement data for individuals in similar age, sex, income, and marital status groups. The amounts of these contributions are indexed to real wage changes after 1983. The annual contribution is constrained not to exceed the maximum contribution allowed under the law. After 1986, the maximum contribution amounts specified in the law are indexed at 80 percent of the CPI over time (actual contribution limits are used for each year through 1986). Individuals

Table 5.8 PROBABILITIES OF CONTRIBUTING TO AN IRA IN A GIVEN YEAR
ONCE SELECTED TO ADOPT AN IRA

Family Earnings Level (1982 dollars)	Pension Coverage Status	
	Covered (%)	Not Covered (%)
Less than $25,000	48.0	60.0
$25,000 or more	84.0	90.0

Source: ICF estimates, based in part upon May 1983 EBRI/HHS CPS pension supplement.

who reported they had an IRA in 1979 were assumed to have an initial balance of $3,000 (in 1982 dollars) in their account.

IMPACT OF TAX REFORM ACT OF 1986

The Tax Reform Act modified the maximum tax deductible amount of contributions to IRAs for active participants in qualified pension, profit-sharing, stock-bonus, tax sheltered annuity, or government plans. Beginning in 1987, the full contribution amount up to the amount deductible under prior tax law (typically $2,000) is deductible for individuals with adjusted gross income (AGI) under $25,000 ($40,000 for joint filers, $0 for married filing separately). The deductibility is phased out over the next $10,000 of AGI for the active participants. Anyone may make a nondeductible contribution to the extent that deductible IRA contributions are not allowed. The IRA deduction for all others is retained in its current form. Beginning in 1987, PRISM assumes that annual contributions to IRAs for pension plan participants will be limited to the maximum deductible amount allowed for taxpayers at their income level.

Assets in Retirement

The model imputes the amount of individuals' assets in retirement based upon the distribution of assets reported in the 1983 Survey of Consumer finances 5.(SC1) data. Separate amounts are estimated for financial assets and home equity. Individuals are assumed to receive an annual income from nonhousing assets equal to about 7 percent of their financial assets. The procedure used to estimate asset stocks and income from assets is described next.

ESTIMATION OF ASSET AMOUNTS

The model assigns family units in PRISM the distribution and level of assets of similar families from the 1983 SCF on the basis of age, marital status, income, and pension receipt status once they attain age 65. Actual records from the 1983 Survey of Consumer Finances, adjusted for inflation, are assigned to individuals simulated in the PRISM model. PRISM imputes the distribution of the level of assets for two types of assets: home equity and all other assets.

CHANGES IN ASSETS DURING RETIREMENT

The assets of elderly families are adjusted over timed to reflect that many of the elderly dissave during retirement. In this step, the model assumes that the value of housing assets increases at the rate of

change in the consumer price index (CPI) over time and the value
of financial assets (i.e., nonhousing) decreases by 2 percent each
year. However, for persons or families with incomes less than $15,000
(in 1982 dollars), the model assumes that the value of financial assets
remains constant. PRISM simulates individuals' use of assets to finance nursing home services.[6] This use of their assets accelerates
the assumed rate of decrease in financial assets. If an individual dies,
his or her spouse is assumed to receive all of his or her assets.

INCOME FROM ASSETS

PRISM assigns an assumed level of income from assets for family
units aged 65 and over. In each year PRISM assumes that income
from nonhousing assets is equal to 7 percent of the value of nonhousing assets. This is the long-run interest rate used in PRISM to
calculate interest on IRAs and defined contribution plans.

Supplemental Security Income Program Benefits

The ICF Retirement Benefit Simulation Model simulates the benefits
from the SSI program in three steps. The model (1) determines which
families and individuals are eligible for SSI benefits using the SSI
assets test, (2) estimates the annual benefit they would be entitled
to receive from both the federal and state SSI programs, and (3)
estimates which eligible families and individuals participate in the
program. The SSI program is simulated in PRISM as described next.

PROGRAM FILING UNIT

To determine the size of program benefits, elderly individuals are
first formed into program "filing units." Each individual forms one
filing unit. Both members of a married couple are treated as a single
filing unit, even if one member of the couple is ineligible (i.e., less
than age 65). An individual under age 65 is assumed to be potentially
eligible for SSI benefits for disabled persons if he or she is simulated
to be disabled under the SSA definition of disability.

ASSET ELIGIBILITY

To be eligible for SSI, individuals must have countable assets no
greater than $1,500 for single individuals and $2,250 for married
couples. This includes stocks, bonds, cash, personal effects in excess
of $1,500, and other nonhousing assets. Home equity is not included
in countable assets. As mandated by the Deficit Reduction Act of
1984 (DEFRA), beginning in 1984, the asset limit for single individ-

uals increases by $100 each year, and the limit for married couples increases by $150 each year until 1989, when the limits will be equal to $2,000 and $3,000, respectively. After 1989, the asset limits are assumed to increase at 50 percent of the rate of increase in the CPI. The model determines asset eligibility by comparing the SSI program filing unit's financial assets, estimated as discussed in the prior section, to the appropriate asset limit.

BENEFIT COMPUTATION

PRISM calculates net countable income for SSI filing units by summing eligible individuals' monthly countable incomes and subtracting allowable deductions. Countable incomes include eligible individuals' cash income from earnings, Social Security, pensions, assets, and income of an ineligible spouse. Allowable deductions include: $20 of unearned income, the first $65 of earnings plus 50 percent of earnings above $65, and earnings income of an ineligible spouse up to one-half the maximum monthly federal benefit for a couple. The benefit amount is equal to the positive difference between the maximum monthly benefit and this monthly net income value. The maximum benefit levels vary by marital status, living situation, the presence of an ineligible spouse, and state of residence (see subsection following).

STATE SUPPLEMENTATION

Forty-one states also provide some form of supplementary SSI benefit to elderly families. However, only 13 of these states provide a supplement to most or all of those who participate in the federal SSI program, while the remaining 28 states do so for only a limited number of elderly facing unusual hardships (e.g., extraordinary expenses such as fire or moving-related costs). PRISM estimates supplemental benefits only for the 13 states that provide supplements to most or all eligible individuals (these supplemental payments account for 88 percent of all state supplemental benefits). These 13 state programs, all of which are administered by the federal government, use the same benefit formula as the one described earlier, with the exception that the maximum benefit is higher in these states.

PARTICIPATION

Not all eligible individuals chose to participate in the SSI program. Thus, only a portion of those simulated to be eligible for SSI are selected to receive these benefits. The SSI participation rates used in PRISM were estimated so as to replicate administrative data on

the number of aged SSI recipients by marital status, family income
level, and size of potential benefit.

ILLUSTRATIVE RESULTS

Given the expected growth in the economy, one would anticipate
continued declines in poverty among the elderly during the next 30
years. To examine the future economic status of the elderly, ICF
conducted a number of simulations using PRISM for the Common-
wealth Fund Commission on Elderly People Living Alone. These
simulations examined the economic status of both the elderly who
live alone and all other elderly. This section of this chapter reviews
some of these results.

As shown in table 5.9, the poverty rate among the elderly living
alone will remain at about 19 percent through the 2001–5 period. It
will then decline to about 15 percent by the 2016–20 period. The
percentage of all elderly families with incomes below the poverty
threshold will decline from about 11.6 percent in 1987 to about 10.9
percent by the turn of the century. By the 2016–20 period, the poverty
rate among all the elderly will decline to about 8.2 percent. The
decline in poverty rates over time will be more pronounced among
elderly living with others. The poverty rate among elderly living
with others will decline from about 6 percent in 1987 to about 3
percent by 2020.

Poverty among Elderly Living Alone

The poverty rates for the elderly living alone are expected to remain
constant during the next 15 years, in part because the poverty rates

Table 5.9 PERCENTAGE OF ELDERLY LIVING ALONE WITH INCOMES BELOW
POVERTY LINE

	Year		
Age	1987 (%)	2001–5 (%)	2016–20 (%)
65–74	16	13	9
75 and over	22	25	23
All elderly living alone	19	19	15

Source: ICF estimates.

for elderly persons living alone who are 75 or over are expected to increase. Table 5.9 indicates that the percentage of elderly living alone aged 75 and over who are poor will increase from about 22 percent in 1987 to about 25 percent by the turn of the century. However, after this point, the poverty rate for those aged 75 and over will decline.

A key question is why the poverty rates among the elderly living alone remain largely unchanged through the turn of the century. There are a number of reasons for this, the most important being demographic. Due to declining mortality rates and a shift in the age structure of the population, the average age of elderly persons living alone will increase between 1987 and 2005. As the aging population depletes their assets and the buying power of their pensions is eroded (few private pensions are fully indexed for inflation), the proportion of elderly living alone with incomes below the poverty line will tend to remain high.

Table 5.10 shows estimates of the total elderly population during the 1987–2020 period. It shows that during the 1987–2005 period, the population aged 65-74 will increase by only 2 percent, while the population aged 75 and over will increase by 48 percent, and the population aged 85 and over will almost double. The 85 and over population will increase for two primary reasons: declines in mortality rates and an increased birth cohort. Thus, the age composition of the elderly population will shift, and the average age of the elderly will increase. Because persons aged 85 and over are the poorest of the elderly, it is not surprising that the poverty rate for the elderly living alone will not decline during the next 15 years.

Table 5.10 GROWTH IN NUMBER OF ELDERLY PERSONS, 1987–2020

	Millions of Persons			Percentage Increase 1987–2005	Percentage Increase 2005–20
Age	1987	2005	2020	(%)	(%)
65–74	17.4	17.7	29.9	2	68
75–84	9.6	12.8	14.5	33	13
85 and over	2.9	5.7	7.1	95	24
Total	29.9	36.2	51.5	21	42

Source: U.S. Bureau of the Census, "Projections of the Population of the United States, by Age, Sex, and Race: 1983 to 2080." Series P-25, no. 952. (Washington, D.C.: Gregory Spencer, 1984).

Income Distributions in Future Years

Although the percentage of the elderly living alone who have incomes below the poverty line will tend to decline slowly over the next 30 years, the percentage who are near-poor will decline more rapidly. As shown in table 5.11, the percentage of elderly living alone with incomes between 100 and 149 percent of the poverty line (i.e., near-poor) will decline from 24.4 percent in 1987 to 19.5 percent by the turn of the century. By the 2016–20 period, the percentage of elderly living alone who are near-poor will further decline to about 16 percent.

Perhaps one of the most interesting findings is that the distribution of retirement income will broaden substantially over time. As shown in table 5.11, while poverty rates decline only modestly for the elderly living alone, the percentage with incomes above 300 percent of the poverty threshold will increase from about 26 percent in 1987 to over 35 percent during the 2016–20 period. This suggests that over time the elderly living alone will contain both a pervasive poor subgroup and a growing affluent subgroup. As discussed in the next section, this dichotomous segmentation of the elderly living alone will occur because many more persons will receive pension income, which will serve to move individuals into higher income groups.

Over time, the percentage of elderly living alone with incomes below 150 percent of the poverty line will decline from about 43 percent in 1987 to about 38 percent during the 2001–5 period, a reduction of about 11 percent. By the period 2016–20, the percentage of the elderly living alone with incomes below 150 percent of the poverty line will further decline to about 31 percent.

Table 5.11 INCOME DISTRIBUTION OF ELDERLY LIVING ALONE

Income as Percentage of Poverty Line	1987 (%)	2001–5 (%)	2016–20 (%)
Less than 100%	18.9	18.9	14.9
100%–149%	24.4	19.5	16.2
150%–199%	13.9	16.7	15.4
200%–299%	17.1	17.8	18.0
300% or more	25.7	27.1	35.5
Total	100.0	100.0	100.0

Source: ICF estimates.

Average Incomes in Future Years

The gap between the incomes of the elderly living alone and other elderly will widen over the next 30 years. The average incomes of the elderly living alone and of the elderly living with others will increase by 26 percent and 31 percent, respectively, over the 1987–2020 period. These estimates are in constant 1987 dollars. For the elderly living alone, the average income will increase from $14,100 in 1987 to $16,400 in the 2001–5 period and $17,800 in the 2016–20 period.

Average incomes for the elderly living with others will increase more rapidly than the average income of the elderly living alone during 1987–2020 period. From 1987 to the 2001–5 period, the average income of the elderly living alone will increase faster than for the elderly living with others. However, as the baby boom generation starts to reach retirement age, after 2010, the average income of the elderly living with others will increase faster than that of the elderly living alone.

A major reason for these increases in future income is a change in the sources of income for the elderly living alone. Specifically, as shown in table 5.12, during the next 30 years, pensions and IRAs will be received by a significantly higher percentage of the elderly, and SSI will be received by fewer elderly. As shown in the table, the percentage of elderly living alone with employment earnings will decline slightly over the next 30 years, while the proportion with asset income will increase.

Table 5.12 PERCENTAGE OF ELDERLY RECEIVING INCOME, BY SOURCE

	Elderly Living Alone			Elderly Living with Others		
Income Source	1987 (%)	2001–5 (%)	2016–20 (%)	1987 (%)	2001–5 (%)	2016–20 (%)
Employment earnings[a]	17	16	15	38	35	37
Social Security	98	98	99	97	98	99
Pensions	35	42	52	53	63	72
Income from assets	71	75	78	81	81	83
SSI	9	8	7	7	3	2
IRAs	1	10	18	3	29	40

Source: ICF estimates.
a. Excludes earnings of family members other than spouse under age 65.

Pension Receipt in Future Years

Pension receipt among the elderly is projected to increase steadily through 2020. As shown in table 5.13, the proportion of elderly living alone receiving a pension will increase from about 35 percent in 1987 to about 42 percent by the turn of the century and to over 52 percent by the 2016–20 period. By comparison, pension receipt among the elderly living with others will increase from about 53 percent in 1987 to about 72 percent by the 2016–20 period. Among elderly widowed females living alone, the percentage receiving pensions will increase from 31 percent in 1987 to about 49 percent by 2020.

This growth in pension receipt can be attributed to a number of factors. First, many more women who retire in the future will have had significant work experience than women who are currently retired. Second, during the 1960s and 1970s, there was a substantial growth in the number of employers offering pensions. Thus, individuals retiring after the turn of the century will have spent most of their working lives in an economy characterized by much higher pension coverage than that which prevailed during the working lives of persons retiring in the 1970s and 1980s. Third, the passage of ERISA in 1974 established minimum standards for pension plans, which greatly increased the likelihood that workers will become participants in a pension plan, become vested, and receive pension benefits. Fourth, the Retirement Equity Act of 1984 (REA) and the Tax Reform Act of 1986 established even stricter minimum standards for private pension plans, which will further increase the number of workers who ultimately receive benefits. Finally, both ERISA and REA will increase the number of spouses who will receive survivor's benefits from pension plans. All of these factors will increase the likelihood that the elderly living alone in the future will receive pension benefits.

Table 5.13 PERCENTAGE OF ELDERLY RECEIVING PENSION INCOME

Year	Elderly Widowed Females Living Alone (%)	Elderly Living Alone (%)	Elderly Living with Others (%)	All Elderly Families (%)
1987	31	35	53	45
2001–5	36	42	63	53
2016–20	49	52	72	63

Source: ICF estimates.

However, one should note that employer pensions will continue to be a relatively small share of the income of the elderly living alone. Even in the 2016–20 period, when 52 percent of the elderly living alone will receive employer pension benefits, the average benefit for those persons receiving benefits will be about $4,800. These benefits will make up approximately 14 percent of the aggregate income of the elderly living alone in this period.

In the future, the elderly living with others will still be more likely to receive a pension than the elderly living alone for two reasons. First, the elderly living with others tend to be younger than the elderly living alone. Hence, they tend to have spent a greater portion of their working lives in a labor force characterized by high pension coverage than have the elderly living alone, who are typically older. Second, most of the elderly living with others are married. Thus, many individuals who do not themselves earn a pension may be married to someone who does earn a pension may be married to someone who does earn such a benefit.

Levels of Income

Table 5.14 shows the average income received by the elderly living alone from the major income sources during the 1987–2020 period. Note that this table shows averages for all elderly living alone, not just those receiving that source. It shows that, on average, Social Security and asset income will continue to be the most important sources of income for the elderly living alone. Together, they account for about 77 percent of the aggregate income of the elderly living alone in 1987. They will account for 74 percent of aggregate income

Table 5.14 AVERAGE INCOME FOR ALL ELDERLY LIVING ALONE (1987 dollars)

Source	1987	2001–5	2016–20
Employment	$ 1,253	$ 1,851	$ 1,925
Social Security	5,676	5,804	6,049
Pensions	1,660	2,151	2,501
Assets	5,131	6,284	6,429
SSI	151	181	147
Other/IRA	179	112	374
Total	$14,090	$16,383	$17,867
Median income	$ 9,400	$10,000	$11,800

Source: ICF estimates.
Note: Averages in table include both recipients and nonrecipients for each source.

in the 2001–5 period and 72 percent in the 2016–20 period. It also shows that, on average, pension and IRA income will increase in importance, whereas SSI income will decline in importance. How will the relative contribution of these income sources change for the elderly living alone? These simulations indicate that over the next 30 years the relative contribution of Social Security will decline, whereas the relative contributions of pensions and IRAs will increase. As shown in table 5.14, the real level of all the major sources except SSI will increase; however, average income from pensions and IRAs will rise more quickly than Social Security income.

Notes

We thank Kevin Hollenbeck for his helpful comments on this chapter.

1. For a detailed description of the PRISM model see Kennell and Sheils (1986).

2. A description of the ICF Macroeconomic-Demographic Model is provided in: ICF Inc.

3. Many plan sponsors provide two separate pension plans for their employees. The first, or primary plan, provides a benefit to all eligible participants. The second plan, known as a secondary plan, is generally an optional plan in which employees' contributions are matched with an employer contribution. For example, some employers provide a basic defined benefit plan that is accompanied by an optional savings and thrift plan.

4. The dynamic aging techniques used in PRISM and DYNASIM differ from other microsimulation models such as TRIM, MATH, and HITSM, which typically use static aging. Static aging models generally age data by adjusting sample weights and inflating reported incomes to be representative of the population in a future year without simulating annual life histories.

5. An individual is "vested" in his or her plan when he or she has earned a nonforfeitable right to receive plan benefits.

6. For a discussion of the nursing home care simulations methodology used in the PRISM simulations, see Kennell and Sheils (1986).

References

Haveman, Robert H., and Jeffrey M. Lacker. Feb. 1984. "Discrepancies in Projecting Future Public and Private Pension Benefits: A Comparison and Critique of Two Micro-Data Simulation Models." Madison: University of Wisconsin-Madison.

ICF., Inc. 1981. *A Macroeconomic-Demographic Model of the U.S. Retirement Income System.* Final report to the National Institute on Aging. Washington, D.C.: ICF.

Kennell, David L., and John F. Sheils. Sept. 1986. *The ICF Pension and Retirement Income Simulation Model (PRISM) with the Brookings/ ICF Long-Term Care Financing Model.* Washington, D.C.: ICF.

Lazear, Edward P. 1979. "Why is There Mandatory Retirement?" *Journal of Political Economy* 87(6): 1261–84.

Chapter Six

A METHOD FOR SIMULATING THE DISTRIBUTION OF COMBINED FEDERAL TAXES USING CENSUS, TAX RETURN, AND EXPENDITURE MICRODATA

Richard A. Kasten and Frank J. Sammartino

The deficiencies of available microdata for distributional analysis have been duly lamented in most past studies of federal tax burdens.[1] Tax return data lack complete information on incomes. Tax filing units are not equivalent to family units. Because many low-income families do not file tax returns, the distribution of incomes from tax return data is incomplete. Census income data are underreported and topcoded. Information is lacking for the highest income families. Some positive and negative components of taxable income are not reported. Both tax-return and census data lack information on family expenditures, which is necessary to compute federal excise taxes; they also lack information on noncash income and accrued but unrealized increases in family wealth, which is necessary for a complete measure of family income.

Faced with these problems, researchers have attempted to match tax-return and census data. Although a few exact matches exist, most analysis has relied on statistical or synthetic matches. In many studies extensive imputations were made to family income microdata to account for missing income information that is unavailable from either tax return or census records. Further adjustments often have been made to adjust measured total family incomes from that data to aggregate national income.[2]

This chapter reports on a more limited analysis of the distribution of federal tax burdens. First, the analysis does not rely on matched data, but, instead, uses microdata from three separate sources to measure family incomes and to simulate federal taxes. Second, income is defined on a cash receipt basis. Noncash income and accrued but unrealized changes in family wealth are not included in our measure of income. Microdata totals for family incomes are not adjusted to national income aggregates.

In the analysis, federal taxes include individual and corporate income taxes, social insurance taxes, and excise taxes except for the windfall profit tax. Although actual tax payments are made by persons, corporations, and noncorporate employers, the economic burden of all taxes ultimately rests with families and individuals. All federal taxes, including the corporate income tax and the employer portion of social insurance payroll taxes, are attributed to particular families.

The distribution of family income and federal taxes is measured for three representative years during the 1975–90 period: 1977, 1984, and 1988. All three years were years of relatively high growth in gross national product, declining unemployment rates, and rising but relatively modest rates of inflation. The similarity of these years reduces the effect of macroeconomic differences on the results. The years chosen for analysis also reflect important changes in federal tax law. In 1977, the Tax Reform Act of 1978 and the Economic Recovery Tax Act of 1981 had not yet been enacted. By 1984, those changes were in place, but payroll tax increases enacted in 1983 and the Tax Reform Act of 1986 were yet to come. By 1988, most changes from the 1986 act were in place.[3]

The second part of this chapter discusses the measurement of family income. The third section explains how the distribution of families' incomes and federal tax burdens was simulated using microdata, followed, in the fourth section, by the results of those simulations.

MEASURING AGGREGATE FAMILY INCOME

One straightforward definition of annual income is cash received during the year. The cash may come as earnings, returns to investment, payments from the government, or retirement income. This simple definition, however, excludes items that may be of considerable monetary value but are not received in the form of cash payments. Among these are certain in-kind transfer payments such as food stamps, rent subsidies, government-sponsored Medicare or Medicaid health insurance, and nonmonetary payments by employers such as health and life insurance premiums.

A more comprehensive definition of annual income that measures the change in total family resources is economic income. Economic income includes not only cash and noncash payments received but also the flow of services from durable items such as houses or automobiles, along with increases in a family's wealth that accrue but are not realized (converted to cash). Under this definition, income includes increases in wealth from appreciation of financial assets such as stocks and bonds, and physical assets such as houses and land. Income also includes the increase in future pension benefits at the time those benefits accrue. Not counted as income in this definition are pension benefits received at retirement and capital gains realized from the sale of stocks, bonds, or physical assets. These activities do not represent new income but only the conversion of existing family wealth into cash.[4]

The individual income tax system generally treats income as cash received. It excludes certain types of cash income, such as welfare benefits and, for the majority of taxpayers, Social Security benefits. Nonmonetary payments such as food stamps, Medicare and Medicaid, and employer-provided health insurance are not included in income. Appreciation of financial and physical assets is taxed only when these gains are realized. Pension benefits are taxed when they are received, rather than as they accrue.

In this chapter, family income is measured on a cash receipts basis, consistent, but not identical, with the way income is counted by the federal tax system. As opposed to the tax system definition, family income includes all cash transfer payments and is measured before all federal taxes. Family income equals the sum of wages, salaries, self-employment income, personal rents, interest, and dividends, plus government cash transfer payments, cash pension benefits, and realized capital gains. Family income excludes accrued but unrealized capital gains, employer contributions to pension funds, in-kind government transfer payments, and other noncash income. Because income is measured before reductions for any federal taxes, employer contributions for federal social insurance and federal corporate income taxes are added to family income. Family income totals from the microdata files are not inflated to match comparable national income aggregates.

Many people incur "paper losses" for tax purposes. To better approximate the economic income of families, rental losses and most partnership losses were not subtracted from family income. All losses of sole proprietorships were allowed.

Using a cash income measure and not adjusting to national income aggregates avoids the difficult problems of valuing noncash and in-kind income, measuring accrued and nonreported income, and assigning these constructed values to the appropriate families in the income distribution. Although these adjustments all are conceptually feasible (although not uncontroversial), they would shift the distribution of income into uncharted regions away from the anchor of reported incomes in the microdata files. Federal taxes computed for these incomes would not correspond to actual tax payments.

SIMULATION METHODS

Estimated distributions of family income for 1977 and 1984, and the projected distribution in 1988, were based on data from three sources. The primary source was the March Current Population Survey (CPS) for 1978 and 1985. The CPS is a monthly survey of approximately 60,000 families conducted by the U.S. Bureau of the Census. Each March, the survey collects detailed information on characteristics of the family and family income in the previous calendar year. The reported data on income from taxable sources from the CPS files were adjusted for consistency with reported income from Statistics of Income (SOI) samples for calendar years 1977 and 1984. (The SOI is an extensive annual sample of actual individual income tax returns.) Data on consumer expenditures were taken from the 1980 and 1984 Consumer Expenditure Survey (CES) Interview Surveys. The CES Interview Survey is a quarterly panel survey conducted by the U.S. Bureau of Labor Statistics that collects detailed data on household expenditures over a 12-month period. The CES data for 1980, the survey year closest to 1977, were adjusted to 1977 levels by changes in per capita expenditures of certain types as reported in the National Income and Product Accounts (NIPA).

Adjustments to the Data

Three major problems with the CPS need to be corrected before simulating taxes and estimating the distribution of tax burdens. First, the CPS does not collect sufficient information for simulating individual income taxes; in particular, it lacks data on deductions and capital gains realizations. Second, high incomes on the CPS are top-coded to maintain confidentiality for families included in the sample. Third, less income from interest and dividends and more income from self-employment is reported on the CPS than on the SOI.

The adjustments for nonreported items and topcoding were relatively straightforward. CPS families were split into tax filing units comparable to those on the SOI. Missing data on deductions and capital gains were assigned to the CPS by imputation. For individual

retirement accounts (IRAs), employee business expenses, and itemized deductions, the SOI was used to determine the probability that
a tax unit had that deduction and the ratio of the deduction to income.
The probabilities and ratios were assigned from a matrix of cells
depending on the level of income, the age of the head, the number
of dependents, and, for certain deductions, other variables such as
the number of earners, receipt of capital income, and state of residence. A similar procedure was used to impute capital gains realizations to the CPS, except that, to better approximate the correct
distribution of capital gains, tax units in a particular cell were assigned a ratio of capital gains to income randomly selected from a
computed distribution of ratios for SOI tax units in that cell, rather
than the single ratio used in the other imputations.

To correct for topcoding, the SOI was used to construct a distribution of incomes at the topcoded level and higher for each type of
income. Any income on the CPS that was at the maximum reported
amount was replaced with an amount randomly selected from the
appropriate SOI high-income distribution.

A more complex procedure was necessary to adjust underreported
incomes on the CPS to match incomes on the SOI. In some cases
this required increasing reported negative as well as positive income
amounts. Because low-income families are not required to file tax
returns, there are many more CPS tax units than SOI units. To make
a valid comparison between the two data sets, CPS units that were
simulated to owe taxes were compared to SOI units with positive
taxes. Each source of income on the CPS was compared to its coun-
terpart on the SOI, and adjustments were made until the level and
distribution of income on the two files was approximately the same.
New recipients were created, and amounts of interest and dividends
were increased for families reporting income from those sources.
After interest income was adjusted upward to match taxable interest
on the SOI, an additional amount of tax-exempt interest was imputed
to the CPS using the 1983 Survey of Consumer Finances. Rental
incomes and incomes from partnerships and sole proprietorships
were adjusted downward; in some cases gains were converted into
losses, and in other cases self-employment losses were added to
records that reported no self-employment income. As a final step,
the weights and incomes of taxpaying families in the top 1 percent
of the income distribution were revised so that the number of such
families and their average income were identical on the two files.

The March 1978 CPS was adjusted for consistency with data from
the SOI for 1977. Similarly, the March 1985 CPS was adjusted for

consistency with the 1984 SOI. Once the CPS files were adjusted, family incomes from the CES were aligned to control totals from the adjusted CPS, by the same process that was used to adjust the CPS to SOI totals.

Aging the Data

Each of the 1984 files was aged to 1988 using actual growth rates in population, income, and expenditures through 1986, and projected growth rates for 1987 and 1988.

CPS and SOI data for 1988 were created using population projections of the Social Security Administration (SSA) and income and employment projections of the Congressional Budget Office (CBO). The SSA forecasts the number of persons by age, sex, and marital status for future years. These forecasts were used to construct separate growth rates for units filing joint, single, and head of household returns. Separate growth rates were constructed for units with at least one member aged 65 or over and for nonelderly units.

Adjustments were also made to reflect the projected growth in the rate of employment. On the SOI, additional single and head of household returns were created. Weights for one-earner couples were lowered, and weights for two-earner couples were increased. On the CPS, weights of nonearners and one-earner couples were lowered, and weights of couples with two earners and other units with earnings were raised.

Once populations weights were adjusted, incomes from each source were inflated by the CBO's projected aggregate growth rate for income from that source. Deductions were raised to be consistent with the projected growth in income.

In every year of the 1980s, through 1985 (the last year for which distributional data are available), incomes—especially earnings and capital gains realizations—of the top 1 percent of taxpayers grew faster than the incomes of other taxpayers. The aging procedure assumed that the trend will continue. From 1984 to 1988, earnings and capital gains realizations of families with incomes in the top 1 percent were projected to grow 20 percent faster than those incomes for families in the rest of the income distribution.

Simulating Combined Federal Taxes

Individual income taxes were simulated using constructed CPS tax filing units after reported CPS incomes had been adjusted to control totals from SOI data. For high-income taxpayers, individual income taxes were simulated using SOI data and then imputed to CPS tax filing units by income classes.

Social Security payroll taxes were simulated using earnings and self-employment income from the adjusted CPS.

Excise taxes were simulated using expenditure data from the adjusted CES. Federal excise taxes were calculated as a percentage of family income for families in different income categories. Those percentages were applied to CPS family incomes.

The corporate income tax was imputed to families in two ways, consistent with assumptions of a greater and a lesser progressive incidence of the tax. In the first alternative, the tax was assigned in proportion to the family's capital income (consisting of positive rents, interest, dividends, and an adjusted amount of realized capital gains).[5] In the second alternative, the tax was assigned in proportion to wages.

Reported pretax family incomes were adjusted to include the amount of the employer share of the Social Security payroll tax, the unemployment insurance payroll tax, and the corporate income tax. The employer share of the Social Security payroll tax and of the unemployment insurance payroll tax were added to family labor incomes. Corporate income taxes were assigned to family incomes consistent with the alternative incidence assumptions. In the first alternative, capital income was increased by the amount of the tax imputed to the family, while in the second alternative, labor income was increased by the amount of the tax.

DISTRIBUTION OF INCOME AND TAXES
IN 1977, 1984, AND 1988

Simulated pretax family income totaled $1,436 billion in 1977 and $2,814 billion in 1984. In each year, pretax family income was equal to 88 percent of aggregate family income computed from the National Income and Product Accounts. Almost the entire difference resulted from variations in the amount of reported capital incomes and proprietor income, but transfer incomes were also lower than their NIPA equivalents. The distribution of income might look different if the missing income could be assigned to the right families. Because some unknown amount of the income may go to families not included in the CPS and because there is no information on where in the income distribution the remaining income should be assigned, rather than changing the distribution of income in an arbitrary manner, the excess total family income reported in the NIPA was left unassigned.

For purposes of comparing the distribution of family incomes in those years, income was divided into four categories: labor income (wages, salaries, and income from self-employment), capital income (rents, interest, dividends, and capital gains), transfer income (Social Security, unemployment insurance, Aid to Families with Dependent Children [AFDC], Supplemental Security Income [SSI], workers' compensation, and veterans' benefits) and other income (alimony, child support, and private pension payments).

Tables 6.1 and 6.2 outline the distribution of total family incomes by population decile and the share received by the top 5 percent and 1 percent of the population in 1977, 1984, and 1988 under the different allocations of the corporate income tax.[6] In these and all subsequent tables, the tenth of the population with the lowest incomes excludes families without positive incomes, although those families are included in the totals.

The share of income in all deciles except the two highest declined between 1977 and 1984 under either allocation of the corporate income tax (see tables 6.1 and 6.2). The share of income in the highest-income decile increased by 10 percent—from a 31.9 percent share to a 35.0 percent share—under the allocation of corporate tax to capital income; and by 12 percent—from a 30.6 percent share to a 34.4 percent share—under the allocation of the tax to labor income. The share of income for the top 1 percent of families increased by 2.5 to 3 percentage points, depending upon the allocation of the corporate tax.

The distribution of separate components of income by family income decile is also outlined in tables 6.1 and 6.2. These results indicate that the increase in the top decile's share of income between 1977 and 1984 resulted from an increase in its share of all types of income. The distribution of family income in 1988 is expected to look much the same as in 1984. The top decile's share of income, however, is expected to increase further.

Tables 6.3 and 6.4 show the distribution of before- and after-tax income and the distribution of separate and total federal taxes under the two allocations of the corporate income tax. Care should be used in comparing the distribution of taxes in different years, because differences reflect changes in the distribution of income as well as in the tax code. Under either allocation of the corporate income tax, the distribution of taxes became less progressive between 1977 and later years. The after-tax income share of the bottom decile shrank

Table 6.1 DISTRIBUTION OF FAMILY INCOME FROM EACH SOURCE OF
INCOME, BY POPULATION DECILE, WITH CORPORATE INCOME TAX
ALLOCATED TO CAPITAL INCOME (in percent)

Decile[a]	Labor	Capital	Transfer	Other	Total
		1977			
First[b]	0.3	0.4	9.5	1.5	1.1
Second	1.2	1.1	17.2	4.2	2.5
Third	2.9	2.3	15.2	7.8	3.9
Fourth	5.1	3.4	11.3	9.7	5.4
Fifth	7.1	4.4	10.0	10.2	7.1
Sixth	9.2	5.2	9.4	11.6	8.7
Seventh	12.0	5.4	7.5	10.3	10.6
Eighth	14.9	6.1	6.3	11.4	12.9
Ninth	18.6	9.6	6.2	13.4	16.2
Tenth	29.1	61.7	6.9	19.5	31.9
Top 5 percent	17.4	53.0	3.7	11.9	21.5
Top 1 percent	5.5	33.4	0.8	2.0	9.2
All deciles[c]	100.0	100.0	100.0	100.0	100.0
		1984			
First[b]	0.3	0.3	7.4	1.5	0.9
Second	1.2	0.8	15.3	3.7	2.3
Third	2.9	1.7	13.3	6.4	3.6
Fourth	4.6	2.8	12.2	8.7	5.0
Fifth	6.5	3.8	11.0	10.3	6.5
Sixth	8.8	4.7	9.6	10.4	8.2
Seventh	11.2	6.1	8.9	11.2	10.1
Eighth	14.6	6.9	7.8	10.8	12.6
Ninth	19.0	9.6	6.6	13.7	16.3
Tenth	31.9	63.0	7.3	22.6	35.0
Top 5 percent	19.7	54.8	4.0	15.0	24.3
Top 1 percent	7.4	36.9	0.8	4.0	11.8
All deciles[c]	100.0	100.0	100.0	100.0	100.0
		1988			
First[b]	0.3	0.3	7.9	1.4	0.9
Second	1.2	0.8	15.5	3.5	2.2
Third	3.0	1.7	13.1	5.8	3.6
Fourth	4.6	2.8	11.8	8.2	5.0
Fifth	6.5	3.8	10.7	10.0	6.5
Sixth	8.7	4.8	9.6	9.9	8.1
Seventh	11.0	6.2	8.7	11.5	10.0
Eighth	14.2	7.1	7.9	11.4	12.5
Ninth	18.6	9.8	6.7	13.9	16.1
Tenth	32.9	62.3	7.5	24.0	35.7
Top 5 percent	21.1	53.7	4.0	15.4	25.1
Top 1 percent	8.8	36.2	0.8	3.4	12.5
All deciles[c]	100.0	100.0	100.0	100.0	100.0

Source: U.S. Congressional Budget Office tax simulation models.
a. Ranked by size of family income.
b. Excludes families with zero or negative incomes.
c. Includes families with zero or negative incomes not shown separately.

Table 6.2 DISTRIBUTION OF FAMILY INCOME FROM EACH SOURCE OF
INCOME, BY POPULATION DECILE, WITH CORPORATE INCOME TAX
ALLOCATED TO LABOR INCOME (in percent)

Decile[a]	Labor	Capital	Transfer	Other	Total
		1977			
First[b]	0.3	0.6	9.9	1.5	1.1
Second	1.1	1.5	17.8	4.3	2.5
Third	2.7	3.2	15.9	8.3	3.9
Fourth	4.7	4.5	12.4	10.9	5.5
Fifth	6.9	5.3	10.2	11.0	7.1
Sixth	9.2	5.8	9.1	12.2	8.9
Seventh	12.0	5.6	6.9	9.9	10.9
Eighth	14.8	7.1	6.1	11.3	13.2
Ninth	18.8	9.5	5.6	12.4	16.6
Tenth	30.0	56.5	5.9	17.7	30.6
Top 5 percent	18.2	48.3	3.2	10.8	20.1
Top 1 percent	5.9	30.5	0.7	2.0	8.1
All deciles[c]	100.0	100.0	100.0	100.0	100.0
		1984			
First[b]	0.3	0.4	7.5	1.5	0.9
Second	1.1	0.9	15.8	3.9	2.3
Third	2.7	2.1	14.0	6.7	3.6
Fourth	4.5	3.1	12.3	9.1	5.0
Fifth	6.5	4.1	11.0	10.2	6.6
Sixth	8.6	5.2	10.1	10.8	8.3
Seventh	11.2	6.1	8.5	11.5	10.2
Eighth	14.6	6.9	7.4	10.9	12.8
Ninth	19.0	9.6	6.4	13.0	16.4
Tenth	32.5	61.3	6.5	21.8	34.4
Top 5 percent	20.2	53.1	3.5	14.3	23.7
Top 1 percent	7.5	36.8	0.8	4.0	11.2
All deciles[c]	100.0	100.0	100.0	100.0	100.0
		1988			
First[b]	0.3	0.4	7.9	1.3	0.9
Second	1.1	1.0	16.3	3.6	2.2
Third	2.8	2.2	13.7	6.1	3.6
Fourth	4.5	3.3	12.2	8.7	5.0
Fifth	6.3	4.4	10.8	10.2	6.5
Sixth	8.5	5.4	9.9	10.6	8.2
Seventh	10.9	6.4	8.6	11.5	10.2
Eighth	14.3	6.9	7.3	11.2	12.7
Ninth	18.6	9.8	6.1	13.6	16.4
Tenth	33.6	59.8	6.6	22.5	34.9
Top 5 percent	21.6	51.5	3.4	14.9	24.2
Top 1 percent	8.9	35.8	0.7	3.3	11.8
All deciles[c]	100.0	100.0	100.0	100.0	100.0

Source: U.S. Congressional Budget Office tax simulation models.
a. Ranked by size of family income.
b. Excludes families with zero or negative incomes.
c. Includes families with zero or negative incomes not shown separately.

Table 6.3 DISTRIBUTION OF FAMILY INCOME AND OF FEDERAL TAX
PAYMENTS BY POPULATION DECILE, WITH CORPORATE INCOME
TAX ALLOCATED TO CAPITAL INCOME (in percent)

Decile[a]	Family Income Before Tax	After Tax	Individual Income	Social Insurance	Excises	Corporate Income	All Taxes
			1977				
First[b]	1.1	1.3	−0.1	0.6	3.2	0.4	0.4
Second	2.5	2.9	0.0	1.6	6.6	1.0	1.0
Third	3.9	4.4	0.6	3.7	6.6	2.2	2.1
Fourth	5.4	5.9	2.1	6.2	8.5	3.3	3.8
Fifth	7.1	7.5	4.0	8.6	8.8	4.2	5.6
Sixth	8.7	9.1	6.1	10.8	10.1	5.0	7.5
Seventh	10.6	10.9	8.8	13.6	11.3	5.3	9.7
Eighth	12.9	13.1	12.3	15.9	12.4	6.0	12.3
Ninth	16.2	16.2	17.1	18.5	14.2	9.5	16.1
Tenth	31.9	29.1	48.9	20.3	17.8	62.8	41.3
Top 5 percent	21.5	18.9	36.5	10.0	9.5	54.0	30.4
Top 1 percent	9.2	7.2	19.2	1.7	2.1	34.3	15.8
All deciles[c]	100.0	100.0	100.0	100.0	100.0	100.0	100.0
			1984				
First[b]	0.9	1.0	0.0	0.5	4.7	0.3	0.4
Second	2.3	2.6	0.1	1.4	5.6	0.9	0.9
Third	3.6	4.0	0.9	3.4	7.0	1.8	2.2
Fourth	5.0	5.4	2.3	5.3	8.0	3.0	3.7
Fifth	6.5	6.8	3.9	7.3	8.7	4.0	5.4
Sixth	8.2	8.4	6.1	9.7	9.5	5.0	7.5
Seventh	10.1	10.3	8.4	12.2	10.7	6.4	9.7
Eighth	12.6	12.6	11.6	15.9	12.1	7.3	12.8
Ninth	16.3	16.0	16.8	19.7	14.1	10.1	17.1
Tenth	35.0	33.6	49.9	24.5	17.8	61.1	40.1
Top 5 percent	24.3	23.2	37.6	12.5	9.8	52.6	28.5
Top 1 percent	11.8	11.0	20.9	2.4	2.6	34.6	14.6
All deciles[c]	100.0	100.0	100.0	100.0	100.0	100.0	100.0
			1988				
First[b]	0.9	1.0	−0.1	0.5	4.5	0.3	0.4
Second	2.2	2.6	−0.1	1.5	5.5	0.9	0.8
Third	3.6	4.0	0.6	3.5	6.7	1.7	2.1
Fourth	5.0	5.4	2.0	5.4	7.9	2.9	3.6
Fifth	6.5	6.8	3.7	7.3	8.4	3.8	5.3
Sixth	8.1	8.4	5.7	9.7	9.4	4.9	7.3
Seventh	10.0	10.2	8.0	12.1	10.7	6.3	9.5
Eighth	12.5	12.5	10.9	15.7	12.1	7.2	12.3
Ninth	16.1	16.0	16.1	19.6	14.3	9.9	16.7
Tenth	35.7	33.9	53.2	24.5	18.6	61.7	41.9
Top 5 percent	25.1	23.5	41.0	12.7	10.3	53.0	30.4
Top 1 percent	12.5	11.5	23.8	2.5	3.5	35.4	16.2
All deciles[c]	100.0	100.0	100.0	100.0	100.0	100.0	100.0

Source: U.S. Congressional Budget Office tax simulation models.
a. Ranked by size of family income.
b. Excludes families with zero or negative incomes.
c. Includes families with zero or negative incomes not shown separately.

Table 6.4 DISTRIBUTION OF FAMILY INCOME AND OF FEDERAL TAX
PAYMENTS BY POPULATION DECILE, WITH CORPORATE INCOME
TAX ALLOCATED TO LABOR INCOME (in percent)

Decile[a]	Family Income Before Tax	Family Income After Tax	Individual Income	Social Insurance	Excises	Corporate Income	All Taxes
			1977				
First[b]	1.1	1.3	0.0	0.5	3.2	0.4	0.4
Second	2.5	2.9	0.0	1.4	6.6	1.1	0.9
Third	3.9	4.5	0.5	3.4	6.5	2.7	2.1
Fourth	5.5	6.0	2.0	5.8	8.5	4.7	3.9
Fifth	7.1	7.5	3.9	8.4	8.7	6.9	6.0
Sixth	8.9	9.1	6.1	10.8	10.2	9.2	8.2
Seventh	10.9	10.8	8.8	13.8	11.2	12.2	11.0
Eighth	13.2	13.1	12.1	15.8	12.4	15.1	13.7
Ninth	16.6	16.2	17.2	18.7	14.3	19.1	17.8
Tenth	30.6	29.1	49.3	21.2	17.9	28.4	35.9
Top 5 percent	20.1	18.9	36.9	10.6	9.7	16.5	24.3
Top 1 percent	8.1	7.2	19.5	1.8	2.1	4.8	10.9
All deciles[c]	100.0	100.0	100.0	100.0	100.0	100.0	100.0
			1984				
First[b]	0.9	1.0	0.0	0.5	4.7	0.4	0.4
Second	2.3	2.6	0.0	1.3	5.6	1.1	0.9
Third	3.6	4.0	0.9	3.2	7.0	2.7	2.2
Fourth	5.0	5.4	2.3	5.1	8.0	4.4	3.8
Fifth	6.6	6.9	3.9	7.3	8.7	6.4	5.6
Sixth	8.3	8.5	6.0	9.5	9.5	8.6	7.7
Seventh	10.2	10.3	8.4	12.2	10.7	11.2	10.2
Eighth	12.8	12.6	11.7	15.9	12.2	14.7	13.6
Ninth	16.4	16.0	16.9	19.8	14.1	19.1	18.0
Tenth	34.4	33.6	50.0	25.0	17.8	31.5	37.5
Top 5 percent	23.7	23.2	37.6	13.0	9.8	19.3	25.4
Top 1 percent	11.2	11.0	21.0	2.5	2.6	6.9	11.9
All deciles[c]	100.0	100.0	100.0	100.0	100.0	100.0	100.0
			1988				
First[b]	0.9	1.0	−0.1	0.5	4.4	0.4	0.4
Second	2.2	2.7	−0.1	1.4	5.5	1.1	0.8
Third	3.6	4.0	0.5	3.3	6.7	2.8	2.1
Fourth	5.0	5.4	1.9	5.2	7.9	4.5	3.7
Fifth	6.5	6.8	3.7	7.2	8.5	6.4	5.5
Sixth	8.2	8.4	5.7	9.5	9.4	8.5	7.6
Seventh	10.2	10.2	8.0	12.0	10.7	11.0	10.0
Eighth	12.7	12.5	10.9	15.8	12.0	14.5	13.2
Ninth	16.4	15.9	16.3	19.7	14.3	18.7	17.8
Tenth	34.9	33.8	53.2	25.2	18.6	32.0	38.6
Top 5 percent	24.2	23.5	40.9	13.2	10.4	20.1	26.6
Top 1 percent	11.8	11.5	23.8	2.6	3.6	8.1	13.0
All deciles[c]	100.0	100.0	100.0	100.0	100.0	100.0	100.0

Source: U.S. Congressional Budget Office tax simulation models.
a. Ranked by size of family income.
b. Excludes families with zero or negative incomes.
c. Includes families with zero or negative incomes not shown separately.

by more than its pretax share, but the after-tax income share of the top decile grew by more than its pretax share.

In all years, the share of income for the lowest decile is larger than its share of all taxes except excise taxes. The highest decile pays a larger share of individual income taxes than its share of family income, but its share of social insurance and excise taxes is smaller. The distribution of the corporate tax is very sensitive to the way it is allocated. The top decile pays about 60 percent of the tax when it is allocated to capital income, but only about 30 percent when it is allocated to labor income.

Notes

Wendell Primus provided comments on this paper at the 1987 microsimulation conference held at The Urban Institute. The views expressed here are those of the authors and do not represent the position of the Congressional Budget Office.

1. See Pechman and Okner (1974), pp. 84–5; Minarik (1980), pp. 3–4; Pechman (1985), pp. 19–20.

2. See Pechman and Okner (1974); Minarik (1980); Pechman (1985); Anderson and Sheils (1985); and Cilke, Nelson, and Wyscarver (1987).

3. The complete elimination of passive losses and the deduction for consumer interest will not be fully phased in until 1991. Taxpayers were allowed to claim 40 percent of these deductions in 1988. They are allowed to claim 20 percent in 1989 and 10 percent in 1990.

4. Ideally, a comprehensive measure of annual income would include the change in the real value of total family resources, rather than the nominal value. Determining income on a real basis requires numerous conceptually and administratively complex adjustments to the accounting systems used by business and the government. These issues are discussed in Steuerle (1985).

5. Total adjusted capital gains in a particular year were computed as a fixed percentage of national income. Each family's share of adjusted gains was assumed to be the same as its share of realized gains. This procedure prevented assignment of a disproportionate share of the corporate tax to capital gains in those years when realizations were especially high.

6. Because family income includes the family's share of the corporate tax, and because the share depends on which allocation method is used, families may have different incomes and may lie in different deciles under the two allocations.

References

Anderson, Joseph M., and John F. Sheils. 1985. *The Household Income and Tax Simulation Model (HITSM): Methodology and Documentation.* Washington, D.C.: ICF.

Cilke, James M., Susan C. Nelson, and Roy A. Wyscarver. 1987. "The Tax Reform Data Base." In *1986 Proceedings of the Seventy-Ninth Annual Conference on Taxation,* edited by Stanley J. Bowers, pp. 201–233. Columbus, Ohio: National Tax Association-Tax Institute of America.

Minarik, Joseph J. 1980. "The Merge 1973 Data File." In *Microeconomic Simulation Models for Public Policy Analysis,* edited by Robert J. Haveman and Kevin Hollenbeck, pp. 3–28. New York: Academic Press.

Pechman, Joseph A. 1985. *Who Paid the Taxes, 1966–85?* Washington, D.C.: Brookings Institution.

Pechman, Joseph A., and Benjamin A. Okner. 1974. *Who Bears the Tax Burden?* Washington, D.C.: Brookings Institution.

Steuerle, Eugene. 1985. *Taxes, Loans, and Inflation: How the Nation's Wealth Becomes Misallocated.* Washington, D.C.: Brookings Institution.

Chapter Seven

MICRO-MACRO LINKAGES IN
ECONOMIC MODELS

Joseph M. Anderson

This chapter discusses the roles of microanalytic modeling and macromodeling in the analysis of income transfer policy. I interpret income transfer policy broadly, to include the provision of in-kind benefits from both public and private sources, such as health care benefits and housing, and the role of tax subsidies in the provision of pensions, health care benefits, housing, and other types of income or categories of expenditure.

By microanalytic modeling I refer to models that are based on analysis and depiction of the condition or behavior of individual economic units. Although the predictions of such models can be weighted, aggregated, and tabulated to provide information about entire populations, subpopulations, or sectors, the behavior that is being analyzed and modeled is that of individual units. In the models discussed in this book, the units are primarily individual persons and households, but they could include individual business enterprises and public agencies.

Microanalysis and simulation usually are based on microdata—observations on individual units collected in a cross-section survey at a specific time (such as the Current Population Survey [CPS]) or over a period of time (such as the Retirement History Survey or the Survey of Income and Program Participation [SIPP]). Behavioral microanalytic models draw on the analytic framework provided by microeconomics—the view that individual units' decisions concerning resource allocation, labor supply, consumption, savings, production, and other behaviors represent the outcomes of rational efforts to achieve the optimal position over a set of well-defined objectives, given complete and accurate information about the resources, costs, and constraints facing the individual.

By macromodeling I mean analysis and depiction of the behavior of aggregate variables, averages, and indexes. These variables generally represent a rather high level of abstraction—for example, GNP, consumption, the average wage rate, the interest rate, the Consumer Price Index (CPI), the noninstitutional population. Macrodata almost always consist of time series observations on aggregates or indexes, and macromodels are almost always time series models. A considerable amount of theory and assumption lies behind the creation of most macroeconomic variables, such as GNP, consumption, or the CPI. No consumer pays the Consumer Price Index for anything. Yet we believe the CPI tells something about the well being of (at least some) households, and may be a useful variable to use in models to predict household consumption behavior and perhaps labor supply, as well as the behavior of businesses and governments. We also can model the determination of the level of, or changes in, the CPI with reference to, say, the rate of unemployment, the size of the money stock, exogenous commodity prices, or other macroeconomic variables.

Macroeconomic models draw on an analytical framework provided by macroeconomic theory. Currently there is great diversity among alternative theoretical approaches in their areas of emphasis, assumptions, predictions, and conclusions. Short-term Keynesian income determination models focus on the determinants of aggregate demand, the relationship between income and expenditure, and the role of lags in adjustment. Monetarist models emphasize the role of the money supply. Neoclassical models focus on the long-term determinants of the growth of real output—factor supplies and technology—and assume that expectations are rational in the sense that they are, on average, fulfilled, that markets work smoothly, and that the economy moves relatively quickly to an equilibrium.

The second part of this chapter reviews why microanalytic models and macromodels are linked currently, and why such linkages might usefully be expanded. The third part discusses several examples of existing micro-macro linkages. The fourth part describes an alternative approach to economic-demographic modeling, that has been developed at Lewin/ICF and combines both micro and macro approaches.

WHY LINK MICROMODELS AND MACROMODELS?

Linkages between micromodels and macromodels are of interest for three, closely related reasons. First, macromodel estimates or predictions of aggregate variables are currently used to provide inputs to microsimulation models and to "control" or align the predictions of microsimulation models. Understanding and improving these linkage methodologies may help improve microsimulation modeling. Second, macro linkages could be used to provide feedbacks and to depict interactions among the variables represented in a microsimulation model at the individual unit level. Through linkages between micro- and macromodels, microsimulation analysis could move closer to a general equilibrium framework, and the accuracy and consistency of microanalysis could be improved. Third, microeconomic data, analysis, and simulation could be used to provide the microeconomic basis for models of aggregate behavior. Although it is recognized that macroeconomic variables generally reflect the aggregate outcomes of the individual behavior of many individual units, it is only relatively recently that widespread attention has been paid to the micro foundations of macroeconomic behavior. To the degree that distributional considerations or socioeconomic composition are important to the determination of macroeconomic variables, or would supplement the information provided by macromodels, such models would be enhanced by use of microeconomic data and/or linkage with micromodels.

Use of Macromodels or Projections to Control Micromodels

Almost all existing microsimulation models are linked in some way to one or more macromodels. In general, the individual behaviors of units in microsimulation models are "controlled," or adjusted, so that the aggregate behavior of the individual units is consistent with external estimates or predictions of the values of those aggregate variables. Microsimulation models are not now sufficiently complete or accurate to provide aggregate predictions of the variables they simulate as accurate as those of macromodels. This is not surprising. Macromodels were designed and developed to simulate the behavior and provide accurate predictions of aggregate variables. They, explicitly or implicitly, should take into account all of the important variables determining the values of their endogenous variables, including variables that cannot be represented in existing microsimulation models. Existing microsimulation models generally represent only one sector of the economy (e.g., the household sector). Macromodel inputs can provide information about the context or environment within which that sector operates.

General Equilibrium Feedbacks and Interactions

A microsimulation model depicts the behaviors or conditions of individual units (such as households). Those behaviors frequently represent the reaction of each of the units to variables or conditions that are considered to be external to their control—for example, general economic and labor market conditions, which are reflected in an average wage rate, a set of unemployment rates, or the rate of inflation. Often these "external" variables reflect the aggregate outcome of the behaviors of the individual units being modeled, as well as the aggregate behaviors of other types of micro units (such as firms). Furthermore, these aggregate variables are determined by the interactions among those aggregate behaviors (e.g., the aggregate supply and demand for labor). These interactions are most completely and accurately represented in a general equilibrium model. The number and complexity of the relationships to be represented are considerable. Until now, no data-driven microsimulation model has been developed that includes endogenously all of the important determinants of the behavior of any one set of micro units. That information has been provided by the projections of a macromodel or another external forecasting methodology.

Two hypothetical examples illustrate this point. Some microsimulation models represent the interaction between employment of household members and receipt of income from transfer programs. Microsimulation models have been used to project the numbers of recipients and the total expenditures of various transfer programs under alternative assumed or projected macroeconomic scenarios, characterized by aggregate employment and unemployment rates. Microsimulation models have also been developed to depict the direct effects of transfer income programs on labor supply and employment. However, important elements and interactions among employment and transfer programs cannot be captured in a microsimulation framework alone. To the degree that increased employment is associated with an expansion in economic activity and tighter labor markets, it may be accompanied by increased wage levels and inflation. Corresponding changes in nominal and real incomes will change eligibility for many transfer programs, and changes in the aggregate price level will change benefit levels of indexed programs. These interactions can be captured only through linkage of a macromodel and a micromodel.

Micromodels have been used to depict the effects on individual households and current and future incomes of changes in labor force participation of various demographic groups. To the degree that changes in labor force participation rates change labor supply, they may affect real wages, factor proportions, production costs, profits, and the aggregate price level. The ways these changes affect aggregate output and household incomes cannot be represented within a microsimulation framework alone, but could be analyzed using a macromodel.

In general, many variables that determine the incomes and other economic conditions or behaviors of individual households are determined in markets by the interaction of supply and demand. Microsimulation models generally depict the components of only one side of any market—such as labor supply, or the supply of savings, or the demand for nursing home beds. Linkage with a macromodel is necessary to provide a representation of the other side of such markets and the general equilibrium outcomes of changes in household conditions or behavior.

Microeconomic Basis of Aggregate Behavior

The behavior of aggregate variables—such as consumption, investment, inflation—is analyzed and depicted, using the tools of macroeconomic theory and macroeconomic models, as though those variables themselves were functions of other aggregative variables—disposable income, interest rates, capacity utilization, and so forth. In fact, every aggregate variable represents a sum, average, or index of variables characterizing the activity of many individual units. The theoretical validity as well as the forecasting accuracy of macromodels could be increased by research into the microeconomic foundations of the aggregative relationships depicted directly in those models. Use of microdata and linkage with microsimulation models could be part of the empirical side of this research.

The treatment of consumer expenditures in macromodels provides an illustration of the potential for useful microanalysis and model linkage. Aggregate consumption expenditures are determined by the individual purchases of each of millions of households. Aggregate consumption expenditures on various categories of consumer goods can be modeled at a macro level with reference to current and past values of aggregate disposable income (representing the sum of the incomes of millions of households, which will not be exactly the same set of households in any two periods), interest rates, aggregate wealth, the aggregate unemployment rate, and other variables. In fact, specific conditions and variables determine the consumption expenditures of each household. In many instances those variables may include the household's particular current and past disposable income levels; its net wealth and the liquidity of its assets; the size, composition, and age of its specific stock of durable goods; the specific rates of return it can earn on its assets or the interest rates it must pay on various forms of debt; the expectations of its members about their future wealth, incomes, and health; and the size of the family, the ages of its members, and other variables.

The validity and usefulness of an aggregate model of consumer expenditures depend on three conditions. First, there must be sufficient similarity among households that the consumer expenditures of a significant number of them can be explained by a limited set of variables of a kindred type from one household to another; and similar variables must have similar effects on the expenditures of many households. For example, a specific category of expenditures for each of many households could be related to that household's current disposable income. This relationship could be similar for a large number of households.

Second, for each of these types of variables, there must exist an aggregate variable, the behavior of which is representative of the behavior of a significant proportion of the individual household variables of that type. For example, the behavior of aggregate disposable income may be fairly representative of the behavior of many households' individual disposable incomes. At any one time some households' incomes will be increasing, others will be decreasing, and others will be unchanged. In general, however, the changes in aggregate disposable income should be representative of the changes in the disposable incomes of a significant number of households.

Third, the aggregative explanatory variable should be systematically related to the aggregative dependent variable in a way that is representative of the relationships between the corresponding individual household explanatory variables and the individual household dependent variables. That is, no important information should be lost or distortions introduced by the process of aggregation. For the relationship between aggregate or average disposable income and aggregate or average consumption, for example, this generally means that changes in the distribution of income over households can be ignored, either because the distribution itself does not influence aggregate consumption or because it can be assumed that significant changes in distribution will not occur as average income levels change. Similar considerations apply to the analysis and depiction of aggregate business investment expenditures, labor force participation, retirement rates, and other aggregative variables.

Microanalysis and simulation of consumer behavior could potentially contribute to improvement of macromodels of consumer expenditures. Potential contributions could be achieved through theoretical and empirical analysis of the micro conditions necessary for the existence and stability of an aggregate consumption function[1] and of the implications of observed or simulated individual consumer behavior for aggregate consumption.[2]

Analysis of microdata and development of microsimulation models contribute to the establishment of the micro foundations of macroeconomic theory and models. It may well be that many macroeconomic variables, such as aggregate consumer expenditures, could be forecast better by a microsimulation model linked to a macroeconomic model than by a macroeconomic model alone.

Linkage to a microsimulation model can enhance a macromodel in other respects. For many analysis and forecasting tasks, distributional information is one of the required outputs. Analysts of pension policy may want to know not only the average or aggregate level of private pension benefits, but the distribution of retirees and retirement income by type of plan, the numbers of beneficiaries with benefits from more than one plan or from various combinations of plans, or the distribution of benefits by income class or other socioeconomic characteristics. Such distributional information can be provided best by a microsimulation model. Where analysis requires both reliable behavioral forecasts of aggregate variables and reliable distributional information, which is mutually consistent, a linked micro and macromodeling system is needed.

EXAMPLES OF MICROMODEL-MACROMODEL LINKAGES

This section reviews several specific applications where macroeconomic and microsimulation modeling were linked. These examples are all taken from projects done at Lewin/ICF, a Washington D.C.-based public policy consulting firm. The first example describes the use of a long-term, annual macroeconomic forecasting model (the Wharton Econometrics Long Term Macroeconomic Model) to adjust or "age" the economic characteristics of households in a static household microsimulation model (the ICF Household Income and Tax

Simulation Model, HITSM). The second example describes a linked modeling system that includes several aggregative energy industry models, a quarterly Keynesian-based macroeconomic forecasting model (the Data Resources Incorporated [DRI] Quarterly U.S. Macroeconomic Model), and a household-based income and energy consumption static microsimulation model (the ICF Household Energy Price Impacts Model, HEPIM). In these two examples the information flow is from the aggregative models to the microsimulation model, although in the second example the process begins with industry sector microeconomic models. The third and fourth examples illustrate the use of microsimulation models to provide data inputs to a macroeconomic model. In the third case, a dynamic pension microsimulation model (ICF Pension and Retirement Income Simulation Model) was used to generate future distributions of retirement income to provide inputs to a macromodel of the retirement income system (the ICF Macroeconomic-Demographic Model—MDM). The fourth example describes an early effort to explore linkages running both ways between a dynamic microsimulation model (The Urban Institute DYNASIM model) and an aggregative model with both micro and macro elements (the ICF MDM).

Household Income and Tax Simulation Model and Wharton Econometrics Long-Term Macroeconomic Model

The first example is an illustration of the use of a macroeconomic forecasting model to "age" or adjust the microdata in a household microsimulation model. For studies of the effects on the incomes of households in various demographic groups of alternative tax reform proposals and federal budget proposals that would affect transfer income programs, ICF used the Household Income and Tax Simulation Model (HITSM), linked with the Wharton Econometrics Long-Term Macroeconomic Model.

THE HOUSEHOLD INCOME AND TAX SIMULATION MODEL

HITSM projects the distribution of disposable income among households of various socioeconomic groups in future years. The model estimates the distribution of employment income among individuals for given macroeconomic model projections of labor force participation, unemployment, wage levels, and inflation. It then estimates the amounts of income received by families from other sources, including various public assistance programs. Finally, HITSM estimates federal and state income taxes and Social Security payroll taxes. These tax payments are subtracted from total cash income to obtain estimates of disposable income.

HITSM can be used to analyze the impact on various subgroups of the population of changes in public assistance eligibility or benefit calculation rules, social insurance benefits, military and federal civil service retirement benefits, Medicare and Medicaid provisions, and other transfer programs. It is also used to analyze the impact of modifications to federal personal income tax laws, such as the elimination of certain tax deductions or changes in tax rates.

HITSM simulations are based upon the March Current Population Survey (CPS).[3] This database is a representative sample of the U.S. noninstitutionalized population, which includes detailed employment and income data for each individual in each of about 60,000 households. ICF statistically matched the CPS data with IRS Statistics of Income (SOI) data from a sample of actual tax returns.[4] These IRS data provide additional information on capital gains and tax deductions, which are not reported in the CPS. The CPS data are then calibrated so that they replicate government agency estimates of incomes received from various sources in the base year (usually the year to which the survey data correspond).

The model adjusts these data so that they reflect projections of the population and economic conditions in a future year (referred to as the simulation year). These data are adjusted to reflect Social Security Administration projections of the population in the simulation year. Hours of work and weeks of unemployment are adjusted to reflect macroeconomic forecasts of labor force participation and unemployment for that year. Incomes are adjusted to reflect these labor market changes and forecasted changes in average wages and prices. HITSM then estimates individuals' incomes from public assistance programs, using the actual eligibility and benefit calculation provisions of these programs. The public assistance programs simulated in HITSM include: Aid to Families with Dependent Children (AFDC), Supplemental Security Income (SSI), food stamps, Low Income Home Energy Assistance Program (LIHEAP), Unemployment Insurance, and in-kind benefit programs including Medicaid, Medicare, housing assistance, and the school lunch program.

Finally, HITSM simulates income taxes paid by individuals in the simulation year. The model calculates federal taxes directly from the CPS and SOI data using the provisions specified in current tax law. It calculates state personal income taxes using the actual tax provisions for each state. The model also calculates Social Security payroll taxes using the procedures specified in the Social Security Act.

The output of this analysis is a database that includes simulation results for each of the individuals in the CPS data. The HITSM simulation results for individuals are combined into family units to permit analyses of either families or individuals in the simulation year. Records for families and/or individuals are tabulated to analyze the distribution of disposable income among various socioeconomic groups. Individuals and/or families may be disaggregated by a wide range of variables, including income, poverty status, age, sex, geographic region, family composition, and marital status.

LINKAGES TO PROJECTIONS OF AGGREGATE EMPLOYMENT AND LABOR FORCE ACTIVITY

HITSM currently uses the March 1988 Current Population Survey database, which reflects the labor market experience of individuals during 1987. In that year, the United States experienced an average weekly unemployment rate of 5.4 percent and an average weekly civilian labor force participation rate of 65.9 percent. The total annual earnings reported by individuals in the CPS data reflected individuals' work experiences during a year when these unemployment and labor force participation rates prevailed. Similarly, the unemployment insurance income reported in the CPS data reflected the unemployment rates during that year.

In future years, average weekly unemployment and labor force participation rates will differ from the levels experienced in 1987. Furthermore, changes in tax laws or federal budget proposals may alter unemployment rates and labor force participation, which, in turn, will affect individuals' hours worked, earnings, weeks of unemployment, and unemployment insurance income during the year.

HITSM modifies the distribution of hours worked annually as reported in the March CPS data to reflect macroeconomic model projections of average weekly labor force participation and unemployment in the selected simulation year. These annual hours-worked distributions are estimated based upon an analysis of historical data concerning the association between the distribution of hours worked and the average weekly labor force participation and unemployment rates. This economic aging methodology also includes an adjustment that corrects the initial CPS data for underreporting of weeks of employment and unemployment.

Annual Hours-Worked Distributions. The Wharton Long-Term Macroeconomic Model was used in these studies to provide forecasts of the average unemployment and labor force participation rates in future years under alternative tax reform laws and budget proposals. These aggregate average rates, however, provide little information on how individual annual household incomes will change as a result of fluctuations in labor force activity.

For most households, annual income is largely determined by the members' earnings during the year. Consequently, it is necessary to estimate the relationship between average aggregate survey week employment data and each individual's work experience during the year. To accomplish this, ICF estimated the relationship between average survey week labor force data—labor force participation, unemployment, and employment rates—and the distribution of individuals by total hours worked during the year, using Census survey data on employment during 1976 through 1986. A set of multinomial logit equations was estimated, expressing the proportion of workers in each of 10 hours-worked groups as a function of the average unemployment rate and labor force participation rate. Equations were estimated for men and women of eight age groups: 14–17, 18–24, 25–34, 35–44, 45–54, 55–64, 65–72, 73 and older.

ICF used these equations to project the proportion of individuals in each of the 10 hours-worked groups, based upon the Wharton macroeconomic model projections of unemployment and labor force participation rates during each simulation year. These projected hours-worked distributions generally result in an aggregate employment rate relatively close to the aggregate employment rate projected by the macromodel for that year. However, a final adjustment is required to replicate the projected aggregate employment rate exactly. This adjustment scales the proportion of individuals in each annual hours group so that in the aggregate, these distributions replicate the number of weeks of employment implicit in the macromodel employment rate estimates for the simulation year. This final stage adjustment generally results in very minor modifications in the logit equation projections of the number of individuals in each annual hours-worked group.

Adjustment of Work Experience in CPS. The HITSM labor force model then modifies the annual work experience information reported by each individual in the CPS data to replicate the projected distribution of individuals by hours worked for each simulation year. The model selects individuals to move from their reported annual hours-worked category to one of the other annual hours worked categories. Individuals selected to change their hours worked are then assigned a set of work experience variables typical of those reported by individuals in the hours-worked category to which they were moved. These annual work experience variables include: hours worked during the year, weeks spent unemployed, full-time/part-time employment status, and the amount of unemployment insurance received. No individual is allowed to move to an hours category more than two categories above or below his or her reported hours-worked group. In general, ICF has found that this approach allows modification of HITSM employment data with a minimum amount of distortion in the underlying socioeconomic composition of families reported in the original CPS.

The algorithm first estimates the number of individuals who must be moved from one hours-worked category to another to achieve the projected hours-worked distribution while minimizing the size of the change in hours worked reported by each individual. This algorithm produces an hours transition matrix that shows the probability that an individual in one hours-worked category in 1987 will be reassigned to another hours-worked category. Separate transition matrices were estimated for males and females in each of the eight age groups previously listed. Based on the transition probabilities, individuals are randomly selected to change from the hours-worked category they reported to another category.

The final step in this procedure is to assign a set of work experience variables to individuals selected to change hours-worked groups. This is accomplished by assigning each of these individuals the values of the set of work experience variables actually reported by an individual in the hours-worked category to which he or she was assigned, who is of the same age and sex and has a similar hourly wage rate. These variables include:

- □ Hours normally worked per week,
- □ weeks worked during the year,
- □ weeks unemployed,
- □ weeks out of labor force,
- □ unemployment compensation received,
- □ employment status at start of year,
- □ employment status at end of year,
- □ number of unemployment spells, and
- □ number of jobs during year.

Matching Macroeconomic Projections of Unemployment. Once this procedure is completed the average weekly labor force participation rate implicit in the adjusted March CPS data replicates the macroeconomic model projection of the labor force participation rate for that simulation year. However, this procedure tends to capture only about 60 percent of the projected change in the average weekly unemployment rate. For example, if we hold the labor force participation rate constant and change the unemployment rate in the logit equations from its 1987 level of 5.4 percent to 8.6 percent, the work experience adjustments alone would yield an implicit average weekly unemployment rate of about 7.3 percent.

The reason for this is that the procedure previously described changes only the annual hours-worked categories for individuals. This understates the change in unemployment, because many individuals may experience changes in unemployment during the year without changing annual hours-worked groups. For example, an individual who is employed full time for 52 weeks in one year remains in the same annual hours-worked category if he is laid off for two weeks in the next year (i.e., 2,000 to 2,080 annual hours). To replicate macroeconomic projections of average weekly unemployment rates, ICF developed a methodology for adding weeks of unemployment to some individuals who are not selected to change their annual hours-worked categories.

An average weekly labor force participation rate cannot be calculated directly from the CPS data, because these data do not report individuals' employment status during each week of the simulation year. The CPS data do, however, provide information on the number of weeks each individual worked during the year as well as the number of weeks he or she was unemployed. Using this and other information on each individual's work experience during the year, one can allocate these weeks of unemployment and employment over the 52 weeks of the year. Once each individual's employment status is estimated for each week of the simulation year, it is straightforward to calculate the implicit average weekly labor force participation, unemployment, and employment rates for the year from the adjusted CPS data.

HITSM adds or deletes weeks of unemployment for individuals not selected to change hours-worked groups in a manner that changes the implicit average unemployment rate so that it matches macroeconomic projections. Individuals within an hours-worked category are selected randomly to be assigned additional weeks of unemployment. Each of these individuals is then matched with an individual in the same hours-worked category who experienced greater unemployment. The selected individual takes on the same number of weeks of unemployment experienced by the individual to which he or she was assigned. As discussed in the previous section, individuals are matched with other workers in the same annual hours-worked group who are similar in age, sex, and hourly wage rate.

Individuals who did not change hours-worked groups are selected to experience additional weeks of unemployment only if they did not report experiencing weeks of unemployment during 1987 (the base year of our data). The probability that an individual will be selected to be assigned weeks of unemployment is estimated so that the total number of unemployment weeks in the simulated HITSM database is equal to the aggregate number of unemployment weeks implicit in the macroeconomic model unemployment rate projections.

The product of this adjustment process is an estimate of the proportion of individuals in each age/sex/hours group who will experience unemployment during the simulation year that is consistent with the aggregate unemployment rate projected for that year. HITSM selects individuals who did not change their hours-worked group to experience additional weeks of unemployment, so that it replicates these projections of unemployment by age, sex, and annual hours of employment.

Interpretation of Modified Employment Data. This procedure for modifying work experience data implicitly assumes that within each hours-worked category, the work experience patterns of individuals will not change from that reported in the March 1988 CPS data. In this analysis, only the proportion of individuals in each hours-worked group is changed. The unemployment, labor force participation, and number of jobs data assigned to an individual changing his or her hours-worked category is on average the same pattern experienced in 1987 by the individual in the hours-worked group to which he or she is assigned.

The variances and covariances among the imputed work experience variables within each hours-worked group are roughly the same as those reported in the 1987 data. The reason for this is that when an hours-worked group changer was matched with an individual in the hours-worked group to which he or she is moving, the hours changer took on the entire set of work experience data reported by the individual to which he or she was matched. Consequently, within each hours-worked group, the covariances among the imputed work experience variables change little from those reported in 1988 for that hours-worked group. Also, because job changes are randomly assigned to individuals within the hours-worked group to which they are assigned, the variances of the variables within that hours-worked group are not changed by the imputation procedure. Finally, because ICF controlled for age, sex, and wage rate when matching individuals, the covariances between age, sex, wage rate, and the imputed work experience data are similar to that reported in the March 1988 CPS.

LINKAGE TO MACROMODEL INFLATION AND WAGE GROWTH ESTIMATES

The March 1988 CPS reports individuals' cash incomes from all sources during 1987. HITSM adjusts these data so that they are representative of the expected level and distribution of income during each simulation year. The model simulates public assistance from SSI, AFDC, food stamps, and other cash and in-kind benefit programs using actual program eligibility and benefit calculation rules. All other forms of income in the CPS data are proportionally adjusted to reflect projected inflation and wage growth between 1987 and the simulation year. All information reported in the 1986 SOI tax data is also adjusted by the growth in wages between 1986 and the simulation year.

Earnings. An individual's annual earnings are the product of the total hours-worked during the year and his or her hourly wage rate. Hours-worked were determined using the economic aging methodology described earlier here. Each individual's 1987 wage rate was proportionally adjusted to correspond to the change in average wages from 1987 to the simulation year.[5] The product of each individual's adjusted wage rate and adjusted hours-worked annually is annual earnings income.

Retirement Incomes. The growth in retirement incomes over time is sensitive to a number of factors. For example, Social Security benefits are indexed annually based upon inflation during the previous year. Consequently, benefit indexation lags the CPI by one year. Average Social Security benefit levels are also affected by new retirees. New retirees benefits are calculated based upon average indexed prior earnings through age 61, which are assumed to grow at the rate of average wage growth, also with a lag. About 8.9 percent of all Social Security recipients in any given year are new beneficiaries.

Similar benefit growth patterns can also be found in pension plans. Some plans provide cost-of-living increases on an automatic or ad hoc basis based upon the prior year's inflation rate. As with Social Security, initial pension benefits will also tend to rise with the general wage level.

To account for this complex pattern in retirement income growth, ICF adjusted pension and Social Security income using a benefit adjustment factor, which is a weighted average of inflation and wage growth lagged one year. The weight applied to the wage growth factor is equal to the average proportion of total Social Security beneficiaries who are receiving benefits for the first time during the year (.089). The weight applied to the inflation factor is equal to 1 minus the proportion of Social Security recipients accepting benefits for the first time (.911). To account for the lagged pattern of benefit increases, ICF used the proportional change in average wages and in the CPI from 1987 through the year prior to the simulation year for which the data were adjusted.

Veterans' and Workers' Compensation. Income from other government programs also tends to grow at the rate of inflation or average wage growth, lagged one year. Veterans' benefits are assumed to increase at the rate of inflation lagged one year. Because unemployment insurance and workers' compensation are based upon prior earnings, these benefits were adjusted by the growth in wages lagged one year.

Investment Income. This analysis assumed that interest income, dividends, rental income, and income from estates and trusts keep pace with the overall level of earnings. Consequently, incomes from these sources were indexed to current wage growth.

Other Income. All other incomes, such as alimony and other regular contributions to the household, were assumed to grow with the price level, without a lag. All employer fringe benefits are indexed to the growth in average weekly wages.

Tax Data. The SOI database currently used in HITSM reports capital gains, capital losses, allowable deductions, and tax credit data for 1986. All of these items are inflated to simulation year levels by the projected growth in average weekly earnings between 1986 and the simulation year.

Using these techniques, the HITSM model adjusts the records of the CPS database to correspond to a data base consistent with the aggregate economic indicators projected by a macroeconomic model, while preserving the distributional information in the original data.

Household Energy Price Impacts Model—Data Resources Incorporated Quarterly Model—ICF Energy Market Models

ICF developed a linked energy market-macroeconomic-household income and energy expenditures modeling system to analyze the effects of energy price changes on households and the economy. This modeling system illustrates the linkage of microeconomic industry sector models (which are not microsimulation models) with a macroeconomic model, which in turn provides inputs to a household microsimulation model. This analysis of the effects of energy price changes (such as may result from crude oil supply disruptions) on households and the economy involved three steps:

1. The effects of world crude oil price changes on the prices and aggregate quantities of petroleum products and other fuels used by households were estimated, using a set of energy market models.
2. The effects of these energy price changes on economic activity, including inflation, employment, and output, were estimated using the Data Resources Incorporated (DRI) Quarterly U.S. Macroeconomic Model.
3. The effects of the changes in fuel prices and economic activity and of government policy measures on individual household energy expenditures and income were estimated using the Household Energy Price Impacts Model.

The linked energy market-macroeconomic-household microsimulation modeling system is shown in figure 7.1

The key analytical tool—the Household Energy Price Impacts Model (HEPIM)—is a large household energy expenditure microdatabase and modeling system. The database consists of 60,000 household records with extensive data on energy expenditures, income from various sources, and demographic and socioeconomic characteristics for each household. A set of algorithms was used to adjust the data for each household to reflect alternative energy price scenarios, policy response measures, and macroeconomic scenarios and to tabulate the simulated data to permit comparisons of the effects on households classified by age of head, income class, and other characteristics. This model has been used to estimate household energy expenditures, income, and employment under a "nondisruption" base case and under alternative oil supply disruption scenarios. The model was also used to simulate the effects on household incomes

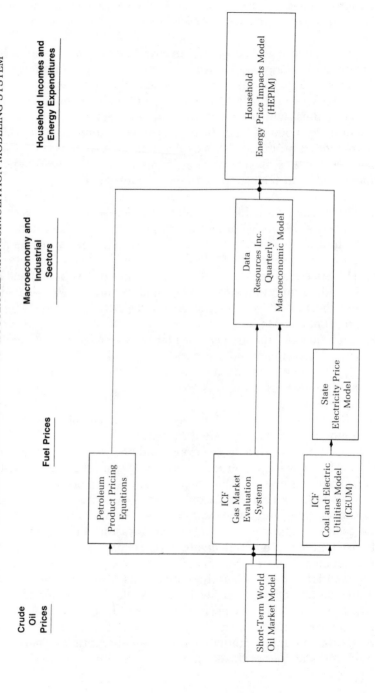

Figure 7.1   LINKED ENERGY MARKET–MACROECONOMIC–HOUSEHOLD MICROSIMULATION MODELING SYSTEM

of alternative government policy response measures under the disruption scenarios. The model simulates the changes in household energy expenditures and incomes, using input data on fuel prices and quantities consumed and on inflation, wages, employment, and other aggregate economic variables.

ENERGY PRICES AND QUANTITIES CONSUMED

Energy prices and aggregate quantities consumed were estimated using a set of models of various energy sectors of the economy. A model of the world petroleum market estimated petroleum product prices and quantities under various oil supply conditions. A structural model of petroleum product prices estimated end-user prices. A detailed model of the North American natural gas market estimated prices of natural gas and quantities consumed by electric utilities, industrial customers, and residential consumers. Because price regulations and transportation costs differ between those states where most domestic natural gas is produced (the intrastate market) and the remaining states (the interstate market), ICF estimated prices for each of these two regions separately.

The changes in electricity prices in each oil price scenario were projected by ICF using estimates of the changes in the prices of residual fuel oil and natural gas, and data on the proportion of each fuel used to generate electricity and on the proportion of electricity costs accounted for by fuel costs. Because the fuel mix and the proportion of total generation costs accounted for by fuel differ in each state, the model provides separate estimates for each state.

These fuel price and quantity estimates, in turn, were used to analyze the effects of each energy price scenario on the economy and on households.

MACROECONOMIC EFFECTS

An oil supply disruption affects households both directly, by increasing the prices and quantities of the fuels they consume, and indirectly by increasing the prices of other goods that use energy in their production or distribution and that are purchased by households and disrupting economic activity, thereby reducing employment and hours-worked. To estimate the effects of an oil supply disruption on households, the Household Energy Price Impacts Model requires information for each year on the rate of inflation, the level of wages, the rate of unemployment, and the average rate of labor force participation, as well as information on changes in fuel prices.

To estimate the affects of energy price changes on macroeconomic activity, ICF simulated the behavior of the economy under alternative energy price scenarios using the DRI Quarterly U.S. Macroeconomic Model. A DRI macromodel simulation was developed for each energy price scenario by exogenously changing the prices of crude oil, gasoline, heating oil, natural gas, and electricity; the quantities of crude oil produced, imported, and drawn from stocks; and the quantities of heating oil and gasoline consumed, to match the estimates generated using the energy market models. The DRI model simulations provided estimates of average wage rates, labor force participation, inflation, and unemployment for each quarter of the simulation period. The model simulations also provided estimates of aggregate household natural gas and electricity consumption. These macroeconomic variables were then used as inputs for the household microsimulation model analysis.

EFFECTS ON HOUSEHOLDS

The effects of an oil supply disruption and of alternative response policy measures on households were estimated using the Household Energy Price Impacts Model. The modeling system consists of a large database containing survey information on incomes, employment, and socioeconomic characteristics, and imputed information on energy use and expenditures for 60,000 households; and an extensive set of algorithms that adjust these data to correspond to alternative energy prices and economic conditions.

The database was created by statistically matching the 1981/82 Residential Energy Consumption Survey (RECS) developed by the U.S. Department of Energy with the March 1982 Current Population Survey conducted by the U.S. Bureau of the Census. In the matching process, data on energy use and expenditures from the 6,000 household records in the RECS were used to impute energy use and expenditures to the 60,000 records in the CPS. This database provides annual information on income from a variety of sources, energy expenditures, employment, and other socioeconomic data for over 60,000 households. The income and public assistance information in this database were calibrated to replicate independent estimates of incomes received from various sources in 1981. The model adjusts these 1981–82 data to be consistent with input assumptions about aggregate income, population, labor force participation, employment, wages, inflation, and energy prices and expenditures for a given base case or alternative energy price scenario for other years. The model then estimates public assistance benefits and tax payments for each household in this year. The economic aging methodology of HEPIM is essentially the same as that of the HITSM, described earlier.

Demographic and Energy Detail. The household model is used to estimate the size of energy price-induced and income-induced changes in each household's expenditures for five fuels: automobile fuel, home heating oil, electricity, natural gas, and liquid petroleum gas. The model estimates the change in each household's disposable income during a disruption due to changes in employment, hours worked, wages, tax collections, public assistance benefit payments, and other factors. The estimated changes in energy expenditures and disposable income can be tabulated for households classified according to various socioeconomic characteristics, such as:

☐ Household disposable income,
☐ poverty status,
☐ age of household head,
☐ region,
☐ urban/rural location,
☐ type of fuel consumed,
☐ primary heating source,
☐ receipt of public assistance, and
☐ employment status.

Public Assistance Programs and Tax Revenues. The household model simulates the impact of an energy supply disruption and other events upon participation and benefit levels in the following income transfer programs:

☐ Aid to Families with Dependent Children;
☐ Supplemental Security Income;
☐ food stamps;
☐ Low Income Home Energy Assistance Program;
☐ unemployment Insurance; and
☐ in-kind benefit programs including Medicaid, Medicare, housing assistance, and school lunch program.

Federal and state income taxes and Social Security payroll taxes are also calculated. The model provides estimates of the impact of energy price changes on both government expenditures and revenues from personal taxes. It provides detailed information on the effects of these programs on households of various incomes and in different demographic groups, while also providing aggregate data on the number of individuals affected, total transfer program costs, and tax revenues.

The model is designed to depict how changes in energy prices and the resulting changes in employment would affect government public assistance payments and tax revenues, as well as to simulate the impact of alternative government policies designed to alleviate the hardships caused by an oil supply disruption. Government response policies that can be simulated include changes in tax policy, changes in the eligibility criteria and benefit levels of existing public assistance programs, or development of new assistance programs based on household energy expenditures or incomes. All of the estimates are annual because the RECS is an annual survey, reporting expenditures for a one-year period, and the March CPS reports incomes and employment experience for a one-year period.

Analysis of Impact of Energy Price Changes. The impact of a specific energy price scenario is estimated by comparing the simulated data for the base case with simulated data for the alternative scenario. The data for each household are first adjusted for each simulation year, assuming a given base case set of energy prices and macroeconomic conditions, and public assistance and tax payments are calculated. The data are then adjusted to correspond to an alternative energy price and supply scenario, with its attendant macroeconomic conditions. The impact of the changes in energy prices and supplies on households is estimated by comparing average income levels, public assistance benefits, energy expenditures, and other data for various socioeconomic groups in the base case simulation with those for the alternative scenario. Alternative policy measures, such as increased energy assistance benefit payments, can be analyzed in the same way by comparing an energy disruption scenario simulation without a policy measure to one in which a particular response policy measure is implemented.

Use of Pension and Retirement Income Microsimulation Model (PRISM) to Calibrate ICF Macroeconomic-Demographic Model

A third application of model linkage provides an example of information flows from a microsimulation model to a macromodel. The ICF Macroeconomic-Demographic Model of the Retirement Income System (MDM) projects labor market experience and average earnings histories for age–sex groups and estimates coverage and participation in various private and public pension systems, including Social Security (OASI and DI), Supplemental Security Income (SSI), private defined benefit and defined contribution plans, individual retirement accounts, the Federal Civil Service Retirement System (CSRS) and Federal Employees Retirement System (FERS), the Military Retirement System, and four types of state and local government retirement systems. Participation in the various types of systems and receipt of benefits are projected by applying estimated and projected age–sex specific participation rates and benefit receipt rates to the projected population. These participation and benefit receipt rates are estimated exogenously and are input data to the model. Given these rates, the MDM calculates numbers of participants, average and total annual contributions to various types of pension funds, numbers of retirees, numbers of beneficiaries from various types of plans, average and total benefit payments, fund asset balances, and other variables characterizing the pension system.

The Pension and Retirement Income Simulation Model is a dynamic microsimulation model designed to project private and public employer pension plan coverage, participation, and vesting for individual workers, and benefit levels and total retirement income from all sources for individuals and families in various birth cohorts. PRISM dynamically ages a microdata base composed of the March and May 1979 Current Population Surveys and Special Pension Supplement data from the May 1983 CPS, matched with Social Security Earnings Records. It uses the ICF Retirement Plan Provisions Database to assign individuals to employer pension plans. PRISM dynamically projects the labor market experience of individuals, including employment and hours worked by industry, unemployment, wages and earnings, pension plan coverage, participation, and vesting by type of plan. PRISM projects individuals' pension benefit receipts by source, based on their benefit accruals during their working lives. A projected PRISM database can be tabulated to provide estimates of average pension benefits by source for various demographic groups for various future years.

PRISM provides much more distributional detail than the MDM. For this reason, ICF uses tabulations of PRISM projections to provide the pension benefit receipt distributions required by MDM. The PRISM simulation is controlled or aligned to be consistent with the MDM projection for which the benefit distributions are provided, with respect to the average wages, participation rates, unemployment rates, and hours worked of age–sex groups. PRISM provides distributions of participants and beneficiaries in several types and combinations of pension plans. These distributions are calculated endogenously in PRISM and reflect trends in the retirement income system, projected economic growth and structural changes, and demographic changes, including data projected by MDM. MDM alone does not contain a methodology to project endogenously changing distributions of retirement benefit receipt over the great variety of sources and combinations, and how these distributions will change as a result of trends in pension plan offerings and coverage and changes in the structure of the economy.

MDM provides counts of total beneficiaries and average benefit amounts, for different age–sex groups, for each of the pension systems identified previously, in each simulation year. PRISM provides distributions of beneficiaries and benefit levels over different combinations of plans (e.g. Social Security plus a private defined benefit plan). Given MDM projections of total beneficiaries by type of plan for each year, PRISM tabulations of distributions over combinations of plans in selected future years can be used to develop such distributions for the MDM projections by a process of iterative scaling (or iterative proportional fitting).

Integrating DYNASIM2 with ICF Macroeconomic-Demographic Model

Another example of micro-macro linkage where information flows both ways is provided by a project carried out jointly by The Urban Institute and ICF with the objective of exploring the feasibility of integrating The Urban Institute's dynamic microsimulation model, DYNASIM, with ICF's Macroeconomic-Demographic Model of the U.S. Retirement Income System.[6]

Both microsimulation models of individual family or household behavior and aggregative models of average behavior of entire systems or of the economy as a whole have been developed and applied to issues concerning the elderly population. The retirement decision and the life-cycle labor force and savings behavior that largely determine retirement income are essentially microeconomic phenomena, and may be best investigated through the application of microeconomic analysis and simulation techniques. Investigation of the distribution of elderly incomes and the distributional consequences of alternative policies requires a microanalytic approach. However, the behavior and well being of the elderly also influence and are influenced by aggregative economic variables—labor force participation rates, average earnings, inflation, and aggregate savings—the behavior of which may best be studied in the aggregate. The major retirement income systems, such as the Social Security system, the private pension system, and the SSI system, can be addressed fruitfully at both the macro and aggregate levels. Because the economic behavior and problems of the elderly involve both aggregative and micro aspects, models using each approach have been developed and applied to these issues.

The insights and information provided by each approach have not been applied fully to the other. In a fully integrated micro-macro model, the values of many aggregate variables could be determined by aggregating the simulated values of the microeconomic variables that are their constituent parts. For example, personal saving would be the sum of each household's savings. At the same time, each household's decisions would be influenced by the values of aggregate variables, determined by aggregating the variables characterizing each household. To be complete, such a model would have to include a microeconomic model of the business sector, in which demand for inputs, such as labor, and the prices and quantities of goods supplied would be determined. Development of such a model represents an extremely ambitious undertaking and does not appear feasible in the near future.

This project represented a first step toward the development of a linked micro-macro model focused on retirement and the retirement income system. The initial objective was to develop a set of simulations of The Urban Institute's DYNASIM microanalytic simulation model and of ICF's Macroeconomic-Demographic Model (MDM) of the retirement income system that were mutually consistent. This was done by aligning the control totals for several DYNASIM variables to the values of aggregates estimated directly by MDM. Estimates of other variables provided by the controlled DYNASIM simulation were then compared to MDM estimates.

The project involved three steps. First, the potential connections between the two models were reviewed. Control variables from MDM, which would guide the DYNASIM simulation, and the common predictions of the models, which could be compared, were selected. The control variables included fertility, mortality, labor force participation, hours worked, earnings, and unemployment. Second, a DYNASIM simulation from 1980 through 1990 was carried out with outputs for the selected variables constrained to match corresponding outputs from MDM. Third, DYNASIM and MDM forecasts were compared, focusing upon variables not explicitly linked via the control process. Comparisons focused on the numbers of Social Security and private pension beneficiaries and the level of benefits they received.

Both models tracked the number of Social Security beneficiaries closely over the historic period. They diverged during the 1980s, with DYNASIM predicting a higher caseload than MDM. This was probably due to DYNASIM's alignment to MDM's declining rates of labor force participation. Declining labor participation rates were associated with higher levels of Social Security benefit receipt rates in the DYNASIM Social Security module than they were in the MDM Social Security module. With respect to benefits, there was less agreement, the most important difference being in the growth in average real benefits.

The private pension comparisons were somewhat disconcerting owing to the wide divergence of results. However, due to the lack of adequate historic data, it was not possible to judge which model was more reliable.

Comparing estimates of the number of pension benefit awards and recipients from DYNASIM and MDM is difficult because the two sets of estimates were developed using very different methods. DYNASIM develops estimates of the total number of pension beneficiaries by simulating the labor market experience of individuals and counting all the individuals who are simulated to receive a benefit. Occurrence of an individual benefit receipt is based on the individual's work history, including industry, job tenure, and wage level, which in turn is based on other demographic and economic characteristics. Because DYNASIM is a micromodel, its major strength is in producing information on the expected distribution of pension benefits rather than in estimating the correct total number of recipients and aggregate pension receipts. MDM projects trends in the aggregate rate of benefit receipt for age–sex groups, which are based on past and projected trends in aggregate age–sex specific private pension coverage and participation.

Another problem in comparing estimates of numbers of pension recipients from each model was that only limited data were available concerning numbers of new beneficiaries and current recipients in the past. Consequently, it was difficult to calibrate and to validate either model. Because of the complicated nature of the comparisons, a summary of the comparisons cannot be provided in this chapter. A complete description of both models and the project is provided in Wertheimer, Zedlewski, Anderson, and Moore (1986).

NIA MACROECONOMIC-DEMOGRAPHIC MODEL—AN AGGREGATIVE, MICROECONOMIC-BASED APPROACH TO ECONOMIC MODELING

This section describes an alternative approach to macro-micro modeling that differs from the examples discussed in the previous section. All of the modeling systems so far discussed here provided examples of links between microsimulation models—models that operate on individual records in microdata bases—and aggregative models (macromodels). The examples included systems where the flows of information were from macro to micro and vice versa. In the early effort to link DYNASIM and MDM, the flows went both ways. However, none of these examples includes a truly integrated micro-macro system with simultaneous feedback in both directions.

The Macroeconomic-Demographic Model of Health Care Expenditures, developed for the National Institute on Aging (NIA) by ICF, provides a new approach to aggregative modeling that achieves many of the objectives of a linked micro-macro model. It is an aggregative simulation model based on microeconomic theory as well as neoclassical macroeconomic growth theory. Its behavioral relationships are estimated using both microdata—large-scale household surveys—and aggregate time series data. It simulates labor market, consumer, and other economic behavior in great demographic detail. It characterizes the average behavior of a large number of demographic groups of households and individuals. However, it is not a true microsimulation model; its simulation system does not operate on an actual microdatabase, and it does not simulate the behavior of individual households.

The major components of MDM and their linkages are shown in figure 7.2. At the core of the model is a macroeconomic growth model—an empirically estimated neoclassical growth model with endogenous household and business sectors and exogenous government and foreign sectors. The growth model has two goods—investment goods and consumer goods—and two factor inputs—labor and capital services. The behavioral equations of both the household sector and the business sector are derived within a microeconomic analytical framework based on assumptions of optimizing behavior subject to constraints. Within this framework, the model depicts the formulation of intertemporal labor supply, consumption, and savings plans by households; and production, investment, and employment plans by business. It characterizes the demand and supply of the two products and the two factors and depicts the equilibration of demand and supply in all four markets by price adjustments and changes in consumption and production decisions. The data for the estimation of the macroeconomic growth model are derived primarily from the National Income and Product Accounts (NIPA).

The model provides considerable demographic detail, both for individuals and families. The population projection system projects

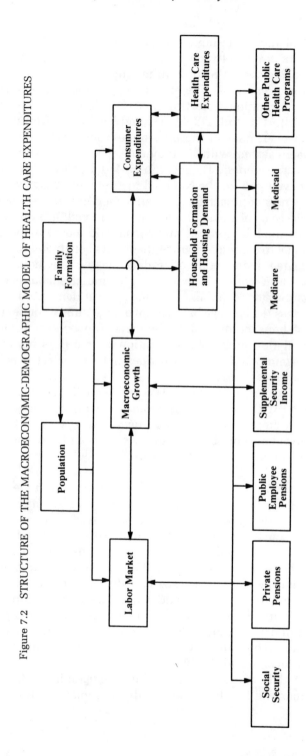

Figure 7.2   STRUCTURE OF THE MACROECONOMIC-DEMOGRAPHIC MODEL OF HEALTH CARE EXPENDITURES

the population by single year of age, race, and sex, based on assumed age–race specific fertility rates, age–race–sex specific mortality rates disaggregated by cause of death, and age–race–sex immigration levels. Based on the population projection, the model projects the number of families, characterized by age, sex, and race of the head, size, region, and urban–rural location. The model projects the numbers of families in each of 1,568 demographic cells, cross-classified by the attributes shown in figure 7.3. Each of these groups is disaggregated into those with and those without health insurance, providing 3,136 groups in all. The model also projects the number of families by housing tenure status.

The model characterizes the economic conditions and activities of both groups of individuals and groups of families. Labor market behavior, earnings, and earnings-based retirement income programs are characterized for individuals. Labor input, defined as total labor hours provided by each of 20 age–sex groups, is determined by the size of the population of each group, its average labor force participation rate, average unemployment rate, average weeks worked per

Figure 7.3 DEMOGRAPHIC GROUPS IN THE MACROECONOMIC-DEMOGRAPHIC MODEL OF HEALTH CARE EXPENDITURES

Family Size	Age of Head of Household
1. One	1. Less than 24
2. Two	2. 25–34
3. Three	3. 35–44
4. Four	4. 45–54
5. Five	5. 55–64
6. Six	6. 65–74
7. More than six	7. 75 +

Sex of Head of Household	Region
1. Male	1. Northeast
2. Female	2. North Central
	3. South
	4. West

Type of Residence	Race
1. Urban	1. Nonwhite
2. Rural	2. White

Private Insurance Coverage

1. Family covered by private health insurance
2. Family not covered by private health insurance

year, and average hours worked per week. These are modeled econometrically, based on the microeconomic theory of labor supply, with reference to income and substitution effects, search costs, and imperfect substitution among age groups.

Demand for labor of various age groups is modeled by estimating the parameters of a translog input cost function, specified to apply to the aggregate U.S. private production sector. This specification focuses on the substitutability among different age groups in production. Labor supply and demand are solved simultaneously for equilibrium labor and capital input and compensation levels, given population, technology, government fiscal behavior, and other exogenous variables.

The labor market model is based on both establishment-level data on employment, hours worked, and compensation of workers, and household-level data on labor force participation, employment, and unemployment of individuals of various ages and sexes, collected by the Bureau of the Census and the Bureau of Labor Statistics. The model estimates average earnings histories for cohorts. Average Social Security and employer pension income levels are estimated for cohorts based on these earnings histories.

Total income and consumer expenditures are characterized for households in the 1,568 demographic groups. Household incomes are related to average labor incomes of individuals in corresponding age groups. Allocations of expenditures over five categories of consumer goods and services and over six categories of health care goods and services, for each of 3,136 groups, are modeled by estimating econometric expenditure share equations derived from a translog preference function within the framework of the microeconomic theory of consumer behavior. The conditions required for the existence of aggregate consumer expenditure equations as functions of individual household consumption equations are derived from the theory of exact aggregation and are utilized to estimate the parameters of the consumer expenditure equations.

The model specifies that consumer expenditures and health care expenditures for each group of households are determined in three stages. In the first stage, households choose whether or not to be covered by health insurance and choose their housing tenure status (own, subsidized rental, unsubsidized rental). In the second stage, households allocate their expenditures over five classes of consumer goods and services—housing, food, health care, other consumer goods, and capital services. In the third stage, households allocate aggregate health care expenditures over six types of health care—hospital services, physician services, dentist services, other professional services, drugs, and eyeglasses and appliances.

The consumer expenditure equations are estimated by pooling time series and cross-section data. The current consumer expenditures and health expenditures model is estimated using the 1984 Consumer Expenditure Survey (CES) and National Income and Product Accounts data for 1948 through 1986 for the consumer expenditures stage and the 1980 National Medical Care Utilization and Expenditure Survey (NMCUES) and the Health Care Financing Administration (HCFA) National Health Accounts (NHA) data for 1948 through 1986 for the health expenditures stage. The effects of demographic attributes on consumer expenditures are estimated using the household CES data, and the effects of price variation are estimated from the time series NIPA data. The effects of both demographic attributes and price variation on health expenditures are estimated using the cross-section NMCUES data, because different households face different consumer prices for health care. Health care price variation is also represented in the time series NHA data.

The NMCUES data are used to characterize the role of public and private health benefits and transfer programs in great detail. Those data were used to estimate a matrix showing the proportion of health care expenditures for each of six types of health care provided from each of 11 sources of payment, for each of the 3,136 demographic and health insurance coverage groups. Based on the estimated expenditure share equations and the matrix of sources of payment, total and average household expenditures on five categories of consumer goods and services and six categories of health care can be projected for 3,136 demographic groups. Health care expenditures for each of the six types of health care, financed by each of 10 other sources of payment, for each demographic group are also projected. These highly disaggregated estimates can be aggregated over demographic subaggregates such as elderly female-headed households, and over health care finance programs such as Medicare, Medicaid, or private insurance.

The elements of the matrix of sources of payment for types of health care can be modified to depict changes in health care finance policies and programs or institutional patterns and practices. In one application, for example, the ICF Household Health Benefits Microsimulation Model was used to estimate changes in payment shares of various sources for individual households that would accompany a proposed reduction in Medicare benefits. These microsimulation model results were tabulated to estimate the average changes in expenditures by type and source that would occur for demographic groups. These estimates were used to modify the matrices showing average proportions of expenditures for various types of health care paid from various sources for different demographic groups. The MDM was then run with the modified payments matrices to estimate the ultimate effects on health care consumption and expenditures for demographic groups, taking into account consumer behavioral responses.

In summary, the Macroeconomic-Demographic Model, with its detailed demographic characterization of consumer expenditures and health care expenditures, combines many elements of macro- and microeconomic models. It represents an aggregative approach, in that it characterizes the average behavior of demographic groups using time series equations. However, those equations are specified within a framework consistent with microeconomic theory. They are estimated using individual household observations from microdatabases, and they characterize the economic behavior of highly detailed demographic groups.

The model is very large. Estimation of its equations was a considerable task requiring the development of new estimation software and consuming large amounts of computer time. Nevertheless, simulation of the model involves far less computer time than even moderate-sized microsimulation models. Therefore, the model can be simulated inexpensively, at an annual frequency, for periods as long as 80 to 90 years. In fact, MDM is typically run for a simulation period of 1980 through 2060. This relative ease of simulation gives it great advantages for scenario analysis and policy analysis. MDM, therefore, provides many of the advantages of a microsimulation approach without suffering one of its major drawbacks—high simulation time requirements and computer costs.

Notes

I am grateful to Richard Michel and other participants at the October 16, 1987, Urban Institute conference on "Software Systems and Income Transfer Policy" for their helpful comments.

1. Work in this area provided the background for the development of the micro-macro modeling system discussed in the last section of this chapter. See Jorgenson and Lau (1979), pp. 115–47; and Jorgenson, Lau and Stoker (1982), pp. 97–238.

2. An early simulation model of consumer behavior based on a micro approach was developed and used by Tobin and Dolde (1971).

3. HITSM currently uses the March 1988 Current Population Survey. However, it is designed to process any March CPS and has been used with most of the March CPS datasets collected in the past 10 years.

4. HITSM currently uses the 1986 SOI data (the most recent currently available). However, it is designed to use any SOI dataset and has been used with several earlier versions of the SOI.

5. These adjustments can be done by industry of employment if projections of industry wage indices are available.

6. This section is based on Wertheimer, Zedlewski et al. (1986), pp. 187–206.

References

Jorgenson, D. W., and L. J. Lau. 1979. "The Integrability of Consumer Demand Functions." *European Economic Review* 12(2) (April): 115–47.

Jorgenson, D. W., L. J. Lau, and T. M. Stoker. 1982. "The Transcendental Logarithmic Model of Aggregate Consumer Behavior." In *Advances in Econometrics*, edited by R. L. Basmann and G. Rhodes, vol. 1: 97–238. Greenwich, Conn.: JAI Press.

Tobin, J., and W. Dolde. June 1971. "Wealth, Liquidity, and Consumption." In *Consumer Spending and Monetary Policy*. Report of Monetary Conference No. 5. Boston: Federal Reserve Bank of Boston.

Wertheimer II, Richard, Sheila R. Zedlewski, Joseph Anderson, and Kristin Moore. 1986 "DYNASIM in Comparison with other Microsimulation Models." In *Microanalytic Simulation Models to Support Social and Financial Policy*, edited by G. H. Orcutt et al., 187–206. Amsterdam: North Holland.

Chapter Eight

MICROSIMULATION AND SIPP: CAN WE USE THE NEW LONGITUDINAL DATA?

Pat Doyle and Harold Beebout

A major new household data collection effort by the U.S. Bureau of the Census has been viewed by most of us in the household microsimulation modeling community as having great potential for improving the information base underlying the models. This data collection effort is the Survey of Income and Program Participation (SIPP), which, in the 1984 panel, followed a sample of approximately 20,000 households, collecting detailed data on economic and household characteristics on a month-by-month basis over two and one-half years.

THE PROMISE OF SIPP

SIPP was anticipated for the promise it held to improve the cross-section microsimulation models such as MATH (Micro Analysis of Transfers to Households) and TRIM (Transfer Income Model) which are widely used to estimate the impacts of changes in tax and transfer programs, through the following features:

☐ It contains monthly data on income and other characteristics corresponding to the accounting period used in determining need in programs such as Aid to Families with Dependent Children (AFDC) and food stamps. In contrast, current models generally use annual income data together with reported data on work patterns and a set of assumptions to infer approximate monthly income streams.
☐ It contains data on most of the household expenses used in determining program eligibility and benefit amounts.
☐ It provides more precise and consistent monthly data on household composition and other household characteristics used in determining categorical and income eligibility for transfer programs.

In contrast, the current model databases provide household composition data as of the March interview and income data for the previous year when household composition may have been quite different than in March.

□ It provides more detailed and precise information on a wider variety of cash and in-kind transfer programs on a consistent monthly basis, allowing examination of patterns of multiple benefit receipt and of the implications for adequacy and equity.

□ It provides more accurate and consistent information for estimating behavioral relationships such as the participation decision and labor supply response.

SIPP also was expected to be a major advance in estimating behavioral relationships at the heart of dynamic microsimulation models, particularly for models with a relatively short time horizon by:

□ Using the monthly longitudinal data on individual and household behavior over the approximately 30-month period covered by each SIPP panel.

□ Incorporating the detailed information on the time pattern of receipt of multiple program benefits in the estimation of household behavior, including program participation and labor supply.

With this introduction to how we had hoped SIPP would allow us to improve the current generation of microsimulation models, let us turn to a brief overview of the survey.

The SIPP Data

SIPP is a nationally representative longitudinal survey of individuals designed to provide detailed information on intrayear fluctuations in income and wealth, poverty status, and transfer income participation (Nelson, McMillen, and Kasprzyk, 1985). It is a multipanel longitudinal survey to which replacement samples (or panels) are added each year. The individuals in each panel are contacted every four months for eight waves (or rounds) of interviewing. The survey instruments are modular in design, consisting of core questions that are constant across waves and topical module questions that are collected once or twice for each panel. The survey is complex and contains extremely detailed information. For example, income is broken down into 50 different sources, in contrast to the 11 sources collected in the Annual Demographic Supplement to the Current

Population Survey (March CPS).[1] Detailed information is obtained and used to construct household and family composition indicators for every month of the survey's reference period. Information on transfer program participation includes both unit composition as well as benefits, and includes over 20 different cash and in-kind transfers.

Challenges and Problems in Using SIPP for Microsimulation

With the great promise of SIPP come many challenges and problems to overcome if the survey is to achieve its potential in advancing microsimulation. The sheer volume and complexity of the survey will severely strain most research budgets unless care is used in designing the database and the access system. There are substantive problems as well. Most important, a number of critical variables for determining program eligibility are not collected regularly as part of the core questionnaire, but are collected once or twice during the course of the panel in topical modules. Worse, these variables are not assembled at one time in one topical module, but are scattered across several different topical modules.[2] Also, the small sample size severely restricts the use of SIPP for many important microsimulation applications. In addition, the data are not aligned according to the calendar periods customarily used for microsimulation models. Other important items, such as medical expenses, are omitted entirely from the questionnaire. In addition to the problems of data volume and survey design, there are problems with response error. Finally, the design of the public-use data products is not optimal for microsimulation purposes.

These problems greatly complicate the use of SIPP for microsimulation. The potential applications and some approaches to overcoming these problems are discussed next.

OVERCOMING PROBLEMS IN MICROSIMULATION APPLICATIONS

SIPP has the potential to advance microsimulation modeling in two ways: indirectly to enhance existing simulation models and directly as a simulation database. SIPP-based research can improve the estimated relationships and assumptions in the current CPS-based microsimulation models. For example, the SIPP asset measures in combination with the SIPP income data could be used to model asset holdings, replacing the current crude estimates of asset holdings used in MATH and TRIM. There are a number of such components of the eligibility determination process not measured in the CPS, and SIPP is an obvious source for developing the statistical relationships needed to model those missing components of transfer program eligibility determination. Similarly, consistent monthly data on income and program participation facilitate the estimation of the behavioral relationships, such as program participation, used in the microsimulation models. Furthermore, the repeated measures of monthly income in SIPP allow refinement of the algorithms in the CPS-based models that allocate annual income to the monthly accounting periods used by most transfer programs.

SIPP has several advantages for use directly as a database for microsimulation, including reported monthly income and employment data that obviate the necessity to construct a typical "month" from annual data. Another advantage is the unmatched richness of detail, allowing cross-section microsimulation models to dispense with many of the assumptions required when using the March CPS. Furthermore, new longitudinal models could be developed that would simulate behavior over time, such as the dynamics of program participation and associated welfare dependency.

Thus, although SIPP does indeed have great promise for microsimulation, it is unfortunately accompanied by far more problems than had been expected. These problems and the efforts made to deal with them are discussed in the subsections following.

Problems in SIPP Applications

Problems in using SIPP for microsimulation studies stem from several aspects of the survey. These include elements of the survey design, the sample size, the design and documentation of the available data products, and the sheer volume of information.

DATA FRAGMENTATION AND LACK OF ALIGNMENT

The Bureau of the Census employs a number of features in the collection of SIPP data that are designed to save costs or improve data quality. Unfortunately, these features greatly complicate use of the data, either directly as a microsimulation database or as a source for the enhancement of microsimulation models based on CPS or other data:

☐ The use of staggered interviewing, whereby each interview wave is administered over a four-month period so that there is only one calendar month in each wave for which data are collected for the full sample.
☐ "Short waves" in the 1984 through 1986 panels, which are administered to only three-fourths of the sample.
☐ The lack of alignment of waves across panels, which affects the ability to combine data from the 1984 through 1986 panels.
☐ The omission of selected items needed for the determination of program eligibility, such as medical expenses.[3]
☐ The fact that important data items for determination of program eligibility are not repeated, including items collected as part of the topical modules as well as characteristics measured only at the first interview, most notably, disability and housing benefits.

The lack of repeated collection of topical and first interview responses is a particularly acute problem for microsimulation. Topical module information—for example, on child care expenses and vehicular assets—is critical for the simulation of eligibility in both the AFDC and Food Stamp programs. However, the information is not collected simultaneously, nor does the survey provide repeated measures for all reference months covered by the survey. (In the 1984 panel, for example, child care expenses were collected in wave 5 and vehicular assets were collected in waves 4 and 7.) The lack of repeated measures of the determinants of eligibility complicates studies of program dynamics because of the absence of measures of how these characteristics change over time. Measures of vehicular (and other) assets were collected twice in all SIPP panels, and two measures of child care expenses were initiated in the 1986 panel. However, although the two repetitions provide some information on the trend of changes, consistent monthly eligibility measures for studies of program dynamics will not exist unless strong assumptions are made regarding monthly variations in these and other topical module items.

The lack of concurrent measurement of the determinants of program eligibility will require that these data be aligned and integrated across waves to simulate program eligibility even for strictly cross-sectional applications. However, although the variables collected in multiple waves can be easily merged, changes in household composition or economic circumstances may result in inconsistencies in the linked data, complicating the simulation of eligibility. The substantive problems faced in the integration of these data and the capture of changes over time are discussed at length in Doyle, Czajka,

Boldin, Beebout, and Hirabayashi (1987). Four of these problems are outlined next.

First, because SIPP follows individual adults, there is the problem of relating topical information that pertains to an adult's household or family in one wave to the adult's household or family situation in other waves. A case in point is the information on shelter costs needed to simulate the Food Stamp Program. These data pertain to the household at the time of the wave 4 interview in the 1984 panel, and their integration with core or topical data in other waves requires either strong assumptions about how moving to a different house affects the level of housing expenses or a statistical model of housing expenses.[4]

Second, SIPP employs varying response units for topical questions, and some are inappropriate for simulation purposes. For example, the reference person of each household in existence at the time of the wave 4 interview is asked to list all vehicles owned by the various members of the dwelling unit. As a result, the survey provides a direct measure of vehicular assets at the household level, rather than individual level. This unit of measurement is inappropriate for the unit as defined by most transfer programs. Vehicles can be assigned to individuals and hence to assistance units within dwelling units, but this requires considerable effort.

Third, there is a problem of capturing change over time in items that are only asked once per panel. Disability measures are a good example. Although not strictly part of a topical module, they are part of a battery of questions administered only once at the time of first interview. Given the implicit assumption of no entry into or exit from disability status, this SIPP questionnaire design feature may lead to a biased estimate of program eligibility for all waves after the first wave, particularly for SSI.

Fourth, there is the problem of dealing adequately with missing information for persons who were not interviewed in the wave or waves in which the topical data were collected. This problem clearly affects the use of core as well as topical information collected in SIPP. However, missing core data resulting from noninterviews are typically accounted for by reduction of the sample and reweighting of the interviewed observations. In many cross-sectional simulation studies, however, elimination of cases that have complete core data for the wave of interest, but are missing data from one or more topical modules, is not likely to be the preferred approach, due to the further reduction of an already small sample size. The other alternative is to impute the missing data.

SAMPLE SIZE

SIPP was intended to include approximately 35,000 sample households in a given month (by combining two concurrent panels), yielding cross-sectional samples of more than half the size of the March CPS. Unfortunately, owing to budget cuts, the combined sample size has been drastically reduced to about 20,000 households, yielding relatively small samples of program participants (for example, approximately 700 sample households participating in AFDC and 800 sample persons receiving Supplemental Security Income (SSI) benefits).[5] These small samples of program participants seriously restrict the use of SIPP for simulation studies examining the effects of proposed program changes. Such examinations of program effects are typically focused on the differential effects across demographic subgroups and income classes. To illustrate the problem, consider a Food Stamp Program change that affects elderly recipients. Assume that in the policy decision regarding the proposed change, the distribution of the impacts across income classes is a critical concern. The August 1984 SIPP file developed from wave 4 of the 1984 panel contains 1,320 sample households reporting receipt of food stamps (Mathematica Policy Research, 1986). Approximately 22 percent of those sample households contain persons aged 60 or older, or 290 sample households. Assuming there were five income classes of interest, each class would on average contain 58 sample households. Since many population subgroups of interest are smaller than the elderly subgroup, many SIPP-based simulation estimates will have very large standard errors.

The types of simulation studies for which SIPP would be uniquely suited, were it not for the sample size restrictions, are analyses of changes to the definition of countable income, assets or expenses targeted to infrequently received income amounts (such as lump-sum payments) or small population groups such as farmers. No other nationally representative data source provides the level of detail needed for such studies. However, the sample size is so small that households exhibiting the desired combinations of characteristics (such as food stamp households with lump-sum payments or farmers receiving food stamps) may not even be captured by the survey, much less be sufficiently represented to support the simulation of these program changes.

DATA FORMAT AND FORM

The Census Bureau provides a series of longitudinal files for each panel and two different cross-sectional files for each interview wave that are substantively the same but differ in structure. As discussed in Doyle, Citro, and Cohen (1987), these file structures present substantial obstacles both for general SIPP access and simulation modeling. Some of these obstacles are:

☐ The use of a cross-sectional file structure whereby monthly information is embedded in household and person records in a way that greatly impedes straightforward development of monthly estimates;

☐ the storage of information on program recipient units that makes it difficult to distinguish multiple program units within households;

☐ the use of questionnaire organization to guide decisions on the file layout, making it difficult, particularly for the complex file structure, to integrate the difference sources of information on income recipiency; and

☐ the lack of both a complete set of responses to the core questions and of topical module data within the longitudinal files.

In addition, simulation of program eligibility is somewhat hampered by concepts that differ between the measures collected by SIPP and those used in determining program eligibility or benefit amounts. For example, unlike the CPS, SIPP measures self-employment in terms of monthly draw. The Food Stamp Program, on the other hand, counts net self-employment earnings, which can be averaged over the period to which they apply (up to 12 months).

The survey also contains a variety of nonsampling errors that affect the measurement of unit composition, duration of program participation, and simulation of eligibility. Doyle and Dalrymple (1987) demonstrate that although edited and imputed data on recipiency in SIPP indicate that almost 5 percent of the households receiving food stamps have multiple recipient units, more than one-fourth of these households represent apparent duplicate reporting of benefits by husbands and wives. Second, Coder et al. (1987) confirm the long-held suspicion that transitions between receipt and nonreceipt of benefits occur more frequently between consecutive waves rather than between consecutive pairs of months within waves. Finally, as is true for all general purpose surveys, SIPP is subjected to underreporting and nonreporting of income and benefits, although reporting is generally better than in comparable surveys such as the CPS. For example, results from the third quarter of 1984 show that the number of reported food stamp recipient households is 90 percent of an independent benchmark; AFDC and Unemployment Compensation benefits are 80 percent of independent benchmarks; and veterans' payments are 76 percent of an independent benchmark (U.S. Bureau of the Census, 1985). The SIPP underreporting problem is less severe than in the CPS where, for example, food stamp recipient households were 68 percent of an independent benchmark, and AFDC and Unemployment Compensation benefits were 76 percent of a benchmark in 1985 (U.S. Bureau of the Census, 1987).

DATA VOLUME AND ACCESS

The richness of the SIPP data on each observation make this survey extremely attractive for microsimulation activities, in spite of the small sample size and the barriers to access already discussed. However, this richness does not come without cost. Access to the data requires a heavy investment in programming time and computing resources. Part of the cost and difficulty of SIPP access result from the design of the public-use cross-sectional files. These files contain substantial redundancies and are inefficient for applications requiring flexibility in the formulation of the unit of analysis. This issue is important, since microsimulation studies typically deal with one or more transfer programs with unit definitions that differ from both the Census family or the household. The design chosen for the three-wave experimental longitudinal research file (U.S. Department of Commerce, 1987) is considerably improved over the cross-sectional files and is in fact well suited for the simulation of a variety of programs as well as other studies.[6] However, as yet the longitudinal products are limited in scope and content, requiring the use of the cross-sectional files for many simulation activities.

There are a number of approaches toward accessing SIPP, many of which are reviewed in Doyle (1989) and Doyle, Citro, and Cohen (1987). These range from use of database management systems such as INGRES and RAPID to traditional sequential access strategies using either procedural languages or the more powerful statistical packages such as SAS or OSIRIS.IV. The selection of the best access approach for simulation studies varies, depending on the nature of the study as well as the capabilities of the institution and its computing environment. Although it is not the object of this chapter to assess these alternatives, it is important to note that the success of any access system for a survey of the size and complexity of SIPP depends heavily on the chosen database design and on how well it supports the specific microsimulation studies undertaken.

The use of SIPP to support the enhancement of CPS-based simulation models and the use of simulation techniques to append uniform eligibility measures to analysis files do not represent unusual access problems beyond those faced in the use of SIPP for descriptive or multivariate studies. However, the development of a SIPP-based generalized microsimulation system presents numerous problems. Model designers need to pay particular attention to the database design both to ensure flexibility in the formulation of program unit definitions and to increase the efficiency with which program reforms can be simulated.

Potential Solutions

In a perfect world we might request changes to the survey design and processing system to correct the problems noted in the preceding section. In fact, we have suggested some changes to SIPP to facilitate microsimulation applications. However, practically speaking, we do not expect to see major changes in the design, particularly in the areas of data fragmentation and alignment, because these features make the survey less costly to implement.

Such problems can be overcome by the user, however. Consider, for example, the problem that selected components of the eligibility determination process are collected once or at most twice per panel, and that these are not collected simultaneously. For both cross-sectional and longitudinal applications, we would like to be able to align these data and to impute them to the time periods for which they were not collected. In so doing we are particularly interested in taking into account changes in circumstances over time.

This problem is not unlike that of longitudinal imputation discussed in Heeringa and Lepkowski (1986). They described five approaches to impute data missing owing to nonresponse in one wave of a longitudinal survey, using reported data from another wave:

☐ Direct substitution of reported values,
☐ deterministic imputation of change,
☐ longitudinal regression imputation,
☐ longitudinal hot deck, and
☐ longitudinal hot deck imputation of change.

The longitudinal regression imputation can be adapted to solve the alignment problem for topical module information collected for individuals, with one significant improvement. For individuals reporting quantitative topical module information in one wave, the data can be expressed as a predicted value based on a regression function plus a residual term calculated as the difference between the reported and predicted values. This residual then represents a measure of the effects of unobserved characteristics of the individual that cause the actual expense to deviate from the fitted expense. This individual-specific residual can be assigned to the individual for each time period in the survey. Then, in waves in which the topical module information was not collected, the value can be imputed as a predicted conditional mean from the regression equation plus the individual specific residual calculated in the topical module wave. (If necessary, the imputed values can be further adjusted for inflation by using a deterministic model.) This method, in effect, results in direct substitution of the topical module data when correlated characteristics remain unchanged. When circumstances do change, the model imputes values that differ from the reported topical module information but that differ in a manner consistent with observed changes in core characteristics.

The preceding approach works well for topical data collected for individuals. However, some pertinent information in SIPP pertains to households at the time of interview. These data cannot be linked straightfowardly across waves, because households cannot be unambiguously defined over time. For the data relevant to the Food Stamp Program, we are fortunate that this situation occurs only in the collection of shelter expenses. Furthermore, these expenses can be associated with addresses, and either a direct substitution model or a deterministic model of change can be employed so long as the address does not change. In the event that the address does change, we can adapt the longitudinal regression approach just discussed if we impose some concept of longitudinality on the household in the SIPP dataset.

In both cases, these approaches address that portion of the sample interviewed in the topical module wave who responded to the questions of interest. For nonrespondents, we are faced with the usual missing data problems compounded by the fact that we need to account for the missing data over time, rather than just in the topical module wave. We recommend the use of a longitudinal regression approach where the regression model is estimated on the sample of reporters in the topical module wave. This regression equation is then used to impute both the missing information in the topical module wave and again in the other wave (or waves) of interest. Ideally, this approach includes the assignment of only one residual term per observation, rather than using a different residual for repeated imputations over time.

Another alternative for this missing data problem is, of course, the elimination of these cases from the sample, with appropriate weight adjustments. However, as noted previously, we do not favor this approach, because the sample size is small. Furthermore, in so doing we lose reported information on other characteristics of these observations.

Cross-Sectional Applications

There are two quite different applications of microsimulation techniques. The most familiar application is the use of the generalized systems such as MATH and TRIM to evaluate the cost and distributional impacts of changes in existing transfer programs. The second application is in studies of participant behavior where simulation techniques are used to develop measures such as eligibility status and potential benefits that cannot be directly observed. Some of the research studies on participant behavior are designed to improve the general purpose microsimulation models, and some have other research objectives. To date, SIPP and its precursor, the 1979 Income Survey Development Program Research Test Panel (ISDP), have been used in several cross-sectional simulation studies of participant behavior.

USES TO DATE

Early studies based on the ISDP (Bickel and MacDonald, 1981; Czajka, 1981; and Fraker and Moffit, 1985) relied on simulations of eligibility for the Food Stamp Program to study program participant behavior. The Czajka study led to improvements in the participation algorithm in the MATH food stamp model (FSTAMP). More recently, a SIPP-based simulation model has been developed for the Food and Nutrition Service (FNS) of the U.S. Department of Agriculture (Doyle, Czajka, Boldin, Beebout, and Hirabayashi, 1987). This model was used to assess the potential improvement in SIPP-based simulations of program eligibles over the current CPS-based simulations. Of particular interest was whether, in spite of its smaller sample size, the improved measurement of income and program participation in SIPP ameliorates some of the technical problems encountered in simulating food stamp participation with the CPS. This model was recently used to develop uniform eligibility measures for the Food Stamp Program to be appended to SIPP-based analysis files needed to support the research agenda of the FNS (Doyle and Post, 1988).

Other applications include work in progress at the Congressional

Budget Office on SIPP-based simulations of AFDC and Food Stamp Program eligibility. The Urban Institute (1987) used simulation techniques with SIPP to examine the impact of the 1985 Farm Bill provision that made pure AFDC and SSI households automatically eligible for food stamps.

POTENTIAL APPLICATIONS

All of the studies that were conducted on the ISDP, including the ones just noted, can be extended with SIPP. In fact, the FNS is currently sponsoring an additional study of labor supply to extend Fraker and Moffit's research to other demographic groups. Beyond that, it is likely that, although SIPP will not replace the CPS as the premier simulation database because of the small SIPP sample size, it will be used to measure the impact of selected program reforms for which the CPS is not suitable. For example, program reforms that affect the asset test cannot be analyzed with CPS, owing to lack of information, and cannot be fully analyzed using administrative data if the reforms introduce new eligibles to the program. On the other hand, detailed data are obtainable from SIPP to support such studies and will most likely be used.

Longitudinal Applications

Microsimulation techniques have not been used extensively in the conduct of longitudinal research. This underutilization is due both to limitations in the available data and to limitations in the state of the art. To date, the longitudinal applications have revolved around the analysis of program dynamics.

USES TO DATE

Carr, Doyle, and Lubitz (1984) and Lubitz and Carr (1985) studied turnover in the Food Stamp Program and events that trigger program transitions, using data from a longitudinal file created from the 1979 ISDP. They employed simulation techniques to measure program eligibility on a monthly basis, and then used this measurement as an explanatory variable in their analysis. Carr and colleagues also presented an analysis of turnover in program eligibility based on these simulated measures. Doyle (1984) analyzed intrayear fluctuations in income receipt based on the ISDP, and the results were used to enhance the allocation of annual income to monthly amounts in the CPS-based MATH model.

POTENTIAL APPLICATIONS

Perhaps the most exciting microsimulation potential is in the modeling of recipiency over time and the modeling of issues such as the degree to which "welfare dependency" is reduced by various policy interventions. The richer SIPP data could potentially improve models such as the one described in Maxfield and Rucci (1986), which is based on the Panel Study of Income Dynamics.

SIPP offers the potential to repeat the ISDP-based studies already noted here and to extend these analyses to other means-tested programs. The survey will also support estimation of the dynamics of program participation, concentrating on the length of time between becoming eligible for a program and deciding to participate. Such studies will be adversely affected by the response error problem, resulting in the tendency to observe transitions in income or benefit receipt between waves. However, it may be possible to ascertain the timing and nature of the decision to participate in various programs.

SIPP may also prove useful in evaluating the effect of a change in program regulations on the program target population. For example, if a change in the benefit reduction rate is legislated to occur in July 1990, then observations from the 1989 and 1990 panels before and after the change can be examined to ascertain if program exit or entry rates deviate and to estimate the effects on benefits and participation levels. Because of the small sample in SIPP, this will only be feasible for program changes that affect a substantial proportion of the participants in a program. Furthermore, because SIPP is not designed to provide small area estimates, changes that are phased in at different times in different geographical areas may not be clearly identified.

CONCLUSIONS AND FUTURE DIRECTIONS

Our review of the issues in using SIPP for microsimulation and of the early applications leads us to the following conclusions:

The promise of SIPP for advancing microsimulation remains, in spite of the difficulties. The five years of operational experience with SIPP have demonstrated that the routine collection of highly detailed monthly longitudinal data, so important to improving our models of transfer programs and household economic status, is feasible. The quality of the SIPP data is generally high in comparison to that of other household surveys such as the CPS, although more work remains to be done on issues such as longitudinal weighting and the timing of transitions.

The potential improvements in microsimulation models arising from the use of SIPP are too important not to solve the problems. As discussed in the first two sections of this chapter, SIPP provides the detailed monthly longitudinal information to eliminate many of the assumptions necessary in the current models and to greatly increase the accuracy and breadth of the models. The remaining problems in data collection design and in SIPP access and use can be solved through the combined efforts of the Census Bureau and the user.

Solving the conceptual data integration and file development problems is too expensive to be routinely replicated. Two critical aspects of making effective use of SIPP for transfer program simulation are: developing a conceptual approach for measuring concepts such as monthly eligibility, where components of the underlying information were not collected monthly; and developing the computer programs to implement the conceptual design and produce a file with monthly eligibility and other constructed measures. Considerable conceptual work on the data integration problem has already been done as it relates to the simulation of Food Stamp Program eligibility as reported in Doyle, Czajka, Boldin, Beebout, and Hirabayashi (1987). Work has been funded to develop SIPP analysis files with component measures of Food Stamp Program eligibility attached. Both of these efforts, supported by the Food and Nutrition Service, are examples of the type of efforts that need to be done to facilitate SIPP use and to reduce the time and resources required for each application.

Modifications in the SIPP data collection design and public-use files are needed. Although some of the problems in using SIPP for microsimulation can be alleviated with efforts of the type discussed previously, progress regarding other limitations requires action by the Bureau of the Census. The following changes would greatly improve SIPP's utility for microsimulation and could be made without increasing either the overall respondent burden or the SIPP budget.

□ Double the effective sample size for the low-income population, either by doubling the overall sample or by oversampling the low-income population. This change is necessary for SIPP to be a practical alternative to the CPS for routine simulation analyses of proposed changes in transfer programs. The cost could be offset by not fielding a new panel every year. A new panel every year is not needed for most analytical purposes. The apparent rationale of increasing the efficiency of measuring year-to-year change could be accomplished by other means.

□ Provide for repeated and consistent measures of the major components of program eligibility not now included in the core questionnaire. This could be accomplished in one of two ways. The key items could be added to the core questionnaire. Alternatively, the questions now scattered across several topical modules could be combined in one topical module, which would be administered at least twice for each panel.

□ Modify the design of the cross-section files, facilitating use for microsimulation and other applications. A revised file structure should reflect the monthly variation inherent in the survey design, should eliminate the large amount of redundancies currently imposed, and should support flexibility in defining units of analysis. In short, the Census Bureau should let analytic use of the data, rather than questionnaire design, guide the choice for organization of the cross-section files. Furthermore, the edit and imputation procedures should be altered to retain more accurately the means and variances of imputed values for low-income households and to account for known relationships between income and the level of means-tested benefits.

□ Enhance the longitudinal processing system so that the effective sample for longitudinal analysis is not reduced to those sample members who were successfully interviewed in eight waves. Kasprzyk (1987) reported that 27 percent of the 44,000 original sample members eligible for eight interviews missed at least one of these. This figure excluded any reference to the roughly 15,000 additional sample members who were associated with the sample for less than the full eight interviews.[7]

With a concerted effort by the users and the Bureau of the Census, SIPP can achieve its promise of advancing the state of microsimulation and of making it a more effective tool for research and policy analysis.

Notes

We gratefully acknowledge the contributions of David McMillen and the anonymous reviewers.

1. Recent versions of the March CPS collect more than 11 different income sources. However, to date, only 11 different types have been identified on the public-use files.

2. Efforts are underway at the Bureau of the Census to correct this problem with the 1989 panel.

3. Consideration is currently being given to the collection of out-of-pocket medical expenses in a future SIPP panel as part of an overall eligibility module.

4. In fact, there is even a problem using topical data on assets within wave 4, because persons may relocate within the reference period.

5. For the first half of each calendar year there are three panels interviewed concurrently. Hence, for those months, the combination of data across these panels will yield a sample size of roughly 30,000 cases.

6. Unfortunately the Bureau of the Census changed this design before releasing the full panel longitudinal file in June 1988. The new approach is less well suited to microsimulation than was its predecessor.

7. This also excludes the roughly 12,000 original sample members who were deleted from the sample between waves 5 and 6 in order to cut the cost of administering the survey.

References

Bickel, M.J., and M. MacDonald. Jan. 1981. *Assets of Low Income Households: New Findings on Food Stamp Participants and Nonparticipants.* Final report to the U.S. Department of Agriculture, Food and Nutrition Service. Washington, D.C.: Mathematica Policy Research.

Carr, T.J., P. Doyle, and I.S. Lubitz. July 1984. *An Analysis of Turnover in the Food Stamp Program.* Final report to the U. S. Department of Agriculture, Food and Nutrition Service. Washington, D.C.: Mathematica Policy Research.

Coder, J.F., D. Burkhead, A. Feldman-Harkins, and J. McNeil. Mar. 1987. *Preliminary Data from the SIPP 1983-84 Longitudinal Research File.* SIPP Working Paper series 8702. Washington, D.C.: U.S. Bureau of the Census.

Czajka, J.L. Nov. 1981. *Determinants of Participation in the Food Stamp Program: Spring 1979.* Final report to the U. S. Department of Agriculture, Food and Nutrition Service. Washington, D.C.: Mathematica Policy Research.

Doyle, P. 1989. "Review of Data Base Strategies for Panel Surveys." In *Panel Surveys,* edited by Daniel Kasprzyk, Greg Duncan, Graham Kalton, and M.P. Singh. New York: John Wiley and Sons.

Doyle, P. July 1984. *An Analysis of Intra-Year Income Receipt.* Final report to the U. S. Department of Agriculture, Food and Nutrition Service. Washington, D.C.: Mathematica Policy Research.

Doyle, P., and R. Dalrymple. 1987. "The Impact of Imputation Procedures on Distributional Characteristics of the Low Income Population." In *Proceedings of the Third Annual Research Conference.* Washington, D.C.: U.S. Bureau of the Census.

Doyle, P., and C. Post. May 1988. "Development of Uniform Eligibility Measures for SIPP-Based Cross-Section Files." Draft report to the U.S. Department of Agriculture, Food and Nutrition Service. Washington, D.C.: Mathematica Policy Research.

Doyle, P., C.F. Citro, and R. Cohen. July 1987. *Feasibility Study of Long Term Access to SIPP.* Final report to the U. S. Department of Agriculture, Food and Nutrition Service. Washington, D.C.: Mathematica Policy Research.

Doyle, P., J. Czajka, P. Boldin, H. Beebout, and S. Hirabayashi. July 1987. *Conceptual Studies of SIPP-Based Simulation of the Food Stamp Program.* Final report to the U. S. Department of Agriculture, Food and Nutrition Service. Washington, D.C.: Mathematica Policy Research.

Fraker, T., and R. Moffit. Mar. 1985. *The Effects of Food Stamp Participation on the Market Labor of Female Heads of Household.* Final report to the U. S. Department of Agriculture, Food and Nutrition Service. Washington, D.C.: Mathematica Policy Research.

Heeringa, S., and J. Lepkowski. 1986. "Longitudinal Imputation for the SIPP." In *Proceedings of the American Statistical Association.* Alexandria, Va.: American Statistical Association.

Kasprzyk, D. Oct. 1987. "Survey of Income and Program Participation Update." Prepared for the Census Advisory Committee on Population Statistics. Washington, D.C.: U.S. Bureau of the Census.

Lubitz, I.S., and T.J. Carr. Feb. 1985. *Turnover in the Food Stamp Program in 1979: The Role of Trigger Events.* Draft report to the U. S. Department of Agriculture, Food and Nutrition Service. Washington, D.C.: Mathematica Policy Research.

Mathematica Policy Research, Inc. Dec. 1986. *Survey of Income and Program Participation 1984 Panel Waves 3, 4, and 5: Household-Month and Calendar-Month Files, Record Format Description.* Final report to the U. S. Department of Agriculture, Food and Nutrition Service. Washington, D.C.: Mathematica Policy Research.

Maxfield, M., and M. Rucci. 1986. *A Simulation Model of Targeted Employment and Training Programs for Long Term Welfare Recipients.* Washington, D.C.: Mathematica Policy Research.

Nelson, D., D. McMillen, and D. Kasprzyk. 1985. *An Overview of the Survey of Income and Program Participation: Update 1.* SIPP Working Paper series 8401. Washington, D.C.: U.S. Bureau of the Census.

Urban Institute, The. 1987. *Impacts of Categorical Food Stamp Program Eligibility for Households Composed Solely of AFDC and SSI Recipients.* Washington, D.C.: Urban Institute.

U.S. Bureau of the Census. 1985. *Economic Characteristics of Households in the United States: Third Quarter 1984.* Current Population Reports, series P-70, no. 5. Washington, D.C.: U.S. Government Printing Office.

U.S. Bureau of the Census. 1987. *Receipt of Selected Noncash Benefits: 1985.* Current Population Reports, series P-60, no. 155. Washington, D.C.: U.S. Government Printing Office.

U.S. Department of Commerce. 1987. "Longitudinal Research File Development Description." Draft. Washington, D.C.: U.S. Department of Commerce, Bureau of the Census.

ABOUT THE EDITORS

Gordon H. Lewis is an associate professor of sociology in the School of Urban and Public Affairs at Carnegic Mellon University and is serving as a visiting scholar at The Urban Institute. His current interests are the analysis of income transfer systems (e.g., taxation and benefit programs), applied decisionmaking, and organizational design. Professor Lewis's work on income transfers has focused on the design and implementation of software for the analysis of systems of transfer programs. The software systems that were developed allow one to assess directly the impact of large numbers of complex and interrelated transfer programs. The approach is especially relevant to the analysis of incentive and equity issues that arise through the interaction of multiple programs at the state and federal level. He is currently a member of the National Research Council's Panel to Evaluate Microsimulation Models for Social Welfare Programs. He served for seven years as editor of the *Journal of Mathematical Sociology.*

Richard C. Michel has been director of the Income and Benefits Policy Center at The Urban Institute since 1983. The Center houses both the Transfer Income Model (TRIM2) and the Dynamic Simulation of Income Model (DYNASIM2) described in this book. Mr. Michel's involvement in microsimulation began in 1975 when he was using the technique to analyze income distribution issues. He became director of the TRIM project at The Urban Institute in 1976. From 1977 to 1979, he was a senior economist in the Office of the Assistant Secretary for Planning and Evaluation in the Department of Health and Human Services and was responsible for coordinating and presenting the official estimates of the Carter Administration's two welfare reform proposals which used the KGB microsimulation model. He returned to The Urban Institute in 1979 and resumed the position of TRIM2 project director which he has held since.

ABOUT THE CONTRIBUTORS

Joseph M. Anderson has been involved with the development and use of both aggregative models and microsimulation models as a professor of economics at Williams College and as a vice president of Lewin/ICF, a Washington, D.C. economic consulting firm. He participated in development of the Lewin/ICF Household Income and Tax Simulation Model (HITSM) and the National Institute on Aging Macroeconomic-Demographic Model (MDM). He has used the models to study the distributional and macroeconomic effects of energy price changes and a wide variety of policy proposals.

Harold Beebout is the director of the Research Division at Mathematica Policy Research (MPR). He played a key role in the development of the TRIM microsimulation model while at The Urban Institute in the early 1970s. After moving to MPR, he led the team that developed the MATH model. Much of his work has focused on making microsimulation models useful as policy analysis tools and improving the data and behavioral content underlying the models.

Anne B. Bergsman is an independent computer software consultant to The Urban Institute. Her involvement in microsimulation modeling began in 1970 as part of the programming team modifying the RIM model daily to estimate the effects of the president's proposed Family Assistance Plan and other proposals. Since then she has been involved in designing, implementing, modifying, and using the TRIM, MATH, Treasury TRIM, and the TRIM2 models for a variety of policy issues.

Pat Doyle is a senior researcher at Mathematica Policy Research specializing in microsimulation and database development. Ms. Doyle directs the development and use of the MATH and FOSTERS microsimulation models and related databases in addition to serving as the architect for several major components of these systems. Her involvement with microsimulation dates back to 1976 with the initial application of the MATH model to simulate the impact of proposed legislated changes on the Food Stamp Program.

Richard A. Kasten has been at the Congressional Budget Office since 1985. He completed his first microsimulation model for his Ph.D. dissertation in 1975. At the U.S. Department of Health and Human Services from 1975 to 1985, he worked on models of welfare reform (the "KGB" model) and social security earnings sharing. In 1986 he joined the Tax Analysis Division, where he forecasts individual income tax revenue and does distributional analyses of the federal tax system.

David L. Kennell is a vice president at Lewin/ICF specializing in microsimulation in the retirement income and long-term care areas. His involvement with microsimulation dates back to 1980 with the initial development of the PRISM model. In recent years he has developed the Brookings/ICF Long-Term Care Financing Model and a microsimulation model of acute health care utilization and expenditures.

Richard J. Morrison has been working on a variety of microsimulation fronts since the mid-1970s. Working primarily for Canada's Department of National Health and Welfare, he has helped to develop several modeling packages that render the construction of microsimulation models quicker and more economical. A major theme running through his work is the importance of looking at equity and incentive effects for comprehensive systems of taxes and benefits.

Frank Sammartino works with the Tax Analysis Division of the Congressional Budget Office (CBO) where he has developed and used microsimulation models to forecast federal individual income tax revenues, and to analyze the distribution of total federal tax burdens. Prior to joining CBO, Mr. Sammartino worked in the Office of Income Security Policy at the U.S. Department of Health and Human Services, where he developed and used microsimulation models to analyze the Old-Age, Survivors, and Disability Insurance Program.

John F. Sheils specializes in microsimulation and database development at Lewin/ICF. He has been working on microsimulation since the mid-1970s. At ICF, he helped develop three microsimulation models: the PRISM model, the HITSM model, and the Brookings/ICF Long-Term Care Financing Model. He is currently working on applications of another microsimulation model which addresses acute health care utilization and expenditures.

Randall L. Webb worked with the TRIM and TRIM2 microsimulation models at The Urban Institute from 1976 through 1988. He was responsible for development of the TRIM2 model from 1979 to 1981 and thereafter supervised the TRIM2 programming staff at The Urban Institute. He is currently assistant director of Computer Services at The Urban Institute and director of Information Systems for The United States Renal Data System, a national database on persons with kidney failure.

Sheila R. Zedlewski is a senior research associate at The Urban Institute, where she specializes in the development and application of microsimulation models. Her involvement with microsimulation dates back to 1972 with the development of DYNASIM. Since 1981, she has overseen the development of DYNASIM2. Ms. Zedlewski has directed a number of studies that have used DYNASIM2 to analyze retirement issues. She also participates as a member of the Institute's TRIM2 team.